Praise for *Psychedelic Bubble Gum*

"Those were truly psychedelic, strange and wonderful times. Reading your book reminded me that I had asked you to participate in the Mad Dogs Tour—as you are one of my favorite soul singers and organists. Your writing style is as entertaining as the rest of your show biz skills."—**LEON RUSSELL,** Rock and Roll Hall of Fame singer, songwriter, musician, and producer

"Few songwriters have planted as many seeds in the public consciousness. *Psychedelic Bubble Gum* is very well written, told with sensitivity, insight and candor. It is an account of Hart's personal and professional challenges and a voyage of spiritual discovery."—**JIM STRAIN,** screenwriter (*Jumanji*) and lecturer, UCLA Department of Film, Television, and Digital Media

"A fast read loaded with practical information and terrific behind the scenes stories of how to make it in the music business. Highly recommended for aspiring songwriters and musicians everywhere."—**MARK WINKLER,** *Downbeat Magazine* 2014 Jazz Male Vocalist

"I read Bobby's book—I liked it! His story is so much like my own that the book is an insight into me. The journey of spiritual liberation means shedding the fear that keeps us from finding out who we really are under the masks we wear. Here, Bobby gives us a peek under the masks."—**PETER TORK,** actor and musician, and singer/ keyboardist/bass player of The Monkees

"Bobby Hart has been a very successful songwriter for many years. The story behind his success is both entertaining and compelling."—**CLIVE DAVIS,** legendary music executive, chief creative officer of Sony Music

"A fascinating story about opportunity and the cost of success. It's about a time in the music business that was magical and will never happen again. Not only a musical journey but a spiritual one as well."—**TOM CAPEK,** studio engineer, keyboardist, composer, and producer

"Is as spiritually juicy as the title suggests. I highly recommend it to anyone who wants to be inspired to fulfill their dreams—whether worldly or spiritual." —**KATIE SILCOX,** author of *Healthy Happy Sexy: Ayurveda Wisdom for Modern Women*

"The enchantment that Bobby creates in his new book is as compelling as the magic in the blink of Jeannie's eyes. I was charmed by Bobby and Tommy when we worked together on the set and the retelling of those cherished years is a complete delight that I'm sure you too will enjoy."—**BARBARA EDEN**, American television icon and star of *I Dream of Jeannie*

"Bobby explains the techniques he used to achieve great financial success. Then, he reveals how he transformed his negative habits through changing his thought patterns. His years of yoga meditation, self discipline and divine love are inspiring. This book is a fascinating story of one man's successful pursuit of happiness."
—**DESIRÉE RUMBAUGH**, creator of the DVD series *Yoga to the Rescue*, holds certifications in Iyengar and Anusara Yoga and leads retreats, workshops, and trainings worldwide.

"I know you are going to be inspired reading Bobby Hart's journey, turning mayhem into miracles. At Sunshine Acres Children's Home we see miracles every day. It was so touching reading the stories he wrote about Sunshine Acres and our work with hurting children."—**CAROL L. WHITWORTH**, President and CEO Sunshine Acres Children's Home

"During the Vietnam war, Bobby was a songwriter while I was a cadet at the Naval Academy. His advocacy to change the U. S. Constitution, allowing 18-year-olds the vote, showed his resolve to give voice to those who carried the rifle. Truly, that may have been his most poignant lyric."—**MICHAEL KUHNE**, U. S. Naval Academy

"Mr. Hart's musical gifts opened the doors that allowed him to become a voice for those less privileged in our society. He distinguished him from others of his generation by seeking out a deeper meaning for his existence. *Psychedelic Bubble Gum* holds a life lesson that is applicable to the 21st Century: Regardless of what you accomplish, it is in the giving that we receive."—**HONORABLE VICTOR REYES**, District Court Judge

"Bobby tells the story of his life and at the same time captures the essence of the turbulent times during the 60s. As an Army Captain, I lead 18-year-old draftees in combat who now were able to vote as a result of the Let Us Vote campaign."
—**DREW DIX**, Congressional Medal of Honor recipient

"Take a ride on that last train to Clarksville for an insider's view of 'sixties pop' and the life of an iconic songwriter."—**PAUL WILLIAMS**, singer, songwriter, actor, author, President and Chairman of the Board of ASCAP

Psychedelic Bubble Gum

Boyce & Hart, The Monkees, and Turning Mayhem into Miracles

*

BOBBY HART

with Glenn Ballantyne

SelectBooks, Inc.
New York

Page 51: *How to Write a Hit Song and Sell It* by Tommy Boyce, used by permission of Caroline Boyce
Page 56: "Lazy Elsie Molly" © 1964 renewed 1992 by Morris Music, Inc.
Pp 59, 60: "Come a Little Bit Closer" © 1964 renewed 1992 by Morris Music, Inc.
Pp 101, 255, 318: "Theme From the Monkees" © Sony/ATV Music Publishing
Page 126: "I Wanna Be Free" © Sony/ATV Music Publishing
Page 180: "L. U. V. (Let Us Vote)" © Sony/ATV Music Publishing
Page 256: "Chicano" © Father Music

This edition published by SelectBooks, Inc.

For information address SelectBooks, Inc., New York, New York.

First Edition

ISBN 978-1-59079-290-2

Library of Congress Cataloging-in-Publication Data

Hart, Bobby.
 Psychedelic bubble gum : Boyce & Hart, the Monkees, and turning Mayhem into miracles / Bobby Hart with Glenn Ballantyne. -- First edition.
     pages cm
 Includes index.
 Summary: "Songwriter, singer, and producer Bobby Hart tells how he and Tommy Boyce created many top hit songs of the sixties and seventies, enabling The Monkees to outsell The Beatles and the Rolling Stones in 1967-68 and Boyce and Hart to become performers and recording artists. He discusses his relationships, political activism, and his religious and spiritual journey"-- Provided by publisher.
 ISBN 978-1-59079-290-2 (hardbound book : alk. paper) 1. Hart, Bobby. 2. Composers--United States--Biography. 3. Boyce, Tommy. 4. Monkees (Musical group) I. Ballantyne, Glenn. II. Title.
 ML410.H2068A3 2015
 782.42164092'2--dc23
 [B]
                                    2014039787

Book design by Janice Benight

Manufactured in the United States of America
10 9 8 7 6 5 4 3 2 1

This narrative is dedicated to
my deathless guru, Paramahansa Yogananda.
His unfathomable love and guidance that has saved my life
also promises to someday lead me to my blissful home in Spirit.
and to
My beautiful wife, friend, and spiritual partner, MaryAnn,
whose love, unwavering support, assistance, and council
have made an undertaking of this magnitude possible.

Contents

❋

Foreword by Micky Dolenz   xi

Introduction: Looking for a Miracle   xiii

1   Anyone Here Play the Banjo?   3

2   You Sound Pretty Good, Kid, But . . .   10

3   Guess What? I Picked Out My Wedding Dress Today!   14

4   Better Keep Your Day Job   20

5   Two Ways to Work the Night Shift   23

6   The Control Room Door Flew Open   28

7   By the Way, I Changed Your Name   33

8   Where'd You Get That Corduroy Suit—Penney's?   38

9   They'd Rather Have the Dancer   43

10   Finally, the Promised Land!   48

11   A Couple More Hits and You Can Hit the Parties with Me   55

❋   **Stepping-Stones thru the Potholes of Life #1: Creativity**   62

12   *Wipe Out!* The Boys in the Bootleg Band   63

13   The Awkward Dazzler   70

14   Doing What Our Egos Wanted and Our Consciences Allowed   75

15   I Need You to Get This Kid Out of Town   81

16   "So Long, Chumps. I'm Getting Out While I Can."   88

17   Soaking Up Our Share of the Peace and Love   93

❇   **Stepping-Stones thru the Potholes of Life #2: Visualization**   99

18   A Grammy or a World Wide Wrestling Federation Award?   100

19   Candy Store Prophets and Disappearing Monkees   109

20   Something About a Train to Somewhere   115

21   Seventeen Songs in the Top-Thirty   123

22   More Records Than The Beatles and Rolling Stones Combined   128

23   They Got What They Wanted, but They Lost What They Had   134

24   Paisley Painted VWs and Limos All Headed for Monterey   140

25   Purple Haze   146

26   Cornering the Sock Market   152

27   Dear God, See You in Nine Days   157

28   In Cities Across America, She'd Find Her Way Backstage   162

29   I Was Never More Proud of Tommy Boyce   168

30   Between Hollywood and Sandalwood   172

❇   **Stepping-Stones thru the Potholes of Life #3: Thoughts**   176

31   If You Hire This Guy I Can't Represent You Anymore   177

32   Changing the US Constitution? How Hard Can That Be?   183

33   Pulling the Hair Out of My Head   190

34   Phantoms of the Opry   197

35   I've Got Steve McQueen with Me   204

36   I've Got a Bad Feeling About This   211

37   Aliens Stood at the Foot of His Bed   217

38   From a Hollywood Somebody to Just Some Body
       in Hollywood   222

39   Well, There You Go, Hart, You Left $200 on the Table   228

40   Sunshine Acres Is On Fire!   233

41   Stopped in Its Tracks by a Tragic Hand of Fate   237

42   No, Really, There *Is* No Budget   242

43   Floating Above the Shroud of My Own Expectations   246

44   No More Back Door, Overcrowded Dreams   251

45   You Took a Gig on Christmas Day?!   257

46   Too Loose to Be Circumscribed by the Mouse and
     His Handlers   262

47   You Say the Queen Was Toasting You?   268

48   I Could Feel Her Mother Go Limp Before I Finished   272

49   A One-Two Punch of Life-Changing Events in Three Days   279

50   I'm Surprised You Guys Don't Suffer from Whiplash!   284

✳   **Stepping-Stones thru the Potholes of Life #4: Willpower**   289

51   I Don't Think God Hears Me Anymore   290

✳   **Stepping-Stones thru the Potholes of Life #5: Your Unique
     Role in Life**   296

52   How Can You Love God If You Never Think About Him?   297

53   Even the Trees Were Bowing in Our Direction   305

     Afterword   313

     Acknowledgments   321

     Index   323

     About the Authors   337

Foreword

by Micky Dolenz

My relationship with Bobby Hart began in April of 1966 at my first recording session with him and Tommy Boyce. Neither of us knew that day would begin the weaving of invisible threads that would tie us together for a lifetime.

I know that Davy, Peter, Mike, and I created a bit of whacky mayhem in the studio when Tommy and Bobby tried to get us to all record at the same time, but looking back, I'm not surprised. After all, the producers of the television show were constantly encouraging us to be whacky. They were actually *training* us to be spontaneous, improvisational, a bit irreverent, and . . . whacky.

But once we started recording the first Monkee album the process became professional and rewarding. I spent many happy hours creating hit records with Bobby and Tommy.

To this day, I always credit them with not only writing many of our biggest hits, but, as producers, being instrumental in creating the unique Monkee sound that we all know and love.

I feel grateful that our stars aligned when and where they did, and that I connected with one of the most successful songwriter/producers ever. Our creative work in the recording studio was so enjoyable, in part, because of Bobby's creativity and professionalism and his ability to help bring out the best in me as a singer.

In the following chapters, Bobby tells the story of his life, vividly revealing his personal and professional struggles, many of which even I wasn't aware of until now. Bobby is basically a private man, and he seldom, if ever, lets others see deeper than his social and business exterior. You will see in the following pages that he fully lets down his guard and tells what was really going on during those mind-altering days and nights when he was busy launching The Monkees off onto our phenomenal musical careers.

Ten years after The Monkees had skyrocketed and faded, Bobby and I were destined to come together again, but this time we were sharing the stage. On July 4th, 1975, Tommy, Bobby, Davy and I played our first concert as Dolenz, Jones, Boyce & Hart in St. Louis to 12,500 screaming fans. For more than a year we traveled across the United States, playing concerts and then touring to Japan, Thailand, Hong Kong, Malaysia, Taiwan, and Singapore. Bobby's low-key and dry sense of humor was often a counterbalance to my own over-the-top, improvisational style of humor when times got tense or we were feeling overtired.

I've never written a foreword for anyone before, but when Bobby asked me, I immediately said yes. He had so much to do with the successes I have enjoyed in my life that I wanted to be a small part of *his* life. His is an extraordinary life that he will share with you in this book.

I've probably introduced more people to Bobby Hart's songs than anyone else. During our long professional relationship we made a lot of musical history together. I'm grateful that Bobby helped me purchase that first-class ticket on the last train to Clarksville, and that he was still sitting next to me on that most amazing trip around the world.

This is a journey you too will share as Bobby navigates the trials and triumphs of his unique life—all the while searching for the high road.

Bon Voyage!

—MICKY DOLENZ
December 18, 2014

Looking for a Miracle

The screams of twenty thousand wild fans were emitting a high-pitched roar that was nearly deafening, but all I could see were the dark silhouette outlines of their faces as I ran onto the stage, blinded by a spotlight that resembled the noon-day sun. The grindege I had felt—from the late night flight, the endless press interviews, eating on the run, visits with radio jocks, and the tedious sound check—was gone in an instant. I ran onto the stage fully energized, my heart reflecting the love that was streaming toward me from the audience. Was this the sweet, hard-won American Dream that I had envisioned for so long?

As far back as I can remember I had a strong desire to somehow distinguish myself from others. I wanted to get out of my suffocatingly small town and create something that people would notice—something that would make me feel empowered, proud, and unique. My mom used the word *distinguished* in another way when she described an actor or a preacher as "elegant" or "distinguished." As for me, I found those traits in the country music stars and deejays that I looked up to as I admired their graciousness, class, and the confident and controlled way in which they carried themselves in public. My American Dream definitely included becoming a "somebody," and it would be a somebody who was distinguished in both senses of the word.

But there was one major obstacle. I was painfully shy and socially introverted. Although I really disliked the feeling of being the invisible boy in the classroom, it was better than the terror I experienced when called on by the teacher. So if I wanted to fulfill my dreams, and obviously I did, I would need to protect myself by finding some nearly invisible and emotionally safe means of going about it. While being totally unaware of the process at the time, I began early on to craft ways to reconcile my handicaps with my ambitions. Still, it felt like for me to become *distinguished*, I'd need to find a miracle!

Music had always been my passion. Alone in my room after school, I would read the lyrics in my *Song Hits* magazine and listen to the records that my favorite country deejay was spinning. By high school, I had made significant strides in coming out of my shell socially, but in the era of Frank Sinatra and his crooning contemporaries, it never entered my mind that someone like me could become a recording artist. Although I dreamed of a career in music, my dream never included singing or performing in front of a live audience.

For me, radio was the perfect solution. On the radio, I reasoned, I could be a star without ever being seen. Beginning in third or fourth grade, I had my own little make-believe radio station in the corner of my room. As I got older, it grew in sophistication into a professional-looking console with twin fourteen-inch turntables, microphones, and a real Webcor tape recorder. I listened to the country stations and emulated the colorful deejays that were bigger than life as they introduced the music that I loved.

Then rock 'n' roll was born, and seemingly overnight, the classically trained vocal skills of singing stars of the forties and early fifties were no longer a prerequisite to stardom. My view of myself was becoming slightly more confident. In the corner of my daydreams, I began to make out a very fuzzy image of myself as a rock 'n' roll star.

On my last day of high school, I mailed off the enrollment papers that I had filled out months before to attend the evening classes at the Don Martin School of Radio in Hollywood. But a more pressing obligation would delay the start of my deejay studies until January of 1958.

Psychedelic
Bubble Gum

CHAPTER 1

Anyone Here Play the Banjo?

The California sun was just a soft red ball hanging well below the tops of the stately palms as I walked west down Hollywood Boulevard to my one room apartment on Whitley Avenue. It was a chilly February evening in 1958, and I was exhausted as I trudged past the seedy bars, Woolworth's, Frederick's of Hollywood, the silent street people with downturned eyes, and the gawking, vocal tourists. It had been an especially long day at the print shop, and I had hoped to get off in time to hang out at the little recording studio near work. Once again that would have to wait for another day.

I remember not even having the energy to attend my evening classes at the Don Martin School of Radio. Becoming a big-time disc jockey had been my dream since childhood, but after a couple of months of trying to make it a reality, that dream had begun to morph into an even more challenging Hollywood aspiration than I had imagined. I told myself "tomorrow will be better, and after all I'm only eighteen."

When I rented the $19-a-week studio apartment, my landlady had been kind enough to loan me a hot plate and a couple of pans so I could heat up some soup and boil water for tea. With my clock radio softly playing top forty hits, I pulled down the Murphy bed from my closet and sank into the mattress.

The disc jockey's voice was an assault on my ears. It seemed manic and insincere, not at all like the down-home style I would try to emulate when I became a jock. Ray Odom, my hero deejay on KHEP country radio, the number one station in Phoenix, would address his unseen audience as "Friends and Neighbors," while these L.A. guys seemed to be talking to themselves, in love with their own voices. Finally, he put a record on and I began to relax. I don't know if it was my long day of work, the ever-present loneliness, or the pure emotion that was streaming through the radio as Elvis sang his new hit "Don't," but gradually I drifted off into a reverie of memories and feelings.

♥

I had known for years that I wanted something unique and way more exciting than a traditional job in my hometown, and I couldn't wait to get started. In my senior year of high school I had signed up with an Army Reserve Unit and had begun attending weekly training sessions at my local armory. The military draft was still in force, and I had always felt a sense of patriotism and loyalty to my country. I realized I could get started pursuing my dreams and at the same time begin serving my country by attending weekly training sessions and two-week summer camps that would go on for seven years.

So, the day after high school graduation, I promised my love forever to Becky Brill, my childhood sweetheart, said a very final "goodbye" to my mom, dad, and two sisters on the tarmac of the Phoenix Sky Harbor Airport and boarded a twin engine Douglas C-53 for Fort Ord, near Monterey, California, to begin my six months of active duty.

I was discharged just in time to spend the holidays with Becky and my folks. Then I caught a ride to California with my high school buddy Benny who was on his way back to college in Pasadena. Benny dropped me off at the corner of Hollywood and Vine on New Year's Day, 1958. I was eighteen and I had come to seek my fortune. I set my duffle bag on the curb and checked my pocket to make sure they were still there: two twenties and a ten.

My body was lying on the bed, but my mind was miles away. As I began reliving my first eight weeks of basic training, I saw the drill sergeant's face pushing me and the rest of the recruits all day long to the limits of our endurance. I felt the endless runs through desert trails, thick with choking dust, and saw myself crawling across barbed-wired infiltration courses while live bullets whizzed above our heads. I involuntarily coughed with the memory of my forays into tear gas-filled buildings without a gas mask. But more terrifying than the bullets and the gas was my loneliness and being an introvert surrounded by a platoon of strangers.

More than anything, I think I survived those grueling weeks by listening to Little Richard, Sam Cooke, and Fats Domino on the local radio station in the evenings and by reading Becky's letters that arrived almost daily. I remember folding one of her letters and slipping it into the chest pocket of my T-shirt to keep it near my heart.

For the final four months of my service, I was assigned to Armed Forces Radio Service and transferred to the beautiful, park-like base called The Presidio in San Francisco. There, in the company of a smaller group, I was able to make some friends. We occupied our days with emceeing the Sixth Army Band syndicated radio show, announcing the titles of endless John Philip Sousa songs. I was finally a real radio announcer.

I soon found a way to steal some quiet time in the evenings. A short walk from my barracks, I discovered a beautiful military cemetery overlooking the Golden Gate Bridge and the angry foam-capped sea. Silently, I would talk to a silent God about my dreams and my fears as I surveyed the acres of rolling green hills garlanded with neat rows of white crosses that would disappear over the horizon, each representing a soul's ultimate sacrifice in the service of our country. I sat in wonder at how a landscape filled with so much sadness could bring me such feelings of peace.

Slowly, I was lured from my daydreams by the sound of boiling water. I sat up and poured hot water into my only cup. I dipped in a tea bag, smiled to myself, and opened the letter from Becky that had arrived that day. She wrote, "I finally talked my folks into giving us permission to get married."

I had always imagined that my heart would soar at this news, but unexpectedly my elation stopped midair, and my smile felt like it had frozen to my face. I thought about how much Becky trusted in our high school love and how much she was depending on me to include her in my dream of becoming a big success in L.A. I knew that I loved her and just hoped that my uneasiness would fade as I digested the unexpected news.

Before going to sleep that night, I wrote a postcard to radio station KHEP requesting Hank Locklin's "Send Me the Pillow That You Dream On" and dedicating it to her. I rested my elbows on the kitchen table to support my head as I heard myself saying a prayer out loud that everything would be all right. Still feeling unsure, I let myself fall into the escape of deep sleep.

On my second day in Hollywood, I had gotten up early, borrowed the Yellow Pages from my landlady, and copied down the addresses of all the print shops whose telephone numbers began with the prefix "HO" for Hollywood. I walked through downtown Hollywood, knocking on the door of each establishment, and by noon I had a job. At home I had learned early from my dad how to set movable type and how to operate the old hand-fed letter presses in our garage, feeding paper in and out of the platens as they quickly opened and closed. Later, I became proficient on the automated Heidelberg press at my after school job.

As I turned from Vine Street onto Santa Monica Boulevard, I noticed a sign that said Record Labels, Inc. When I entered the shop, I saw a heavyset lady with thick glasses sitting at a table, punching out the perforated holes in the center of record labels with a rubber hammer and a punch that looked like a screwdriver. She was very friendly and told me that I should talk to the owner, whose name was Mr. Rose, and motioned me in his direction.

An affable older gentleman greeted me warmly, pointed to a row of Heidelberg automatic presses and asked, "You know how to run one of these things?" I summoned up my most confident voice and told him "Sure, Heidelberg presses are my specialty," and he hired me on the spot. I said, "Thanks a lot, Mr. Rose." "Everyone calls me 'Rosey,'" he retorted. Rosey soon became a father figure to me and a source of security and trust. It made me eager to please him, and I did my best to hold up my end of the deal.

At my new job I learned to keep several presses operating at once, printing silver or black ink onto colorful sheets of paper and then die cutting them into round record labels with big holes in the middle for 45s and small ones for the long playing albums. We printed labels for Specialty, Chess, Checker, Imperial, Era, Gone, Ember, Del-Fi, and most of the other independent record companies that had proliferated since the advent of rock 'n' roll, springing up like mining towns during the gold rush.

So every morning I'd pack a brown paper bag, rationed with one lonely cheese sandwich, and walk the two miles to work, down Hollywood Boulevard, south on Vine Street, and east on Santa Monica Boulevard. The giant clock on the top of the Hollywood Ranch Market, with hands that spun around in triple time over the famous words "We Never Close," never failed to bring an involuntary smile to my face as I approached it each day. This kind of supermarket glamour had been missing from my Arizona experience. As I passed by the Ranch Market's sidewalk counter, I would purchase a three-cent frosted doughnut and drop it into the bag to keep the sandwich company.

♥

But it was a much smaller sign, glaring conspicuously in my line of vision as I walked to and from work every morning and evening, that began to inflame my interest. On a theater-style marquee that hung over the door of a small recording studio on Vine Street, someone had arranged the letters to read "Come In & See What Your Voice Sounds Like—$10." Every day, as I passed by, the sign would silently call to me. I'd sometimes turn and look back at it as I walked on. After a few days, I became intrigued by the sign and its implications. Soon intrigue turned to obsession!

One Saturday morning I got up my nerve and booked ten dollars worth of studio time. My heart pounding, I started with something I knew I could do: I laid down a Jerry Lee Lewis style piano track. Then, by sheer willpower, I forced myself to over dub some background vocals and sang lead on my version of "You Are My Sunshine." Although I was totally unaware of the musical influences that were flowing out of my mouth and into the microphone, as I look back, I'm sure they must have been a combination of the great country, black gospel, and R & B artists that had brought such joyful feelings into my young life—everyone from Fats Domino to Ricky Nelson.

When the sound engineer signaled me into the control booth I could feel my face turn beet red, but when he played the record back for me, I couldn't believe my ears. He had equalized the tracks and blended my voices together with tape echo. A wave of excitement broke over my fantasy that the tape sounded like a record I might hear on the radio. From that moment I was hooked. It was only weeks before I dropped out of disc jockey school and was spending every Saturday, and nearly all the money I was earning at the print shop, making music at Fidelity Recorders.

One day, a fellow stuck his head in the studio door and asked, "Anyone in here play the banjo?" I raised my hand involuntarily and managed a shy, "I do." I quickly stifled the flutter of apprehension that I might not be able to fulfill the man's expectations and followed him down the street to Music City, the famous music store on the corner of Sunset and Vine where the man rented a tenor banjo.

Then he took me to another little studio across the street from Fidelity, where he set up a microphone and instructed me to strum along on the banjo as I sang "Red River Valley" and "Oh, Susanna." More than likely, it was a lucrative movie or TV background score for the producer, but he handed me a ten spot after the session and I left with my head in the air. "Yippee!" I thought to myself, "I just turned professional!"

These were just a couple of the old folk songs I had learned around a campfire at Pine Flats Camp Grounds in Northern Arizona's Oak Creek Canyon. Before I turned eighteen, every year in June, our family friends, the Kidds—Bob Kidd, his wife, Leota Kidd, and their two Kidd kids, Clyde and Christina—would set up their summer quarters. It was a compound of tents, picnic tables, and campfire pits in the beautiful red-rock country near Sedona.

In Phoenix in 1948, there was no central air conditioning. The only weapon we had to use against temperatures that climbed into triple digits on summer days was an old swamp cooler. Even then the temperatures indoors would be full of humidity and in the high nineties. So, when

"Uncle Bob" would call on a Thursday evening to invite me to spend a few weeks with his family in cool Oak Creek, I'd lie awake most of the night in eager anticipation.

It was an idyllic time for me. Leota would make mounds of pancakes, eggs, and bacon and then send us off on our own for endless hours of roaming, playing, fishing, and mountain climbing. In the evenings, around the campfire, Leota would strum her guitar and lead us in camp songs. Then we would roast marshmallows and trade ghost stories on into the night.

Had the river of circumstance flowed another way, Leota could well have been another Tammy Wynette or Loretta Lynn. She had that kind of sincere, pure, soulful Oklahoma voice that cut through the evening air and made you feel the truth in every emotion she sang. She was probably my first real musical influence.

CHAPTER 2

You Sound Pretty Good, Kid, But . . .

My earliest school years were flavored by religious underpinnings, nurtured by my devout parents and the church we all attended regularly. Right from the first grade, as I walked the mile from our little house down Central Avenue to Osborn School I would spend the time softly singing and talking to God from my heart. I was a young believer in the spiritual way of life that I would hear espoused from our church pulpit.

But as I grew older, I also became secretly fascinated by supernatural ideas that were far beyond the confines of our church orthodoxy. I remember one day stumbling on a small ad in the back of my dad's *Popular Science* magazine: "Ancient searchers for truth uncover amazing discoveries of laws that unlock the inner powers that reside within you."

My imagination was sparked by the mystical sounding Rosicrucian ad and the implications that there may be something more to life than I was hearing in church three times a week. Without telling my parents, I filled out the little form and sent it off for my free copy of *The Mastery of Life*.

I never shared my Rosicrucian connection with anyone, but I held to the hope that it could help me find that part of me I felt was somehow missing. The principles of Rosicrucianism opened me even more to looking for my own source of inner wisdom and guidance. Unseen by anyone, I began to look at life in a different light—one coming from the possibility that I had power and wisdom enough to create my own future.

Throughout early grade school, I preferred to keep to myself, both physically and emotionally. Mom was my world. Always hyperaware of how she was being perceived, she expected exemplary behavior from me, and I would do anything not to disappoint her. She had given me so much love, positive reinforcement, and praise during my pre-school days that it took me a couple of years to adjust to the real world of public school. During my earliest school years, even the slightest hint of criticism from my teachers would start an involuntary flow of tears rolling down my young cheeks.

It was that positive self-image that my mom's support had helped develop in me during those formative years that I have drawn on throughout my life. It always made me feel that if I worked hard enough, I could do anything I set my mind to. And, over the years, it was that constant effort that gradually allowed me to strengthen my immature emotions and start to emerge from my protective shell.

I took a giant leap forward my first year at Phoenix Christian High School. In private school, I didn't seem so geeky. I now had a cute girl-friend and soon became good friends with a small circle of hang-out buddies. Benny Lindsay had a lot to do with that. He was the all-state star of our basketball team and drove a '57 blue Mercury, the nicest car driven by anyone in our grade. Everyone wanted to ride with Benny, and he would usually let me be one of the five guys in the car, whether attending school events or dragging Central Avenue on the weekends. One of my favorite pastimes in my lonely Hollywood apartment was reminiscing about those days. But I remember catching myself one evening thinking, "High school's over now, and it's time to set my mind on my future."

♥

After a few weeks, some people around the little recording studio began to take notice of the music I was making there on Saturday mornings. One day, a kind stranger told me, "You should go down and see this record producer by the name of Jesse Hodges. He's had pretty good luck at getting labels to sign his singers, and I think he'll like the way you sound."

With a mix of apprehension and excitement, after work the next day I took the stranger's advice and walked the ten blocks down Sunset Boulevard to an office mall of quaint little freestanding English-style houses called *Crossroads of the World*. There were several music business listings on the directory. But I soon found the number I was looking for and walked into Jesse's small office.

Jesse Hodges was a young man, about thirty years old, who smoked cigars and spoke with an easy Southern drawl. I looked down at my shoes in trepidation for the entire time as he listened to "You Are My Sunshine" coming from the resin-coated metal disc they called an acetate. When it was finished, he smiled and said, "You sound pretty good, kid, but what I'm looking for are singers who have their own material. Go home and write some songs and then come back and see me."

I entertained no feeling of rejection from this critique. Far from it, I left Jesse's office thinking I was just one hit song away from stardom. I didn't know it then, but that was some of the best advice I ever got. Learning how to create a musical piece out of thin air was a new concept to me. My self-image had taken me as far as creating my own vocal recording of somebody else's song, but now I had been challenged with opening my mind to the value and possibilities of becoming the creator of unique products and services. Jesse was planting life-long perennial seeds of success in the heart of a future songwriter/producer.

Well, I had never written a song before, but Jesse said to do it, so I went to my apartment, picked up my guitar and started writing. A couple of nights later, I took my guitar out into the hallway, inserted some coins into the public phone on the wall, dialed Becky's number and played her the songs. One, I had written in her honor, an up-tempo, three chord, Elvis-style rocker called "Becky Baby."

As the final chord rang out, I ventured an excited "What do you think?" hoping for some encouragement from my first audience. The line was silent for a moment and then Becky said, "The song is beautiful and you sound great on it. I will remember this moment forever. I just know you're gonna make it, and I can't wait till I'm there to share it with you."

When I was satisfied with my three new rockabilly "masterpieces" I booked some recording time at Fidelity Studios. I called a young drummer I had met there and hired him to help me cut the demonstration records. This would be my debut at playing the role of record producer. I asked, "It's going to be just the two of us, so can you give me a lot of drums?" He understood immediately and filled up all the empty spaces between the words with raucous D. J. Fontana-style drum licks.

Looking back now, the songs seem pretty amateurish, but when I played them for Jesse, his face lit up like he had won the lottery. He signed me to a management/recording artist contract on the spot. Then he said, "You're part of the family now, so feel free to stop by the office whenever you like."

I called "Becky Baby" back in Arizona to tell her the news: I had been signed as a recording artist within four months of hitting town. I was an exploding comet of energy when Becky and I talked. It wasn't until hours after we hung up that I began to sense that, although her excitement for me was sincere, it was not the only thing she wanted to talk about that evening. Although I knew I should call her back, the thought kept getting crowded out by my excited visions of pop stardom. I put off making the call until the hour was too late.

CHAPTER 3

Guess What? I Picked Out My Wedding Dress Today!

The music business turned out to be more complicated than I realized. At our next meeting, Jesse Hodges laid out his unique business scheme. In one three-hour union recording session, using top musicians and studios, he would produce four songs: an "A" side and a "B" side for two different singers. But the rub was that the two singers, and all the co-writers of the four songs, were expected to pony up $400 each to fund the recording date.

By mid-summer Jesse had scheduled my recording session. There was only one problem. My prospects of coming up with four hundred dollars were about as good as Jesse's chances of winning the lottery. When I talked to my parents that month, I never mentioned my dilemma. I also knew that they really didn't have it to give. I had chosen my own independent path and my parents' well-being was more valuable than any shortcut on the way to my dream.

A month earlier, I had taken on a roommate, a friend from Arizona who had also come to Hollywood to go to disc jockey school. When he heard about my dilemma, he was determined that I would not miss my big opportunity for stardom. At the last moment, he called his parents. They said they would like to help, and the most they could lend me was $250.

A couple of weeks before the big day, I went to Jesse's office with my head held low and dejectedly told him that we would have to cancel the session. "Hey," he said, "don't worry about it, we'll find the rest of the money somewhere." My new manager/producer was the first of many music business personalities over the years who would play the part of protagonist or antagonist in my own personal drama. Heroes or villains, they all would become enlightening examples or teachers in my education of not only how variable and crazy the music world can be, but also in the action adventure-love story that was unfolding as my life.

That evening I took a long walk down the Boulevard. In 1958 Hollywood Boulevard was (and still is) the Times Square of the West, seedy and glamorous at the same time. At the street level, drunks, transients, and hustlers walked the dirty sidewalks a decade before the Walk of Fame stars were carved into them. But you only had to lift your eyes skyward to find the glitter and glitz of brightly lit billboards, swirling spotlights illuminating the evening sky, and the flashing animated neon signs that hawked Coca-Cola and Chesterfields until the sun came up.

The world of Hollywood seemed to revolve a universe away from the Pentecostal Church in Phoenix where I grew up. I attended church with my family several times a week, and I couldn't wait to go. It was tambourine-shaking Southern gospel—spirited, soulful, and one of the main breeding grounds for what was soon to be known as "rock 'n' roll." My dad played the tenor banjo in the church orchestra, and he taught me some chords. It was the first instrument I played just for fun. Later, I got a tenor guitar for my birthday. It had four strings and tuned the same way as the banjo so I could play it right away.

Ours was a lower middle class family. We were well off enough to have a small, detached garage behind our home and poor enough that the garage door opener was me. Dad always seemed to earn enough money for our necessities, but in the early days we rarely ate in restaurants. In my childhood, twin bicycles were dad and mom's mode of transportation and my seat would be one of the baskets on their handlebars. I was in my teens before the family could afford a used Chevy Impala.

One evening when I was about seven or eight, a door-to-door salesman from a national music school called at our Lexington Avenue home. He asked, "Wouldn't you like to learn how to play a musical instrument, Sonny?" When I was told I could pick any instrument I wanted, I chose the six-string electric guitar. But the salesman said, "The guitar is a very difficult instrument for a beginner. Why don't you start with something easier like the violin?" My parents were not sophisticated enough to notice the absurdity of this argument, so they signed me up. Of course, we later found out that the school only taught violin classes.

My piano teacher did me one better. After years of trying to teach me to sight-read classical pieces one note at a time, she finally took pity on me and gave me a book that showed how to play simple triad chords. A whole new world opened up for me that day. I learned three chords, and right away I could play my favorite songs from the radio. Later, during my high school years, I studied stride piano from veteran jazzman Sharon Pease, paying for my own lessons. I learned more in six months from him than I had in six years of classical instruction.

One summer when I was around fourteen, I drove with my family in our friend's pickup truck to attend a week of revival meetings at a sister church in Lubbock, Texas. During the services, I immediately zeroed in on a very attractive "older" lady—she was probably in her thirties—and the exciting soulful music she was making on the church organ. Thus began my lifelong romance with the Hammond B-3. My folks arranged for her to give me three or four lessons during the week we were there, and the Hammond B-3 organ has been my instrument of choice ever since.

By my teens, our minister would often call on me to play the church piano or the Hammond B-3 for the congregational singing, and almost as often he would admonish me afterwards to tone down the rock 'n' roll treatment I'd be giving to the old hymns. I had found the passkey to more fully expressing myself.

♥

Finally, the big day arrived. I guess you could say I was floating on air as I entered Radio Recorders for my first session as a professional singer. Jesse had coached me in his office the day before, and I did some last minute practicing, singing out loud as I walked down Santa Monica Boulevard from the print shop to the studio. Jesse had not only booked a first-class studio, but as I was about to learn, also a top flight crew of musicians. Through the glass in the sound booth, Jesse pointed out the session players who were tuning up their instruments in the large studio, and I couldn't believe that these guys would be playing on *my* session.

There was Earl Palmer, the great New Orleans drummer who had played on hits for Fats Domino, the Everly Brothers, James Brown, Ray Charles, and Pat Boone, who was tuning up his kit to play on *my* record. And set up in a row on his left were three phenomenal guitarists. For years I had watched Neil Lavang play his electric guitar every Saturday evening on *The Lawrence Welk Show* and, to me, he was a star. And, playing twin acoustic six-string guitars were Rockabilly pioneers, Johnny and Dorsey Burnette, generally recognized (along with Elvis and Gene Vincent) as being the fathers of rockabilly.

The number one tune on the Billboard charts that week was an infectious instrumental that sounded like it came straight out of a smoky Tijuana nightclub. It was called "Tequila." And rounding out my session players was one of the men responsible for creating it: Danny Flores (aka Chuck Rio) of the Champs. It's his caricature voice that can be heard reciting the title, "Tequila!" at the drum breaks.

Jesse put me in the glass-walled vocal booth along with his partner, Donnie Brooks, who stood about twelve inches in front of my face, energetically mouthing the words to the songs in an effort to animate my performances. I had not written "Love, Whatcha Doin' To Me" and "Stop Talkin, Start Lovin," the songs that Jesse selected for my session, but I tried to put everything I had into my rendition of them. When I finished, everyone seemed very pleased with my performance.

In the next weeks, as I waited for Jesse to place my record with a label, I hung around his office and became friends with Donnie Brooks and the Burnette Brothers. Donnie, three years my senior, had been recording since he was twenty-one, finally finding success with a top-ten song called "Mission Bell." Donnie became like a big brother and a mentor to me. Hanging out with guys already successful in the business was a boost to my self-esteem, and more and more I started to believe that I could make it too.

Soon Jesse Hodges' fertile mind spawned yet another creative marketing idea. In those years, it wasn't unusual for several artists to record the same song. And under the song titles on the *Billboard* and *Cashbox* top 100 charts, *all* of the singers who had released the song would be listed, no matter which one had recorded the hit version. Jesse decided that he could get some great publicity for his artists simply by having them record a song that was already on the charts and releasing it on the "B" sides of their next singles. Voila! His artists' names would immediately appear on the charts.

At my nine to five job, I was learning a lot about the record business. By the size of the label orders, I could easily tell what records were breaking to become hits, even before the trade magazines knew. Jesse explained his plan and I agreed to help by keeping a sharp eye on the printing orders. Soon I reported back to Jesse that the new Ritchie Valens single, "Come On Let's Go," was taking off like gangbusters. Jesse had a green light to put his new scheme into action.

A few mornings later, as I walked into work, Rosey motioned me into his tiny office with a solemn stare. Word had somehow leaked out of Jesse's plan and my involvement. The owner of the record pressing plant next door, our biggest client, had already been in to see Rosey and he had demanded my termination. I tried to protest that our scheme was just a harmless way to get some publicity, but Rosey explained that Ritchie Valens' record company hadn't seen it that way.

Mercifully, he chose to give me a stern lecture about the questionable ethics of "insider trading," and a second chance. I grew up a little bit that scary morning. Rosey had taught me an important lesson about loyalty by defining for me the difference between being a communicator and a snitch. But most of all, it was the example of his loyalty and trust in me that changed me for the better in many ways.

Arriving home from the print shop one evening in late October, I retrieved one of Becky's regular letters from the mailbox. I laid it on the table, picked up my guitar and began working on a new song that had been rolling around in my head. Later, when I opened her letter, Becky's first words shocked me out of my musical daydreams and squarely back into reality.

"Guess what, Mom and I went down and picked out my wedding dress today," she wrote, "and my folks said we could have the wedding next month." I had loved her since she was twelve, and we had always talked about getting married someday. But four hundred miles away in Hollywood, with my head in the clouds over my budding new singing career, those teenage conversations seemed to have faded far into the past, and "someday" had slipped into the distant future.

I walked out to the hall payphone and called Becky to discuss the situation. "I know we always talked about getting married," I began, "and you know I love you, but . . ." She was crestfallen and I could tell that she was silently crying on the other end of the phone. I said "I'm sorry, Baby. Of course, I want to marry you." We set the date for November 15th.

I broke the news to Jesse the next day that I would be driving to Phoenix in a couple of weeks to marry my high school sweetheart. I knew he would think that this was not a good business move for his new artist. In the early sixties, recording stars were expected to be cute, young, and available, and maintaining this image was a source of employment for many a public relations agent. I braced myself for a fierce argument, but Jesse just smiled and said, "Congratulations!"

Better Keep Your Day Job

Becky looked beautiful when I picked her up for breakfast and some last minute shopping the morning of our wedding. Her eyes were dancing with happiness, and once again I remembered how deeply and how long I had loved her.

We met when she was twelve and I was fourteen at a Sunday afternoon revival meeting at a Phoenix church called Fellowship Tabernacle. She was sitting with her sisters four or five rows ahead, and she turned around, smiled, and winked at me! No member of the opposite sex had ever shown me that kind of attention before. I was smitten. After that, of course, I began attending Becky's church as much as possible, arriving (with permission from my dad but not the Department of Motor Vehicles) on his little, red Cushman motor scooter.

Our time together was limited to church meetings and telephone conversations until I was old enough to drive. Then, when Becky attended Phoenix Christian High a year behind me, I picked her up each morning for school and the romance began to heat up. Our relationship had its ups and downs, and we had maintained varying degrees of closeness in the five years that had passed. But in my whole life, I had never considered anyone else to be my girlfriend.

Becky and her father appeared at the back of the church and the lady playing the organ began the wedding march. My heart started pounding so loudly in my chest that I suspected my best man Benny could hear it, too. As they approached, Becky looked long and deep at me, her eyes shining with innocence and youth. A wave of love and gratitude washed over me, overwhelming my nervousness, as I took in the magical moment.

Becky's dad gave me a warm smile and gestured for me to take her hand, breaking the spell and reviving my anxiety as he began the ceremony.

Flying through the midnight desert in Benny's Mercury with Becky snuggled close, her head on my shoulder and her arms around me, felt like the freest moment of my life. The loneliness of my first year of living in a seedy part of a big city was behind me, and I now had someone I loved to share my adventure with. We got a few hours of sleep at a motel in Blythe and still made it to Hollywood by Sunday noon. I had rented us an apartment with an Olympic size pool in a large new complex called the Beachcomber. It was nicer than my first apartment building and closer to the print shop.

♥

The glow of our honeymoon was still shimmering brightly in the spring of 1959 when I finally got the call I had been waiting for. Jesse had sold my record to a small independent company called Radio Records. It was owned by Fabor Robinson, a southern gentleman who had garnered some success, mostly with country acts like Bonnie Guitar and Jim Reeves, and he was now venturing into rockabilly artists. Although I didn't know it at the time, I guess that's what I was. Becky squealed when I told her the news: I had my first label deal!

When Jesse handed me the Radio Records contract, I thought I was supposed to sign my full legal name. So I wrote "Robert Luke Harshman." In our family, Robert was my dad. Everyone had always called me Luke. But once I started recording, Becky and I thought that a good stage name for me would be Bobby Harshman. So when my record was released on my birthday in February of 1959 I was surprised to see that the label read "Love Whatcha' Doin' To Me," by Robert Luke Harshman."

One day on my lunch hour, I broke the news to Rosey that Fabor Robinson had organized a weeklong promotion tour. Although he had grudgingly let me use his presses to print fliers and Bobby Harshman Fan Club membership cards, Rosey had always been suspicious of my dreams of stardom. I suspect he had seen too many wide-eyed Hollywood hopefuls come and go. Now my dreams were interfering with his production line.

I pleaded that I needed only one week off, but he took a hard line and asked me to choose between my only means of support and my "fictitious" career. I gave him my notice without hesitation. Seeing the disappointment in Rosey's eyes made me feel like I was losing a friend, one who had put his trust in me when I needed a job and even stood by me during the Ritchie Vallens incident. I sensed that Rosey was sure he was only looking out for my best interests. But my dream was starting to materialize like a red balloon floating above, and for me, there was no other choice but to follow it.

The tour consisted of driving in Fabor's late model black Cadillac sedan from L.A. to San Francisco and stopping at every radio transmission tower we spotted on the horizon. He was the driver; I was the lookout. Fabor gave me a short tutorial on how a star should look and act. He showed me how I should carry myself in public and even patiently gave me a lesson in how to manicure my fingernails, under which were probably still embedded the traces of black printer's ink.

During a rest stop alongside the highway, Fabor demonstrated how "stars" walk into a room, flash a roguish smile to the girls in the radio station, and create mystery by not really giving straight answers during interviews. It was like a different language to me, disingenuous and foreign to my nature, but I smiled shyly, trying to picture myself in this new role. Then Fabor commented in that world-wise way of his, "With a little more practice, you could learn to do it just as well as James Dean."

I thought I was on my way to stardom. I did my mysterious interviews, and the deejays would give my record a spin on the air right then and there. But when we left town, they'd go back to playing the Platters, the McGuire Sisters, or the Everly Brothers. A week later I was back with Becky in L.A., without a hit, without a job, disappointed, and a little concerned about our immediate survival. Someone had stuck a pin in my shiny red balloon.

CHAPTER 5

Two Ways to Work the Night Shift

A day before, I'd been speeding toward my dreams in a golden halo of light and excitement. Now, back in L.A., I'd been dropped into a deep, dark pit of fear and despondency. I had no career, no job, no prospects. After a couple of days, I'd had enough! For a year now, I'd been out on my own, dreaming my own dreams and calling all the shots. This was my time, and there was no way I would give myself permission to be faint of heart.

Becky had always encouraged my dreams, no matter how fanciful. And now her unconditional support and the sense of humor that had always been our connection jolted me out of my slump. It took every ounce of determination that I could muster to renounce the fear, pry myself off the floor, and place my concentration on trying to pick up the pieces of my life. "It's a new day," I told myself. "Let me just start over."

I jumped onto an early morning city bus to downtown L.A. and sat alone in the rear where I could feel more comfortable saying a prayer for deliverance from the financial mess I had put myself in. I soon found the showroom of the distributor where they sold Heidelberg printing presses. I was happy when a friendly salesman told me that they had a waiting list for someone with my rare expertise in running their machines. Beginning on that day, he would send me out to print shops in the greater Los Angeles area. When the work ran out or the commute proved to be too long, he'd give me another address for the next day.

I'd leave bright and early, ride the bus to the print shop du jour, work all day, and ride the bus home. Becky would spend her days as most housewives of the 1950s did, doing laundry, cleaning, and being ready to welcome her husband home with a nice meal. After a few months, Rosey called and asked if I'd come back to Record Labels, Inc. to work the evening shift. I was grateful for the opportunity to return his gesture of loyalty and immediately said yes.

On some weekends, the Burnette Brothers would pick me up in their late model Cadillac, and we'd drive the hundred miles to Bakersfield or Fresno where we would perform at the barn dance shows with other rockabilly acts like Bobby Lee Trammell and Johnny Russell. My knees were a little wobbly at first, but it was a great opportunity to hone my fledgling performance skills in front of a live band and a livelier audience. It was an eye-opening experience to live the life of a traveling musician, and I awkwardly tried to fit in while avoiding the booze, blood, and bad jokes.

After five hours of performing, listening to great music, and watching the couples dance and drink and drink and dance, more often than not the obligatory bar-room fistfight would be our cue to jump into the car. Then we would fly like the wind, heading home to Hollywood, just barely beating the sunrise.

♥

As a kid, I was fascinated by everything that came over my little radio. But it was the *music* on my radio that really made me feel something. I had never identified with what they called popular music in the early fifties. I found it to be sanitized and soulless, so I listened exclusively to the country stations. I loved T. Texas Tyler singing "Remember Me" and Web Pierce's "There Stands the Glass." When Elvis Presley created a whole new musical genre in 1955, KHEP, my local country station, was the first to play his records. My favorite deejay, Ray Odom, played Carl Perkins, Buddy Knox, Gene Vincent, Sanford Clark, and all the rockabilly guys.

As a young teenager, I was also heavy into groups like the Moonglows and the Penguins and soloists like Fats Domino and LaVern Baker. To hear their recordings I would have to go out of my way, driving to the record stores in the black section of South Phoenix or listening to a local station that played what they were calling "race music." It was there that I was introduced to and fell in love with black gospel music and its great proponents like Professor Alex Bradford and Sister Rosetta Tharpe.

When I heard snippets of news about the civil rights movement and how Rosa Parks had refused to give up her seat to a white man on a bus in Montgomery, Alabama, I somehow felt a kinship with the victims of racism because of my love for this great music and these wonderful black artists. There were no African-American kids at Phoenix Christian High, and I don't pretend that I was fully tuned in to the civil rights situation locally or nationally, but I know that I felt something was wrong about it all and that it created a feeling of connection between the black music artists and me.

♥

My string of ordinary days at the print shop was suddenly broken one morning when I got a call from Jesse. He said, "I just heard about this rockabilly tour of three cities in West Texas that's gonna happen next weekend. I pulled some favors and got you booked on it." The concert promoter had chartered an airplane to fly a bevy of California rockers to perform shows in El Paso, Amarillo, and Midland-Odessa. I felt the blood rush to my heart, excited for the break, but a little nervous because this time I'd be touring with the stars.

By Sunday we had arrived in Midland-Odessa to perform our last show of the tour. At the airport I was assigned a driver to look after me while I was in town. He flashed a big smile and said "Hi, I'm Joe Melson. If there's anything I can do for you, just let me know." He was a friendly, outgoing Texan who looked to be about my age. He treated me like royalty, and throughout the day we spent together he acted more like a fan than a personal assistant.

As we drove from the airport, it couldn't have been more than five minutes before I suddenly heard my voice coming over the radio. Apparently the local radio stations had been playing my songs in heavy rotation to promote the show. It's hard to explain what it's like to hear your record on the air for the first time. I kept my cool on the outside, but fireworks were going off inside.

Joe told me how much he loved my music. He said that my records were really big in Midland-Odessa, and he must have assumed it was the same all over the country. I think he honestly believed that I was a big star.

That evening, I sang my two songs to an enthusiastic Texas audience. Before going on, I had watched from the wings as the deejay/emcee introduced a young local singer who had been booked to open the show. He was dressed in black and wore horn-rimmed glasses, which led me to think that Buddy Holly must also have been one of his heroes. Unlike most of our crew of rockers from California, he didn't move around much when he performed. He just stood there, strumming his guitar and singing "Whole Lot of Shakin' Goin' On" and a couple of other cover songs. But, even now, I remember being struck by his vocal range and the clear-throated sound that was distinctly his own.

The next time I heard that amazing voice was early the following year when Roy Orbison's first Monument record, *Uptown,* was released. In the next two years Roy Orbison would offer to the world an amazing catalog of work that would firmly establish forever his own unique genre of music: unmistakable, haunting, crystal-clear vocals that would soar to a crescendo over cleverly constructed chord progressions and three-minute lyrical stories, more operetta than pop song. My opening act was now one of rock's most enduring superstars.

It was years before it hit me: One evening while browsing at Tower Records, I began reading the writer's credits on a vinyl Roy Orbison greatest hits LP. I noticed that Orbison had a co-writer on his classic hit songs, "Uptown," "Only the Lonely," "Blue Angel," "I'm Hurtin'," "Crying," "The Crowd," "Blue Bayou" and, yes, on "Running Scared." On the writer's credit line, in parentheses under every one of these great songs, were the words: (Roy Orbison/Joe Melson)

I don't know if Joe Melson, my personal driver, had already met Roy Orbison by the time I got to Odessa for the show, or if they hooked up shortly after. I do know that their first collaboration was on the charts just a few months later. And I like to fantasize that Joe got to talking with Roy while I was singing "Love Whatcha Doin' To Me" on that stage in Odessa, Texas, in the summer of 1959.

♥

In June, Fabor Robinson decided it was time to record my second single. He picked two songs that had been hits a decade before, "Girl of My Dreams" and "Is You Is or Is You Ain't My Baby." Fabor booked Western Studio One on a Sunday, my day off from work, and hired a band of great country/rockabilly musicians. When I got to the studio, I discovered that Fabor had also hired a family group called the Blackwells to sing the background parts. Dewayne Blackwell and his two sisters had a very commercial, tight sound, and their friendly personalities gave me moral support as I tried to put a new spin on two old songs that I wasn't too sure were right for a nineteen year old rock 'n' roller.

As I sang my lead vocals, Becky and the two Blackwell girls smiled and cheered me on from behind the glass control room window. Fabor protested at one point when he thought I was trying to "Elvis the song up" a little too much, but his objections were overruled by the girls' screams of approval.

By the time my second record came out, Fabor had sold his company to a New York firm with national distribution, so "Girl Of My Dreams" came out on Guyden Records. It didn't help. I promptly had another bomb. This time, I kept my day job and was grateful to have it. My fledgling confidence and faith in myself as a singer had taken a substantial hit, but once again, I forced myself to see it as only a momentary setback. I steeled my resolve to never stop trusting that my talent, sacrifices, and hard work would pay off for Becky and me. I kept on praying and trying. What else could I do?

CHAPTER 6

The Control Room Door Flew Open

"Hey, Bobby! I want you to meet my friend, Curtis Lee. He sings really good and I thought since you're a big star now, with a recording contract and all, maybe you could help Curt get discovered." Our best man, Benny, was at the door of our Beachcomber apartment, and standing just behind him was a tall, good-looking fellow with blond hair and cut muscles popping through his T-shirt.

Benny had developed the habit of driving over from Pasadena College on the weekends to hang out with Becky and me in "glamorous" Hollywood. Our apartment was basically one room, but Becky was a good sport. She made up pallets on the kitchen floor, just over the open bar counter from the sofa bed where we slept, so the guys could stay overnight, heads facing the other side of the sink.

Curtis was outgoing and fun-loving. While Becky brought out the iced tea he told me that he was from Yuma and had been singing all his life in church. Benny said he had heard Curt solo with the school choir and been impressed. I let the two of them know that I'd be happy to introduce Curtis to my record producer/manager. After a pizza lunch, Benny, Curtis, Becky, and I tracked Jesse down at a little studio near Sunset and Gower where he was producing a demo of a new song.

As we walked in from the bright July sunlight, it took a few minutes for our eyes to adjust to the subdued lighting that seems to come standard in all studios. Jesse was seated at the console between the sound engineer and another gentleman, preparing to add a lead vocal to his freshly recorded music track. Jesse looked up, giving us a friendly nod, and I quickly introduced him to Benny and Curtis. Jesse, in turn, introduced us to pioneering rock songwriter, John Marascalco, who had written the song they were recording that day. We stood quietly against the back wall of the control room as Jesse asked the engineer to roll the track for the artist in the vocal booth.

We couldn't see the singer from where we standing, and as the catchy, up-tempo intro played, we waited to hear what would come out of the darkened studio. As soon as the first verse started, Becky, Benny, Curtis, and I shot each other nods and glances of approval of the smooth, energetic, youthful voice that was streaming like a ribbon of sunshine from the control room's loud speakers. After only a couple of takes, Jesse seemed pleased. He pushed the talkback button and asked the singer to come in and take a listen.

The heavy control room door flew open like a sheet in the wind, and a smiling, excited, slight teenager bounded into the room. Our eyes were glued on him as he approached. He quickly scanned the room, acknowledging the four strangers with a quick nod as his eyes passed ours. Jesse hit play on the master tape and everyone was totally silent during the playback. When it finished, the group gave out simultaneous expressions of appreciation. Jesse stood up and introduced us to his singer. "Everyone, I'd like you to meet Tommy Boyce." Jesse told Tommy that I was one of his recording artists and that my second single was out on Guyden Records. Before we left, Tommy said, "Good luck with the record, man." Then he invited us all to attend a party that evening at the house of one of his friends.

It had taken only a few moments in the studio to notice that Tommy Boyce possessed a very unusual personality, spontaneous and extroverted, yet very cool at the same time. He carried himself with the confidence of an established rock star and yet his fast-paced speech came in unrehearsed fits of irrepressible charm. Tommy had a genuine smile and a confident handshake, but he also had a cockiness about him that was a little over-the-top for four laid-back kids from Arizona.

Benny, Curtis, Becky, and I found the address in the foothills above Franklin and under the Hollywood sign. It was the first time any of us had ever attended a Hollywood party, and everyone was very excited. I tried to look casual from halfway across the room as I watched and listened to Tommy holding court. Just as in the studio, his demeanor, body language, and charismatic energy communicated that he was the "star" in the room. He and I didn't speak much that evening, although he did ask Becky to dance and she was quite charmed by him. Tommy and Curtis seemed to hit it off right away.

I listened as Tommy told a couple of girls how his parents had first met. He said his dad had dreamed of stardom for himself, but he didn't have much of a voice. So the first time he heard Evelyn's beautiful singing voice, he asked her to marry him, thinking that with her voice and his skills at self-promotion, the two of them could conceive a superstar kid.

Later in the evening, someone asked Tommy to sing. Feigning shyness while appreciating that every eye was on him, he "reluctantly" made his way to the old upright piano in the corner where he played and sang a couple of up-tempo songs. I watched with admiration at how he captivated the attention of the group—especially the girls. I wondered to myself why I could be so much more comfortable performing on stage in front of a large crowd than I could ever be singing to just a few people at a party. I supposed that the answer had something to do with the amount of distance between me and my audience. I was also surprised to see that the obvious contrast between my personality and Tommy's was bringing out feelings of insecurity that I was sure I had already conquered.

After that night, I would run into Tommy Boyce from time to time at Jesse's office. Tommy was my age my height and build. Fresh out of high school, he was still living in the L.A. suburb of Highland Park with his mother Evelyn and his city-bus driver father, a true Southern character who called himself "Sid the Virginia Kid." He talked freely about how his early musical influences had really been his father's heroes: Ernest Tubb, Hank Williams, and the old blues yodeler, Jimmie Rodgers. But a turning point in his life came when his mother, who worked in the ticket window of the local movie theater, took Tommy along on a Saturday, where he watched *The Al Jolson Story* six times in a row. From that point on, he began to see himself as an entertainer with a wider audience than just the country market.

Sid was Tommy's biggest supporter. On his days off he would hit the streets of Hollywood, pounding on the doors of record companies and managers to promote his son. On weekends Sid would take Tommy around to the local talent shows, and then he'd work the back of the room, organizing a contingency of young ladies to scream their approval when Tommy would appear.

Soon after his first big weekend in Hollywood, Curtis Lee played hooky from Pasadena College and had a meeting with Jesse Hodges who offered him his standard deal. Within a few weeks Curtis had elicited some financial help from his folks and made his first record with Jesse producing. Before I knew it, he had dropped out of college and rented a room above a paint store in a dilapidated old building on the corner of St. Monica Boulevard and Vine, half a block from where I worked and a couple of blocks from where we lived. We'd often see Curt on the weekends, especially when Benny came to see us.

That spring Benny returned to Phoenix where he enrolled in Grand Canyon College to continue his higher education. Then over the summer months Curtis began to hang out more and more with Tommy. I think maybe the two bachelors figured that when it came to meeting girls, they could do better on their own without the "old" married couple around. On most weekends Tommy would drive his dad's car in from Highland Park to Hollywood, and sometimes Becky and I would run into him and Curtis on the Boulevard.

♥

On a chilly October evening in 1959, Becky and I were enjoying our usual stroll down Hollywood Boulevard. The circus of extremes for the senses with its bright lights and colorful characters was still about the only form of entertainment that we could afford. As we passed Johnny's Steak House, we ran into Curtis and Tommy, who were enjoying the same affordable pastime. We told them our good news; we had just found out that Becky and I were expecting our first child!

Then, Curt told us Tommy's good news: one of his songs had been recorded by rock 'n' roll legend and one of my high school heroes,

Fats Domino! Becky and I were elated at the news and the four of us exchanged spirited congratulations. That elusive dream of success in the music business, which until that moment had seemed so far away, was finally becoming a reality for one of our own young crowd. Somehow, that made it seem more attainable for all of us.

CHAPTER 7

By the Way, I Changed Your Name

Tommy and Curtis stopped by the apartment one evening early in the following year. When Curt asked me if I had written anything lately, I brought out my guitar and played them something I had just finished called "Dr. Heartache." Curt got really excited about the song and asked me if he could record it. Tommy didn't say much, but I could tell that it might have been the first time he was a little impressed by my abilities as a songsmith. He seemed to look at me in a different light after that.

When Curtis went home to Yuma that summer, Tommy began spending time with Becky and me on the weekends. Hanging out with Tommy was always a blast! In contrast to my own laid-back nature, Tommy's energy level was always engaging and full throttle. He had a distinctive, machine-gun style of speaking that would inevitably be picked up and emulated by anyone who hung around with him. Sometimes his brain would spin so fast that his mouth couldn't keep up, and he'd start to stutter, then catch himself and break into his infectious trademark laugh. One of Tommy's most endearing qualities was his ability to laugh at himself.

On the weekends Tommy, Becky, and I would often have dinner together in Hollywood, walk the Boulevard, and then head back to our apartment to work on each other's songs. I helped him with his, and he helped me with mine, with neither of us taking co-writing credit on the other's songs. More and more he was becoming like family. When our first son, Bobby Jr., was born July 8, 1960, Tommy went with me to be with Becky in the hospital.

A few weeks before Bobby Jr.'s arrival, we ran into an artist manager named Lee Silver on the street outside Capitol Records, and Tommy introduced me to him. One Saturday afternoon in August, as Tommy and I were lounging on the floor of the apartment, guitars and yellow pads at the ready, there was a call from Lee. He said he had heard good things about me and wanted to sign me to a personal management contract. After I hung up, Tommy told me that Lee knew a lot of people in the business and could definitely open some doors for me. But he was puzzled as to why Silver was so interested in me when he had never offered to sign *him* up!

Unfortunately, Curtis's record of "Dr. Heartache" had not been a hit. So Lee Silver, my new manager, took the song over to an A & R man at Capitol Records who thought it would be great for Tommy Sands. The Sands recording only made it into the nineties and was on the *Cashbox* charts for just a couple of weeks. But at last I could say I had written a song that had made it onto the national pop song charts.

Like Curtis, I had long since been dropped from my record label. But Lee Silver liked a couple of the songs that Tommy had helped me finish, and in December he took me into the studio to record "Girl in the Window" and "Journey of Love." He hired a bass player, a drummer, and an inventive piano player for the session. Tommy had agreed to play acoustic guitar, and when he showed up at the studio he brought along with him a new friend, Nino Tempo.

Tommy had met Nino on the set of the popular TV series *Peter Gunn*, where the two of them had bit parts playing musicians in a recent episode. Nino was one of the top session saxophone players in town. He brought along his horn and played some great solos on my recordings. Then Tommy and Nino sang the background parts, and I did the lead vocals. Lee wasted no time mixing the recordings and shopping them around to try to get me a record deal.

Silver pressed up some copies of "Girl in the Window" on his own label and slyly released it on December 15th, taking advantage of the fact that during the holidays there wouldn't be much competition from other radio promoters during the last two weeks of the year. He was able to get the record designated as "Pick to Click" and "Pick of the Week" respectively on the two local Top Forty stations, KRLA and KFWB. When "Girl in the Window" made the L.A. charts, Lee made a deal to lease the masters to Era Records, an established label with national distribution.

Just before the record was to come out, Lee called and asked me to meet him at Aldo's Coffee Shop on Hollywood Boulevard. It was a hangout for music promotion men because it was located directly under the KFWB second floor studios. As Lee slid into the booth, he tossed a box of my new 45s to me across the table and broke the news that I was now back on a national record label. I couldn't believe that he had made it happen so quickly. Then, just as I reached into the box to inspect my new record, Lee added, "By the way, your name was way too long for the kids to remember, so I changed it. From now on, you're *Bobby Hart*."

♥

One day near the end of 1960 I overruled my natural shyness and made a cold call, managing to get an appointment with veteran music publisher, Lester Sill. On my lunch hour I took the bus up Western Avenue and found his small office on Argyle. Now, a hundred disappointments later, I would be meeting with a new music man only a few blocks from Crossroads of the World and Jesse Hodges' office. While I waited in the outer office I struck up a conversation with a young man who was also waiting to see Mr. Sill. He was wearing the standard L.A. wardrobe of jeans, white T-shirt, and black boots and looked to be about my age. I managed a low-key "How ya' doin'," and he introduced himself as Phil Spector. I recognized the name. I had printed the record labels for "To Know Him Is to Love Him" by the Teddy Bears and knew that he had written the song and was a member of the group.

Just to make conversation, I asked what he had been doing since his big hit three years earlier. Spector seemed to take offense, thinking that I was implying that by now he should have had a lot more successes to tell me about. He said something like "Hey, Man, I've only been out of high school for two years." Then, he told me that he wanted to go to New York and get into producing. A few minutes later he was invited into Lester

Sill's office. I sat there in the silence of the empty lobby with this increasingly more frequent feeling of being left behind.

♥

The last Saturday evening of October 1960 (seven months before the birth of our second son, Bret) Becky and I got a babysitter for Bobby Jr. Tommy borrowed his dad's car and picked us up at our apartment for the hour-long drive down to the Long Beach Municipal Auditorium. Curtis Lee was appearing in a big rock 'n' roll show, and we were there to cheer our friend on.

While we were out front watching Curtis perform a great show, Stan Schulman, the owner of Dunes Records, was watching him from the wings of the stage. After the show he cornered Curt backstage and immediately offered him what could only be a golden opportunity for an unknown artist: a management and recording contract with Dunes Records. Wasting no time, Schulman sent him home to pack for his journey to fame, fortune, and the Big Apple.

As Tommy, Becky, and I headed back to Hollywood that night, still buzzing with excitement over Curtis's big break, a drunk driver crossed over the center divider of the Santa Ana Freeway and struck us head on. Our car spun around and came to a stop on the embankment. After making sure Becky was all right, Tommy and I ran to see if the driver of the other car was okay. He was fine, having been well insulated from the blow by the spirits he had recently imbibed.

When the Highway Patrol arrived, they insisted that Becky wait in the car while they wrote out their report. Then, without warning, another vehicle came careening through all the red safety flares that the patrolmen had strung along the freeway and plowed directly into our car a second time, knocking my pregnant wife out of the car and onto the pavement. Watching helplessly from across the freeway, as if in slow motion, I saw her head bounce as she landed. With an intense prayer on my lips, I ran the fifty yards to her. Incredibly, she, and all of us, were fine. Our second son, Bret Harshman, was born perfectly healthy on Memorial Day, 1961.

It took Curtis Lee only a couple of months in New York to convince his new manager, Stan, that what was missing from the Dunes Records creative team was songwriter Tommy Boyce. And so, in January 1961 during one of New York's coldest winters in years, Tommy Boyce arrived to take the town by storm. When Curtis and Ray Peterson picked him up at the airport, they said he was wearing a thin leather jacket and a neck brace!

Stan Schulman moved Tommy into Curt's small quarters in a dingy, midtown hotel, where they were expected to stay in the room and write songs all day. Boyce settled in, braving the New York cold and the discipline of Stan's work schedule. Together, these added up to a jarring new lifestyle that the twenty-one-year-old had not expected, but one that quickly paid off for him and Curt. By April, Boyce had written both sides of the new Ray Peterson chart single.

In July Tommy scored his second top-ten record, Curtis Lee's first Dunes release, "Pretty Little Angel Eyes." Written by Curtis and Tommy, the record climbed all the way to #7 on the *Billboard* charts. Curtis followed up his hit with another Boyce/Lee composition and Phil Spector production, "Under the Moon of Love," which charted in late October.

Meanwhile, there I was, stuck in L.A., printing the record labels for Tommy and Curtis's hits. For three long years I had continually mustered the courage to keep on trying to win the million-to-one lottery of success in the tricky world of music. Becky and I had lived on faith, sacrifice, and persistence as over and over we watched so many promising opportunities fall through. And now my friends were moving on without me.

One night when Becky was away visiting her folks in Phoenix, I was in no hurry to get home after a late shift at the print shop. I sat alone in a small neighborhood café where Tommy, Curtis, Becky, and I had shared so many laughter-filled evenings. Without the others it felt totally cold and empty, and for the first time ever, I wondered if I had what it takes to make it in this crazy, unpredictable business.

CHAPTER 8

Where'd You Get That
Corduroy Suit—Penney's?

It was the summer of 1962. Joey Dee & the Starliters had lines around the block at the Peppermint Lounge in Manhattan, and Chubby Checker was twisting again like he had done the previous summer. The newspapers were full of John Kennedy establishing the Peace Corps, Nelson Mandela being acquitted of treason after a four-year trial, and Jaguar ads for a cool new sports car called the XK-E. As for me, it seemed like I was still spinning my wheels and stuck in first gear.

About a year after signing with Era Records, I was dropped from the label because they had not been able to spread the success of my records beyond the L.A. city limits. Becky was well aware of my elusive dreams of stardom, but the dreams of success in the music business were mine, not hers. She loved me and was more than happy to be the wife of a factory worker.

After he played on my record, Tommy, Becky, and I became good friends with Nino Tempo and his sister, who recorded under the name of April Stevens. Ever since we met at my recording session, Nino had seemed to like the way I sang, and sometimes he would pay me a few bucks to sing on his song demos. Nino taught me a lot about working in the studio, including how to sing a "triplet," the basic riff that made almost any word sound hipper by turning one syllable into three notes. The few extra dollars meant a lot to Becky and me and our budget. Now, just at the right time, Nino would come to our rescue again.

Nino suggested me as an up-and-coming talent to his friend, Don Costa, the legendary arranger/producer. Best known for his later work with Frank Sinatra, Costa was producing pop hits in New York at the time. I guess by now, Costa fully respected Nino's musical taste, since another talent he had recommended to Don had resulted in immediate success and, ultimately, over a dozen chart records for Don Costa and his artist, Trini Lopez.

Within a few weeks, the exclusive singer/songwriter contract came in the mail. Costa signed me to South Mountain Music, the publishing company he owned with Teddy Randazzo, and to DCP, his record production company. The deal was made "sight unseen," never having heard, met, or even talked to me on the phone. His office started sending me a check for fifty dollars every month. In return, I would mail them back original songs.

♥

The previous year, when "Girl in the Window" had become a local hit in L.A., I was asked to perform at rock 'n' roll shows sponsored by radio stations KFWB and KRLA. Nearly every weekend a disc jockey or a record promoter would pick me up at our apartment and drive me to some Southern California high school auditorium, where I would perform as a thank you for the radio exposure I had received. Now, a year later, I was still saying my weekly "thank yous" to the local radio stations. I was happy to know that even though I wasn't getting paid, someone wanted me up there on their stage. And over the months of work, my performance trepidation had nearly evaporated.

I would perform while sandwiched between other local acts like Jan & Dean, the Righteous Brothers, the Coasters or any big name artists who were in town and wanted to get their records played on L.A. radio. The Beach Boys would often be the backup band for all the other acts on the show. Still in their teens, the Beach Boys were fun loving and very accommodating. They knew the arrangements to "I Got a Woman," "Johnny B. Goode," or practically any other song I would call out just as I hit the stage. When they performed their own sets, their young voices provided only a hint of the unique vocal blend that would make them one of the most beloved and enduring of American musical groups.

On an unseasonably hot October Saturday night, a local promoter picked me up at the apartment and we drove the thirty miles to the Los Virgines High School in Malibu where I was set to perform with a number of other record acts at one of those rock 'n' roll hops. As I finished my set, a tall, skinny kid in a shiny silk suit introduced himself to me backstage. He was a nineteen-year-old Anthony Perkins look-alike who radiated coolness and in-your-face confidence. "Hey," he said in a deep voice, "I'm Barry Richards." I shook his hand.

"You sounded pretty good out there. Where'd you get that corduroy suit, Penney's?" I glanced down at the newly purchased suit that Becky had picked out for me and considered taking offense, but by the time I looked up, I saw a smile on his face and he had already moved on to another topic. I figured that this must be a preview of the stranger's strange sense of humor. "How long you been doing these shows?" he asked. "Over a year, now," I surmised. Then my new acquaintance straightened his ultrathin Bobby Darin tie and volunteered, "You know, I'm really an actor. I just do these shows on the weekends to meet girls . . . and for the ten bucks." I heard myself blurting out, "What ten bucks?"

It seemed like at nearly every show after that night in Malibu, I would run into Barry Richards. I must say he made me laugh more than anyone I had ever met. He could imitate the voices of Jimmy Stewart, Clark Gable, Henry Fonda, and a dozen other celebrities with the expertise of any top impressionist of the day. I could do a pretty good WC Fields, one voice not in Barry's repertoire, and we could walk the streets of Hollywood for blocks without ever reverting to our own personas.

Since I still couldn't afford a car, Barry would often give me a ride home from the weekend hops. One night, zooming down the 101 Freeway back to Hollywood in Barry's tiny MGA roadster convertible, I remember yelling over the freeway noise, "You know, man, some people actually get *paid* for doing what we do every weekend." Barry yelled back, "What do you mean?" "Nightclubs!" I ventured, not realizing that he had not yet turned twenty-one. "I can play the Hammond B-3 organ, and I know how to play the bass pedals with my feet, so we wouldn't have to hire a bass player. What can you play?" Barry thought for a moment, and then, with a twinkle in his eye, he shouted, "I can play the tambourine!"

Barry called the Musicians Union the next afternoon and got the numbers of some out-of-work drummers and guitar players. Then he called to tell me about the first of endless, clever promotional plots I have watched him devise over our many years of friendship. "Look," he began, "neither one of us has the money to hire an audition hall. Your place is too small, and I know my dad would never let us do it here at his house. But I told him that we already had our new band together, and that we'd be happy to entertain for free at his Toastmasters party this Saturday night."

When our prospective band members showed up at Barry's family home in Encino that weekend, we escorted them to the pool deck, explaining that we'd do a few numbers together and then there would be free food waiting for them after our set.

Serendipitously, the two musicians who walked through the door that night were just the right fit. First to arrive was a great southern guitar player named Lonnie Dobro followed quickly by a heavy young drummer who had the name "Jimmy Abbott" painted on his kick drum. Barry told Jimmy he had the job, as long as he was willing to replace his drum logo with the words Barry Richards & Bobby Hart, and we were in business.

By Tuesday, Barry had convinced the owner of a small jazz club in the Valley that the only way to make a killing in the 1962 club market was with the latest craze, *twist music*. He agreed to come down to the Musicians Union organ practice room to audition "the hottest new twist band on the West Coast!" Barry Richards and Bobby Hart were signed to play for one week at the Prelude on Lankershim Boulevard in North Hollywood.

We sang "Money (That's What I Want)," "Whad I Say," and "Slow Down." By the weekend, word had spread, the place was jumping, and there were lines outside waiting to get in! As we were packing up at the end of our first Saturday evening performance, the club owner informed us that he was extending our contract indefinitely. After a week of working nine to five at Perry Printing and then nine to two a.m. at the Prelude, I strolled into Mr. Perry's office early Monday morning and gave him my official notice, leaving behind my print shop life forever.

About ten o'clock on our second night performing in the club, from out of nowhere, a young Leslie Caron type with short brunette hair and a white fringe chemise dress jumped onto the stage and began doing the twist like nobody's business. Unbeknownst to us, the club owner had hired a twist girl, and she performed with us every night for the rest of the engagement. "Mary Ann, the Twisting Doll," as she billed herself, had an expressive face and an exuberance that was captivating.

Each night when the club closed at 2 a.m., Barry and I and the rest of the band, including Mary Ann, would drive from the San Fernando Valley to the International House of Pancakes on Sunset on the Hollywood side of the hill to unwind.

Mary Ann and I hit it off right away, and after a few evenings, our conversations began to last later and later into the night as, one by one, our band mates drifted away from the table. She liked my singing and encouraged me to become more soulful in my style and learn some of the great blues songs that she had been exposed to while working with some southern soul bands. At one of the rehearsals, she brought some records with her and turned me on to "Turn On Your Love Light," the great Bobby "Blue" Bland single that became my signature song in clubs for years after.

I was finally a full-time working musician, which is what I had wanted for so long. It felt great, releasing my emotions through my voice every night and enjoying the resulting adulation from the crowds. But my new chosen profession, and the relationships that came with it, would soon impact my life in ways that I had neither the foresight to envision nor the ability to handle.

CHAPTER 9

They'd Rather Have the Dancer

For four years my life with Becky had been routine and predictable. Up at seven, ride the bus to work, eight hours on the job, and take the bus home. Becky would have the kids clean, dinner ready, and in the evenings we'd hang out together—chips and dip in front of the TV, walks down the boulevard, and once in a while, when we could afford it, pizza at Micelli's.

Now everything was different. We were finally able to buy our first car. A white '59 Chevy Impala with red vinyl interior and chrome wheels. And for the first time, we could afford to move into a small, detached house in the hills near Lake Hollywood. On a typical day, I'd sleep until after noon, drive to the club to rehearse, have dinner with Becky and the kids, perform from nine until two, and then hang out with the band and the after-hours crowd until four or five in the morning.

Becky was stuck at home with the boys while I was spending more time with the band than I was with her. This was not the marriage she had bargained for. From the beginning, she knew I wanted to be a professional musician. But in those days, we were thinking in terms of teen idols and hit records, not smoke-filled nightclubs. Becky tried her best to be happy for me, but for our marriage my new club life marked the beginning of the end.

As we approached the final weeks of our long run at the Prelude Lounge, I kept asking Barry to get on the phone and get us another gig. At barely twenty-one, and with his pockets full of cash, Barry Richards was more interested in spending some quality time at the beach. I, on the other hand, had quit my day job and had a family to support. The more I pressed the issue, the more Barry made it clear the he was disinclined to be taking on a second gig so soon after our upcoming hiatus. With only a week or two left before the end of our engagement, time was finally running out for making plans.

For several weeks Mary Ann's booking agent, David, had been calling me to say that he could get the band work in a stable of nightclubs, lounges and honky-tonks that he represented around the greater Los Angeles area. But the rub was, as he explained it, "These club owners don't want to pay for a second singer who doesn't play an instrument. They'd rather have the dancer."

On the Monday night of our last week at the Prelude, I took Barry aside before we started our set. "I don't know how to tell you this, man. I'm so sorry, but I'm going to have to take these gigs that David's been offering me. I know you could use some time off, but I've got Becky and the kids to support and I just can't be out of work." At the time he seemed fine with it, shrugging his shoulders with a smile as he said, "Hey, do what you gotta do."

Over the years, of course, Barry has never failed to remind me of that conversation whenever he thinks I need a shot of guilt to bring me down to size: "Yeah, remember that time when you abandoned your partner after I had pulled you out of the print shop, set you up in the music business and turned your whole life around?"

Now, with this new configuration of the band, Mary Ann was not only the dancer, but also my business partner as co-leader of the group. We decided to call our new band the Ascots. For the next few months, we played all over the greater Los Angeles area in places like the Forge in El Monte, the Redwood Lounge in Long Beach, and the Bowl-O-Rama in Norwalk.

But with the longer commutes added on to the long nights with the band, the strain of spending so much time with Mary Ann began to ramp up the tension at home, taking an additional toll on Becky and our marriage. For the first time since we had met as children, our arguments quickly become louder and more frequent. In early 1963 the band and I drove off for an engagement in Kansas City. To avoid another fight, I didn't tell her that we'd be taking Mary Ann with us for the Missouri club job.

After the gig, while the band finished breakfast at a roadside diner, I found a phone booth outside in the snow and called Don Costa's office collect. He came right on the phone and greeted me warmly. "I'm halfway to New York," I said, "and since you have me signed as a recording artist, do you think we could cut some records if I drove on in to the city?" "Sure," he said, "come on back. I'll book the studio."

After dropping Mary Ann at her mother's home in upstate New York, I headed to the big city to hook up with my record producer, whom I'd yet to meet in person. After circling the Manhattan block for what seemed like an hour, I found a parking spot and took the elevator to the nineteenth floor offices of Don Costa Productions at 1650 Broadway. I was told that Costa had left for the day, but the receptionist promised to give him a message first thing in the morning. When she asked where I was staying, I confided that I had just driven into town and was pretty low on cash. She said, "I think it'll be all right if you want to crash on the couch here in the waiting room for the night."

Of course, I was still in the waiting room and probably looking a bit rumpled when Costa arrived the next morning. A balding Italian-American, slightly overweight and with a great smile, he looked to be only a few years older than me. Costa greeted me warmly and told me that my session was arranged for the following Tuesday. Then he asked what songs I wanted to record. I hadn't thought of that! But Don liked a song I had previously sent in, called "Wind Me Up and Watch Me Cry." And, I suggested a Bobby Vee vocal treatment of "Bluebirds Over the Mountain."

Don had his secretary slip me a few dollars and arrange for me to sleep at an unfurnished empty flat on 61st Street that Costa only used as a get-away when he needed peace and quiet to write his musical arrangements. I slid beneath a heavy pile of window drapes that were lying on the floor and slept quite warmly there.

Arriving at Bell Sound, one of New York's premier studios, I found Don already rehearsing the orchestra. None of my records had ever had a string section, let alone one playing a Don Costa arrangement. He was easy to work with and made some great tracks. For backup, Costa had hired three girls whose record, "My Boyfriend's Back," was just charting. They called themselves the Angels. Then, just as I was heading into the booth to begin my vocals, I was told that there was a phone call for me. I walked out into the stairwell where the pay phone was located to take the call. It was Becky.

She said, "David, your agent called and told me everything. I know you're back there with her. It's over with us." I choked back the emotion that seemed to be rising from my stomach to my throat while a million thoughts chased each other in my mind. I had known for months that someday this moment would come; still I was unprepared and stunned! As the blood rushed to my head, I heard myself saying "No! No, I'll call and tell her she's not coming back with me. Please! I'm in the middle of my big session right now, but I'll start home first thing in the morning. I don't want to lose you and the kids."

I staggered back into the studio and walked to the microphone in a fog. "I'm a professional," I kept telling myself, as I somehow made it through the vocals, but the thrill of my first big orchestra session had evaporated. The painful and conflicting feelings spinning inside my head at that moment were the worst I had ever experienced. Unfortunately, getting those emotions out of my body and onto the record didn't seem possible that day. Another big opportunity had been squandered. Lost in a cloud of guilt, I was hit by the realization that this time, I could only blame the tangled web that I had created for myself.

After a sleepless night I grabbed some snack foods, filled up the tank and aimed my '59 Chevy toward Hollywood. I began the three thousand mile journey west with the desire and faith that I could win my family back. But every turnoff for at least a thousand miles would witness a fierce wrestling match with myself over whether to turn the car around and head back to Mary Ann. I tried to drown out the voices in my head by listening to the hits all the way along America's scenic roadways, but my mind and my heart were disconnected and my body was on autopilot.

Becky let me back into the house, and over the next few weeks we really tried to return to "normal." But one side of me was hopelessly attached to Mary Ann, while at the same time I couldn't conceive of living without my wife and family. Over the past few months, all the self-discipline and integrity that a twenty-three-year-old could create had not been enough to keep me from falling into the worst psychological jam of my life. And try as I might, I seemed powerless to pull myself out of the tangled mess.

On my third trip back to L.A. from New York, I found Becky and the kids in a small apartment in North Hollywood. From the moment she opened the door, I could see on her face that everything had changed. Her eyes were no longer dancing with innocence and youth. They were sad and tired from crying. I had pushed her too far. She had moved on, and this time the walls she had built for her own survival could not be breached.

On the return ride to Manhattan in the darkened back seat of the half-empty Greyhound, alone with my thoughts and my guitar, I wrote a song called "Reputation." It had taken five three-thousand-mile journeys, running on borrowed credit cards and adrenaline-fueled emotions, before I finally realized that I had lost the love of the two women in my life who I was sure I couldn't live without.

Through the rain splattered windshield, I watched the on-coming headlights diffuse into long blurry rays and move down the walls of the bus, illuminating me in a flash, then abandoning me just as quickly into the darkness. As I sat quietly, I realized that even more than my loss, my rejection, and my loneliness, this intense pain was coming from the feeling that I didn't much like who I had become.

CHAPTER 10

Finally, the Promised Land

I disembarked at Port Authority early on a grey, rainy morning and made a call. I found Tommy Boyce living with an NYU professor named Susan Hudson in a beautiful apartment in the upscale New York City suburb of Riverdale. Following Tommy's directions, I found the subway and sat mesmerized by the passing panorama through Harlem and the Bronx and on into Riverdale, where he met me at the station.

I spent the night on their couch and after breakfast on a bright, crisp May morning, Tommy brought me into town to show me around and get me settled. We took the D train from Riverdale, got off on Broadway and walked to 53rd Street. It felt really good hanging out with my old friend again.

My first impression of living in Manhattan was: this is Disneyland for adults! You walk everywhere you go, and everywhere you go there's something entertaining to see. For a twenty-four-year-old unknown songwriter, New York was Mecca, the goal of my pilgrimage. Virtually the entire music business was located in just two buildings, 1650 Broadway, and catty-cornered across the street, the storied Brill Building at 1619 Broadway. Tommy and I turned a corner, and there we were in the Promised Land—"Tin Pan Alley."

New York was electric! The air itself seemed to exude creative energy. From the first day, there was a vibe in the air that shot through me like adrenaline. I found it physically impossible to walk down a Manhattan street at my usual cactus-strewn Phoenix or laid-back Hollywood pace. Once you entered the sidewalk, you walked or got walked on. You kept up with the hundreds of fellow pedestrians who half-walked, half-ran down the street, or you got swept aside. Although the city held the entertaining excitement of an amusement park, there was a slight sense of danger, just enough to keep your senses sharp and just the impetus I needed to jump start my career.

Tommy was glad to see me too, and although no one said it out loud, it looked like the timing was finally right for Boyce and Hart to become writing partners in earnest. He told me that Curtis Lee had become totally disillusioned with the record business when it came time for him to receive his first royalty check. Although he had charted two big hits, after the record company had deducted two years of his living expenses and all the recording costs, Curt had ended up with no royalties at all. Curtis had returned to Yuma and had gone to work in his father's construction business.

Tommy took me around and showed me a couple of cheap hotels that he knew. We walked down Seventh Avenue and turned east onto Forty-Ninth Street where Tommy pointed out a weather-worn sign that read *Chesterfield Hotel.* The lobby was drab and dingy, but when the day clerk told me the rent was $21 a week, I signed on the dotted line. When the World's Fair opened the following summer, the price shot up to $34. It was a shabby 6' by 6' cell, just big enough for a cot-sized bed, one straight-backed chair, and a small sink. There was a window from which to watch the snow fall and the red neon sign on the adjacent building that flashed "HOTEL BRISTOL" all night long through the threadbare curtains and into my room.

I shared the bathroom down the hall with the twenty-some other tenants on the 21st floor, most of whom were well over three times my age. At night, some of my more sanity-challenged hotel mates would wander the halls babbling incoherently. Large chunks of plaster would fall from the ceiling over my bed during the night. It didn't take long for me to learn to sleep with my head under the blanket.

On a typical day, I would roll out of bed, clean up, and walk the half a block down Forty-Ninth Street to a small diner where I'd sit at the counter for breakfast. After a few days, as soon as I sat down the waitress, who was at least thirty years older than me, would pour me a cup of coffee and look me straight in the eyes asking, "Usual?" Somehow it gave me a slight feeling of being taken care of, and although I was totally unaccustomed to her brusque big-city style of serving, it was comforting to know that I was familiar to at least one person in this faceless city.

Tommy would take the subway into Manhattan and meet me mid-morning at the offices of South Mountain Music. By now Don Costa had kindly increased my advance to fifty dollars a week. The publishing company's floor plan included a row of closet-sized cubicles, each furnished with one chair and a piano, and we would work all day in one of these tiny rooms, sandwiched in between other teams of songwriters in their own cubicles.

As we had done back in Los Angeles, Tommy and I fell into an easy rhythm of writing together. Others have called it chemistry, but I think I know some of the elements that made our partnership work. Instinctively, we both had learned to listen: first to top forty radio, which streamed out ever-changing, instant updates on the kind of music the kids were loving and buying at any given moment; and secondly, we had learned to listen to conversations, our own and others, our subconscious minds constantly scanning the soundtracks of our lives for that elusive song title or catchy line.

Melodically, Tommy and I were always searching our minds for great hooks: tunes that anyone could sing along with, melodies that would roll around in your mind long after you had turned off the radio. I had learned a great lesson from my nightclub days. I remembered that we had always picked songs to learn and play that featured infectious instrumental riffs that lent immediate recognition to the records, right from the intro.

Many of the writing teams around us had teamed up to showcase their differences and respective strengths. But we hadn't sought each other out because I thought Tommy was a great melody writer or because he thought I was a brilliant lyricist. He could write words and I could compose melodies, and we'd both had years of experience writing alone. Sure, we respected each other's abilities, but the real reason we wanted to be partners was because it was so much more fun doing it *together*.

Tommy and I made each other laugh every day, and it wasn't necessarily because we always shared the same sense of humor. I would break up at the totally unexpected musings that would pop out of Tommy's mind as he observed someone or something going on around us. My brand of humor was more cerebral. I liked puns and word play. When Tommy would hit me with a particularly stinging critique of one of my many shortcomings, I could invariably turn the tables on him with a quick jab of wit that would have him on the defensive and dissolving into laugher.

When we wrote, Tommy would always make it obvious that he valued my input, and that gave me the confidence to be forthcoming with even my most dubious of suggestions. There was this strange sense of security I would feel when writing with him. I trusted Boyce's instincts almost as much as *he* did when it came to which elements may or may not be commercial in a song. Don't get me wrong; there were plenty of shoving matches when searching for that perfect word or turn of phrase. But both of us knew that our common goal was whatever would achieve the best outcome for the song.

Part of my contribution to the partnership was my pragmatism and more grounded focus. In our writing sessions, when Tommy would be tossing out lines a mile a minute, I was often the one who would sit back, picking out the good ideas from the mundane and organizing them into a cohesive story. I was never satisfied until there was a definite feeling, philosophy, or message behind each song.

In his 1974 book, *How to Write a Hit Song and Sell It,* Tommy described our writing partnership this way: "There was no set pattern of work, no yardstick for measuring the relative contribution of each, and, most importantly, no assertion of ego. That's what made it such a pleasant and workable partnership."

In our cubicle at South Mountain Music, Tommy and I would work on melodies and lyrics and talk about life until we were famished in the late afternoon. Then, Tommy would disappear down the hall to catch his train home to Susan and their luxury apartment in Riverdale, leaving me on my own in a big city where I knew virtually no one.

♥

During the previous two years, Tommy had often accompanied Curtis Lee on his road tours, playing guitar and conducting the band, and that's where the two of them had gotten to know a number of other pop acts. Some great voices stood out from among the commercial teen idols in the world of pop music in the first half of the sixties, before The Beatles changed everything. But in 1963, I got to know three of the best.

Brian Hyland had burst onto the pop scene in 1960 as a sixteen-year-old high school sophomore with his number one first record, "Itsy Bitsy Teenie Weenie Yellow Polka Dot Bikini." His teenage novelty voice had mellowed into a velvet pop sound by the time "Sealed with a Kiss" had reached #3, two years before Tommy introduced me to Brian in 1963.

He had just returned from a tour of England when Tommy and I visited him in his hotel. Brian excitedly told us about this new British group called The Beatles that was making the girls crazy across the pond. He had memorized their singles and he pulled out his guitar and sang for us flawless versions of "Please Please Me," "She Loves You," and "I Want to Hold Your Hand," complete with the high falsettos.

Stopping by the publisher's office one day to pick up my check, we ran into Tommy's old friend, Del Shannon. I had been a fan ever since the first time I heard "Runaway" in 1961. Like Brian, Del was just back from England, where in earlier days The Beatles had been his opening act. Some months later, Del took Tommy and me on an extended weekend drive to his Detroit neighborhood, where he was still known as Charlie Westover. It was four days of laughing, strumming, and singing harmonies. Del, Brian, Tommy, and I all shared a love of country music.

One day at a publisher's office in the Brill Building I ran into teen idol, Lou Christie. Just a few months earlier, at age nineteen, he had charted his first big hit, "The Gypsy Cried," and now his current record, "Two Faces Have I," was in the top ten. He was in town to record a new album. Over egg rolls and black tea, Lou told me that he had been writing his songs with a real gypsy lady. She was thirty years older than he was, had flaming red hair, and was a self-described clairvoyant and mystic. Lou said she had been able to predict which of their songs would become hits.

It all seemed very mysterious to me, a boy from a fundamentalist Christian background. But having always been curious about the spiritual unknown, I was fascinated by all the intrigue that seemed to surround him. I was glad that I had a writing partner who was my own age, one who I could relate to on the same level and a buddy that was fun to hang out with.

♥

Now and then, Susan would invite me to take the subway with Tommy back to their apartment for dinner, and on those occasions I'd usually stay overnight. It soon became apparent why she had captured Tommy's heart. Not only was she sweet, pretty, and a college professor, she was more world-wise and sophisticated than we were. She'd serve us candlelight dinners with nice china and wine glasses. Tommy and I would have great fun late into the evening, remembering the days when we were hang-out buddies in Hollywood, and filling each other in on what had transpired in our lives between those days and the present. We would pretend to be telling the stories to Susan, but in reality we were the ones getting high from rehashing the tales that we both already knew.

For the first time since I had known him, I could see that Tommy was in a serious relationship. I teased him about finally getting caught, but I really liked that Susan seemed to genuinely care about Tommy. And she listened sympathetically when the conversation came around to me and how much I was missing my family. Susan was easy to talk to, and after a while we began to develop a friendship.

Every week when I got my publishing advances I'd make my pilgrimage to the drug store on the corner of Forty-Ninth and Broadway, where I'd buy a fifty-dollar money order to send back to Becky. Although I was trying not to, I would sometimes lay in bed thinking about her in the late night hours when my loneliness became overpowering. She and the boys were spending more time in Phoenix with her folks. Once in a while I'd try to reach her on the telephone. The conversations then would be short and cautious. She was learning how to protect her heart, and I was still trying to understand mine.

So once again, every evening would find me alone, walking up and down Broadway just like I had done on Hollywood Boulevard five years earlier. I would walk until I was so tired that when I came in, I could fall right to sleep without having to look around at my meager accommodations. The noisy canyons of concrete and steel were a long way from the peaceful ones of my Oak Creek Canyon youth, and I can't say that they ever came to feel like home. But there was no doubt in my mind that in the summer of 1963 I was right where I was supposed to be. I could feel the hot breath of success creeping up on me and it was gaining speed.

CHAPTER 11

A Couple More Hits and You Can Hit the Parties with Me

I t was a freezing March morning in 1964, and I clasped the arms of my thin cotton jacket for warmth as Tommy and I fought our way, block by block, through the snow flurries. Thankful to have finally reached our destination, we ducked into the lobby of 1650 Broadway and punched the elevator button. In a moment, its silver doors glided open to frame a lone, elegant figure facing us from the center of the car, bathed in the warm glow of the overhead spotlight. Tommy greeted him by name and introduced him to me. "Wes, this is Bobby Hart, my new writing partner."

"Hey, how ya doin'?" The handsome young man in the expensive-looking business suit shook my hand without the slightest pause in his stream of conversation. "Listen, have you guys got anything for Chubby Checker? He's recording in a couple of weeks and I'm taking the train down to Philly tonight to play him some songs."

The thirty-floor ascent to Wes Farrell's office took maybe thirty seconds. As he was making his brisk exit, and just before the elevator doors closed behind him, Tommy called out, "We'll try to come up with something, Wes!" Tommy pushed the down button, and forgetting our previous appointment, we headed for my room at the Chesterfield. As we rushed back down the busy streets a sliver of sun broke through the clouds, but my mind was already whirling into the future, propelled by the urgency of the mission we had just accepted.

I had written with Tommy long enough to know that his number one rule of songwriting was: "Never start a song until you have a great title to anchor it on!" My pragmatic mind was running over the titles of Chubby Checker's most recent hits, desperately searching for a formula. Somehow, in my head, "Loddy Lo," "Hooka Tooka," and "Hey, Bobba Needle" all sounded to me like nursery rhymes. On the fly, I explained my reasoning to Tommy in shorthand as we passed a midtown bookstore so he wouldn't think I was crazy as I dashed in. He followed me inside and watched as I purchased a collection of children's nursery rhymes.

The Chesterfield Hotel elevator was probably about a hundred years older than the one at 1650 and it took much longer to negotiate the 21 floors. As we entered my tiny room, Tommy grabbed his guitar and sat on the edge of my rickety bed. Thoughtfully, he began strumming a Calypso beat while I thumbed through the book, calling out nursery rhyme titles. I found an eighteenth-century English verse I had never heard of called "Lazy Elsie Marley" that we both liked. I calmed down right away as we started having fun topping each other's creative efforts to come up with a lyrical story that would complement Tommy's rhythm.

Elsie Marley turned out to be a coal miner who didn't want to get up to go to work in the mine. We fabricated a romance between Elsie and "Gentleman Jack" who bought her expensive presents like "a wig and a purple gown," making her "the best dressed miner in town." Finally, we plugged in a sing-along chorus,

> *Lazy, lazy Elsie Marley, put the pack back on your back,*
> *Lazy, lazy Elsie Marley, carry it on down by the railroad track*

Tommy grabbed his guitar and we were out the door. By two o'clock that afternoon, we were back at 1650 Broadway, bursting through the doors of Wes's office at Picturetone Music and playing him our new song.

Although only about our age, Wes Farrell had already enjoyed major success. But from nine to five Wes would trade in his knit sweater for a business suit as he worked his day gig as professional manager of Picturetone Music, which he ran for Phil Kohl and Joe Kohlsky, two old-time Tin Pan Alley publishers who owned the company. Kohl and Kohlsky were brothers. Phil had shortened his last name; Joe decided to keep his family's Russian second syllable.

Wes loved our song. "This is great!" he said. "Phil and Joe have to hear this." He rushed us into the larger office next door to his, where the brothers were sitting behind twin desks. We sang "Elsie Marley" again for them, this time with even more confidence.

As we signed the publishing contracts we noticed that they had typed the title as, "Lazy Elsie *Molly*." Between the brothers' New York accents and our own West Coastese, something got lost in translation. We sang Marley; they heard Molly. When we pointed out the mistake, Phil and Joe insisted that Molly was much more commercial. But since we had spent over two hours with Elsie, addressing her by name, we thought if anybody knew what her name was, it should have been us. In hushed tones Tommy and I talked it over in a corner of the outer office, and seeing how adamant the brothers were, we decided to accept the change. They were right, of course.

An hour later Tommy, Wes, and I were making a rough demo recording of the song in the small studio in the basement of 1650. And, as promised, later that night Wes took the train down to Philadelphia and played it for Chubby Checker.

The next day, I went to meet Tommy at a Nedik's hot dog stand on 42nd Street that we frequented. From the counter stool where I sat, I could see Tommy and Susan approaching, hand in hand. While still about a hundred feet away, Tommy broke loose and ran up to me, yelling the news. "We've got Chubby Checker's next single!" Tommy's face was radiating his youthful excitement and he had both his thumbs thrust high in the air. "Wes called early this morning and he said that Chubby loved "Lazy Elsie Molly."

Though it seemed much longer as Tommy and I impatiently waited, Chubby's new single was on the streets within a month. Every Monday after that, we would visit the office of Picturetone Music and scan the *Billboard* magazine in the reception area. Week by week, we excitedly watched as our song climbed up the charts. I was, of course, ecstatic to have my first hit in the top forty. So it was quite a letdown when the Kohl/Kohlsky publisher brothers told us one morning how disappointed they were that the record had peaked at only the number #39 position.

They made it clear that from now on, they would only be interested in signing *top ten* songs.

I was confused and offended, but my mind quickly started throwing water on my emotional fire, keeping it within limits. As I walked Tommy to the station that evening, I was still complaining, "We didn't have any control of our song's success once it was recorded and in the hands of the label's promotion department. After all, it had been Chubby Checker who had picked our song from all the others that had been submitted to him. "'Lazy Elsie Molly' *should* have gone top ten," I said, "and it wasn't our fault that it didn't! Maybe, if they hadn't forced us to change the title . . ." Tommy didn't seem to hear a word I said. He quietly stepped onto the train, then turned and nodded goodbye, leaving me alone at the station.

Although we still spent most of our time writing in our South Mountain Music cubicle, the weekly advances they had been paying me had dried up. As we passed Don Costa in the hallway one afternoon, he offered a line that made Tommy and me smile. "I've gotta find some "fresh money," he said.

So most Fridays would find Tommy and me waiting in Wes Farrell's reception area until late afternoon when he would be able to slip into our publisher's office and try to cajole Phil and Joe into giving us a fifty dollar advance on our writer royalties. The brothers would make us sweat it out until closing time, but then they usually came through with enough to get us through one more week.

Wes Farrell possessed a charming, exuberant personality, and he loved to laugh. In professional situations he spoke with speed and confidence. Wes had been open and cordial to me since our first meeting; still behind the charm there was always a slight air of superiority. One Monday afternoon when we stopped by his office, he told us the colorful story of his weekend and the great party he had attended on Saturday night. Then he added, "As soon as you guys write just a couple more hits, I'll be able to take you with me to some of these spectacular affairs."

Just as we were ready to leave his office, Wes took a call. When he hung up he confided, "Listen, guys, I just talked to Artie Ripp at UA.

He's looking for songs for Jay and the Americans. He's taking them into the studio next week. If you guys want to hang around until closing time, the three of us could try to write something for the group. What do you think?" "Sure," Tommy said, "we'll see you around five."

Tommy and I had nothing to do and no one to see, so we hung out in front of the building, talking and watching the endless stream of passersby on Broadway. We had a good chuckle recalling Wes' crack about us still being a couple of rungs down the ladder from his social level, but we were really jazzed that Wes had thought enough of our writing abilities to want to work with us. We wolfed down a couple of street vendor burgers and headed back upstairs a few minutes after five. When Phil and Joe turned out the lights and left for the evening, Wes welcomed us into his small office.

I soon learned that Wes Farrell had a no-nonsense style of working; he was quick and to the point. If Tommy's manner had been energetic, Wes was New York driven! Within less than ten minutes, the three of us had tossed around a number of ideas and finally agreed on trying to come up with a lyric story along the lines of the Marty Robbins country hit, "El Paso," but in the style of an American pop song. If Tommy was uncomfortable that we were moving ahead without a strong title, he hid it well as he experimented with different Latin riffs on his guitar. I ventured what seemed like a generic opening line to set the scene, "In a little café, just the other side of the border," and Wes immediately set it to a melody as Tommy strummed his chords.

Wes continued on into a second line of melody with the lyric already built in: "She was sitting there giving me looks that made my mouth water." It was a line I never would have written, too off the wall to be commercial, I surmised, and besides, *water* didn't rhyme with *border*. But observing how pleased both Wes and Tommy were with the provocative image, I held my tongue. The two pros were unknowingly teaching me that catchy content always trumps rhyme. And upon second hearing, the way Wes sang the two words, "warder" *did* rhyme with border.

Well, in short order we had come up with an exotic setting and two main characters who were already embroiled in a charged situation. Now we needed the antagonist. Tommy said we should introduce a bandito. Wes remembered our Gentleman Jack character from "Lazy Elsie Molly" and proposed his counterpart, "How about, 'Bad Man José?'"

We continued to blurt out lines, mixing and matching each other's ideas and collectively building a colorful story. Tommy decided that the guitar player in the cafe needed to warn the singer that the girl belongs to Bad Man José.

Then I heard the guitar player say, "She belongs to Bad Man José"
And I knew, yes I knew I should leave but then I heard her say . . .
Come A Little Bit Closer.

Finally, we had our title. Then, as the two shared a dance and a kiss, José approaches the cafe, and the guitar player needs to blurt out one last warning.

"What's the Spanish word for 'split outta here quick?'" Wes asked, desperate for some magic word to instantly appear. "Vamoose!" I shot back, "José's on his way, vamoose!" Wes stopped mid-sentence, paused, and looked at Tommy and then at me. "Is that really a word?" "That's how we say it in Arizona," I replied. So "vamoose" it was. When the music stops and the singer looks up to see the bandito in person, that's enough to make him drop his drink and "vamoose," taking off through the parted window curtains, running for his life. As he does so, in the background he hears the girl whispering those same seductive words to Bad Man José:

Come a little bit closer, you're my kind of man, so big and so strong,
Come a little bit closer, I'm all alone and the night is so long.

It was probably the most well-crafted song I had been a part of to date, and it was certainly the most humorous. We sang, and laughed as we added the polishing touches. Tommy must have played his guitar nonstop for hours that night. So pleased with ourselves and with our creation, we would continue to sing it over and over long after the writing process had ended. And just when we thought we were done, one of us would start it up again from the top. It was a magical night and I left feeling that we had created something special. Maybe more important to me, was the satisfaction of knowing that I had been able to "keep up with the big boys."

Within a week we were invited to the session to watch as Jay & the Americans' producer, Artie Ripp, cut a great record of our song. As he recorded the instrumental tracks, we got to meet the group and then watch Jay Black add his powerful tenor lead vocal.

To the delight of Tommy Boyce, Bobby Hart, and Wes Farrell, in September of 1964 "Come A Little Bit Closer" reached the #3 position on the charts, becoming Jay and the Americans all-time biggest selling record of their eighteen hits. As for me, I'll always remember the thrill of finally scoring my first top-ten record. I immediately felt it providing a much-needed boost to my confidence. The whipped cream on the sundae came one afternoon at Picturetone Music when Phil and Joe congratulated Tommy and me, heartily shaking our hands and grinning from ear to grizzled ear.

So, with two hit songs in as many months, I would wake up every morning feeling like I was finally a real professional songwriter, which only inspired me to work harder and write more songs. But this fact hadn't had time to make much of an impact on my financial situation. I was still struggling to get by. Even though every hit record starts with a great song, songwriters pretty much float at the bottom of the music business food chain. I learned that for my top-three song, I would split with my two co-writers a royalty of one cent per record sold. And I was told that my first royalty check from the publisher shouldn't be expected for a year or more.

Fortunately, the Universe had already devised a backup plan to keep a few bucks rolling in as I waited for my royalties to arrive. As I was to find out many times in my life, there was more than one way to draw a paycheck.

CREATIVITY

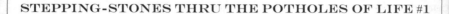

(1) YOU HAVE IT—EMBRACE IT!

From childhood, creativity has always come naturally to me. Later, I realized that even though we each have differing levels of confidence in our own creative abilities, EVERY BRAIN HAS A CONSTANT FLOW OF CREATIVITY FLOWING THROUGH IT. Otherwise, you wouldn't be able to think of an excuse when you're late or do a crossword puzzle. The fact that your creation doesn't look like everyone else's is proof in itself that your mind is capable of creating something unique. VISUALIZE YOUR GOAL, BUT DON'T SHARE IT WITH ANYONE ELSE—It's hard enough to keep your own mind positive and focused. You may have to CHANGE YOUR ENVIRON-MENT. If your friends aren't supportive, get new friends.

(2) START!

GET SOME OIL ON THE CANVAS. If you're writing, put some words on the page. When I write lyrics, I use a yellow pad and pencil. Sometimes I fill the whole page before I find that one line that inspires me. Then I go back and replace everything that doesn't come up to the level of my breakthrough line. The eraser is always gone long before the lead.

(3) FIND YOUR TOOLS & LEARN YOUR CRAFT

PAY YOUR DUES. You can't make a song swing without years on your instrument practicing the boring stuff like scales and chords. Don't fall for the popular idea that you can make it on your PR. You need PR, but back it up with real usefulness. If you want to become a great engineer, hang out with great engineers. If you want to break into Hollywood, don't stay in Podunk. PAY ATTENTION. Every soul who crosses your path has something to teach you.

(4) DON'T STOP!

It can be a spiritual and humbling experience to face a blank page, not knowing what will materialize. PERSERVERANCE may be the most important ingredient in bring-ing any dream to fulfillment. Stay true to your mission: CALM YOURSELF in order to better receive the best thoughts that are flowing through the Universal Stream. BE GRATEFUL and resist the temptation to take all the credit when the good ones come.

CHAPTER 12

Wipe Out!
The Boys in the Bootleg Band

The door to our writing cubicle flew open, catching Tommy and me by surprise and interrupting our feeble struggle to find some inspiration for a new song. Don Costa showed his face and then walked away while still speaking. "Bobby, could you come into my office for a minute," he asked, his voice trailing him down the hall. As I entered the room Don said, "I got a call today from Teddy at the Thunderbird." I knew he must have been talking about Teddy Randazzo, the co-owner of his publishing operation who always seemed to be away on the road performing. Don continued "One of Randazzo's background singers is leaving next month to get married. How would you like to fly out to Vegas in a few weeks and join the group?"

In a heartbeat, my mind did a flashback to one year earlier. Back in L.A., Barry Richards and I were packing the Prelude Club with our twist band. *Dance Panorama* magazine had asked if on our day off we would serve as judges for their big dance contest to be held at the Thunderbird Hotel in Las Vegas.

On September 8th, 1962, we climbed on a Greyhound for the five-hour ride. Once there, we stayed up all night in the casino since we couldn't afford a room.

I remember standing in the back of a packed Thunderbird Lounge at three o'clock in the morning watching the Teddy Randazzo Show. Teddy sat at the piano singing one dance number after another while his *Dazzlers*, three handsome boy singers in black mohair suits, fronted a stand-up mic, stage right, doing rhythm steps and singing oohs, ahs, and harmonies. Then the lights came down, Teddy left the stage, and the band broke into a grooving blues instrumental.

I saw that the incredible instrumental sound that had been backing the vocalists and Teddy's piano was coming from just a trio of musicians. I watched them in awe along with some other L.A. club musicians who stood with me in the back of the room. After a few minutes, one of them reverentially whispered the player's names.

Gerry McGee was standing on stage with his back to the audience, lost in the Louisiana riverbank swamp guitar style that was uniquely his, as he played his hypnotizing tribute to John Lee Hooker. It must have gone on for fifteen minutes. Larry (the Mole) Taylor, Randazzo's incredible young bass player, was grimacing and jerking his head with every pull of the strings on his electric bass—and finally, laying down an explosive beat and keeping time like a metronome, was drummer Billy Lewis. I had never seen a more exciting trio of musicians than Gerry McGee and the Cajuns.

Sure, Barry and I had fibbed: "Direct from Las Vegas" on the fliers that we handed out for our engagement at the Prelude. But here were three musicians who were the real deal, good enough to play in the entertainment capital of the world. I could feel my heart rate increasing from the music they were making and the wave of inspiration that was flowing from the stage to the back of the room. Somewhere in my subconscious mind that night a strong desire must have been lodged, a desire that somehow, someday, I could rise to the level of excellence of these three musicians.

It took me several paragraphs to tell you about it, but in Don Costa's office, the full epic memory of that night in Las Vegas had played itself out in only a few seconds. Recovering from my reverie, I looked up to find that he was waiting for an answer.

Did I want to be one of Teddy Randazzo's Dazzlers? Silently I asked myself, "Do I want to trade my Manhattan flophouse and the blizzards of New York for some golden sunshine and warm desert air? Do I want to perform in the entertainment capital of the world with Gerry McGee and the Cajuns?" Not wanting to sound too anxious I said, "Let me think about it," but I'm sure my uncontrollable grin must have given me away.

♥

On my way to Vegas in May 1963 I drove first to L.A. for one last try at picking up the pieces of my marriage. It was too little, too late. Becky had already packed up the kids and moved back to Phoenix with her folks. My old friend, Donnie Brooks, kindly let me sleep on the floor of the tiny Sunset Boulevard motel he and his girlfriend Penny were renting by the night. His record career having long since peaked, Donnie was now booking pop acts in small concert venues to try to make ends meet, and by day I helped him by making calls to artists and bookers.

One day Donnie and I stopped by the shoddy Sunset Strip office of one of the booking agents Donnie sometimes worked with. The infectious drum solo record "Wipe Out," by the Surfaris, was flying up the charts that month. The agent tossed a *Billboard* magazine across the desk at us and said, "Hey, I can book this act in the Upper Midwest. It's an instrumental group, and nobody knows what these kids look like. Put together some musicians and make up some 8 by 10 glossies with the words "the Surfaris" printed at the bottom, and I'll line you up a tour."

Now today, everybody knows the word "karma," the cause and effect precept shared by all the world's religions that can be most succinctly described as "you reap what you sow." Although some still think it's a philosophy created in the seventies by John Lennon in his song, "Instant Karma," I can definitely attest to the fact that the law of karma was already being fully enforced in 1963.

The caper started off smoothly enough. It wasn't hard to find four really good musicians who needed the work and were willing to take on a job as "identity thieves." We had them pose for a photo as the agent had suggested. John Maus was a guitar player/singer I had known from my nightclub days a year earlier when he was playing Pandora's Box with his sister, under the name of John & Judy. Scott Engel became our bass player/second singer and we added a keyboardist and a young drummer. The agent lined up two weeks of one-nighters in Wyoming, South Dakota, and Nebraska, and Donnie designated me to go along as the road manager.

We packed up my '59 Chevy Impala and took off for the long drive across Arizona and Utah. The first two high school auditorium gigs in Wyoming went off without a hitch. The agent had booked us in small towns where the kids were starved for entertainment. Everyone had a great time and really seemed to enjoy the bogus Surfaris. It wasn't until the fourth day of our trip that the karma police began to catch up to us.

The night was pitch-black, illuminated only by the weak fifty-nine Chevy's headlights. A hard rain was falling on the lonely two-lane highway as we crossed over into Nebraska. I had driven all day and was struggling to stay awake. Our young drummer professed to be wide-awake and was eager to take over behind the wheel, so I pulled over and traded places with him. Though I'd known him for only a few days, he had seemed like a fairly mature, responsible guy. I had no idea then that he was only sixteen years old! I settled into the back seat between John and Scott, and was out like a light.

In a flash of terror, I awoke to the feeling of the Impala in free fall as it silently tumbled, end over end, over a high cliff. I remember bouncing off the seat, hitting the ceiling of the car, then being thrown back to the seat again before the mass of metal, musical instruments, and human bodies finally came to a hard landing. The Impala bounced, skidded and came to a rest, upside down in a dark, wet canyon. I could smell the mix of gas, oil, rain, and sagebrush.

In the silent darkness, one by one we began to collect our senses and talk about how to get out of the car. We helped each other by pushing and pulling until the four of us stood, shaking and cold, beside the flattened wreckage. We knew that nobody would ever see us down in the ravine so we agreed to climb the muddy canyon walls up to the highway. When we finally reached the road, we all sat down and tried to extricate the mud and twigs from our shirts, pants, and shoes, hoping that the steady rain would wash away the mixture of blood and dirt from our faces.

After what felt like an hour, a very long and silent hour, we finally saw a vehicle coming, so we all stood in the middle of the road making sure it didn't pass us by. A trucker slowly pulled to a stop and begrudgingly agreed to take us all to the next town. Remembering it was my Impala and my role as road manager, I agreed to stay behind with the car and the instruments to wait for the Highway Patrol.

Since it was the only shelter from the pounding storm, I slid back down the hill and crawled into the upside down car where I waited for over an hour in the cold and the dark. Finally, I heard the sound of a tow truck arriving and saw the flashlight of its driver shining down at me. He threw me a chain and skillfully pulled the car up from the ravine to the road. Once the driver had cinched the carcass up onto his flatbed, he asked me to take off my shoes and coat before getting into his tow truck. He dragged my once beautiful Impala twelve miles into the little town of Crawford, Nebraska. The shaken, fake Surfaris and I would spend the next seven days of our lives in what could only be described as a time warp worthy of *The Twilight Zone.*

The next morning I needed to go see my beloved, two-tone Impala one last time. I was speechless to see that it was totaled. The roof was so flat that it made me wonder how we had all lived through the crash, and I quickly gave up hope of ever driving it again. The local mechanic said he could sell us a 1941 hearse. The hearse was the only vehicle for sale that was big enough to hold our luggage, guitars, drums, and us. I purchased the car with some of the cash we had collected from the shows. We all climbed in as the sun began to set and listened to the whine of the big V8 as it sped us out of Crawford in the direction of our next gig.

I was cruising at about 60 mph with my arm out the window, listening to AM country radio when, about twelve miles on the other side of Crawford, I suddenly lost all power and heard a loud knocking in the engine. The motor in the old hearse had thrown a rod. By now, it was starting to feel like a page from a policy and procedure book as the band got a ride back to Crawford and I waited in the hearse for a tow truck.

The same tow truck driver from the day before pulled up, and with fewer than a dozen words we chained up the hearse, climbed in the tow truck, and drove back into Crawford to the same mechanic's garage. We checked into the same little hotel and went to see the mechanic.

Incredibly, he said he had a second hearse for sale, just like the first one, and that he could exchange the broken parts. "It'll take me a day or two," he said.

The next few nights, we paid young local citizens to drive us the fifty to one hundred miles to the towns where we were booked to play our shows and then back to our little Crawford hotel rooms. Our local hosts were thrilled to do it, not so much for the few bucks they earned, but because it was probably the most excitement they had seen in years. And we were turning into local celebrities of sorts.

At the end of the week, our mechanic friend was still saying that he would need a day or two more. After all, he had to take care of his regular customers first. Finally, my time had run out. I had to report to the Thunderbird Hotel in Las Vegas and my new job with Teddy Randazzo the next day. I divvied up with the four musicians the dwindling cash that was left from our gigs and got a ride to Chadron, Nebraska, thirty miles away, where there was a small airport, and purchased a one-way ticket to Las Vegas.

Boarding the twenty-passenger, twin-engine plane, I settled back into my narrow seat. As I started to relax for the first time in days, I became aware of how much tension I had been holding in my body. I straightened my back to relieve the pain around my cracked ribs and allowed the roar of the engines to drown out my surroundings, leaving me alone with my thoughts. I felt the blood return to my frozen face as I slowly shook my head, reflecting on what had just happened to me and how naively Donnie Brooks and I had walked into our karmic ambush.

Neither the booking agent who plotted it, Donnie who produced it, nor I, the road manager, made a dime from our ill-fated business venture. I lost my car and nearly died; and the three musicians were left stranded in a little Nebraska town that had become a prison of sorts for the boys in the bootleg band.

I never saw them again and never learned how they got back to California. For over a year I harbored a great deal of guilt whenever I thought about my abandoning the boys. After all, I had been the road manager and somewhat responsible for them.

But that changed when I learned that at least two members of the group had indeed made it back. They, like me, had not been about to give up on their dreams of success in the music business—no matter how risky that business can be.

In 1964 John Maus and Scott Engel teamed up with Gary Leeds, formed a band, and moved to England. By then their matured voices and Phil Spector-influenced record production style had added up to nine top-thirty records in the U.K. and two top-twenty hits back home in the U.S. The phony Surfaris had become the Walker Brothers!

And so, here I was back in Las Vegas. It was one year, almost to the day, since I had stood in the back of the room mesmerized by the Teddy Randazzo Show. But this time, instead of watching from the back, I would be right up there with them on stage.

CHAPTER 13

The Awkward Dazzler

I landed at McCarran Airport before midnight and took a cab to the Thunderbird Hotel and Casino on the Strip. The thousand-watt marquee in front said "Teddy Randazzo and the Dazzlers." I walked through the glass double doors, found my way into the lounge, and once again, there they were—Teddy, singing lead from behind the piano, Gerry McGee and the Cajuns providing the grooving instrumental parts, and the Dazzlers dancing behind a floor mike like Joey Dee & the Starliters, doing background parts and sometimes singing some complicated late-night, tight "Four Freshmen" harmonies straight out of the forties.

I caught Teddy coming off stage after the first set and introduced myself. The good-looking Italian-American appeared to be a little older than me with straight salt and pepper hair, and he greeted me as if we were old friends. Teddy showed me to a closet-sized dressing room backstage where I was to learn my harmony parts from a pre-recorded tape while they did the rest of their shows. Sometime before dawn, I fell asleep with my head slumped over a tape recorder. But by the time the group had finished the last show of their closing night in Vegas, I had most of my vocal parts memorized.

The next night, after the four-hour drive to Reno, we opened at the Golden Hotel and Casino without rehearsal. At a band meeting the following morning, I found out that Randazzo had noticed my singing and really liked it. He even instructed the other two singers, who were from New York, to emulate the country way I slurred into the oohs and aahs. But when it came to my dancing—now that was a very different story. You see, we didn't have dances at Phoenix Christian High School and I had never learned. Then, once I started performing, I was usually sitting on a bench behind a Hammond B-3 organ.

Teddy took me to a local music store and bought me an acoustic guitar. He said "Tonight, you'll stand in the back with the musicians and sing your parts into a mic from there." A couple of days later when we got a chance to rehearse, he worked with me for several minutes, showing me some side-to-side rhythm steps and how to smoothly blend my movements with the other two singers. I spent my off-hours in front of my motel room mirror working on my steps, and by the second week I made my way back up to the front of the stage with the other Dazzlers.

Teddy's next booking was to be at a supper club called the Holiday House in Milwaukee, coming up in November. But November was two months away. While Teddy and the other Dazzlers headed back to New York, I accepted an invitation to ride back to Los Angeles with the Cajuns where they intended to try lining up some club gigs to keep bodies and souls together during the hiatus. The three musicians suggested I could play keyboards with them and sing the vocals.

Within a few days, we were working at the AM/PM nightclub on La Cienega Boulevard, from 9 to 2 weeknights and after-hours until 8 a.m. on the weekends. Belting out a raspy version of Marvin Gaye's "Hitch Hike" in the wee hours of a weekend morning, my weary mind was jolted by a sobering thought: It had taken less than a year for my subconscious desire to materialize. I was the lead singer of the Gerry McGee and the Cajuns band. What great fun it was working those two months with some of the greatest musicians in the world, developing my confidence and building my chops.

♥

There were two big surprises waiting for me in mid-November when we flew back to New York to hook up with Teddy before making our way on to the Milwaukee gig. The first was that Tommy Boyce had been hired to join the Randazzo group, replacing one of the Dazzlers who was unavailable for that booking. But the big shock came when Don Costa called me into his office to tell me that when the regular backup singer rejoined the group for the following engagement at New York's Copacabana, I was the one who would be the odd man out . . . something about my limited dancing ability. Surprise number one, Tommy would be a Dazzler. Surprise number two, I would soon be unemployed.

On Friday, November 22, 1963, we all piled into a Greyhound bus and headed for Chicago, where we would stay overnight before continuing on to Milwaukee. I noticed a definite air of sadness in the lobby as we checked into our small Chicago hotel. I asked the young girl behind the check-in desk, "Why is everybody so gloomy?" She said, "The president's been shot." "The president of the hotel? " I asked incredulously, my head in a fog. "No!" she replied. "The president! . . . the president of the United States."

We took our bags and climbed the stairs to our rooms in stunned silence. By the time Tommy and I reached the television set, Walter Cronkite was announcing that John F. Kennedy had been confirmed dead at one p. m. at Parkland Hospital in Dallas, the apparent victim of an assassin. I remembered as a kid when my mother's radio soap opera was interrupted to announce the death of FDR. But this was different. This was the young "movie star" president who was in his prime and was loved by the world. Tommy and I went out to buy the newspapers. People were crying in the streets. To them, and to us, this was personal.

The wind had been knocked out of Tommy, who had been an especially big fan of J.F.K. He gathered up and saved everything he could find in print about the assassination. He trained his 8mm movie camera on the TV and recorded the news coverage. He called Susan. While I felt a deep sorrow at the loss of our president and a strong sense of apprehension about the future, I knew that Tommy was always susceptible to highs and lows that went beyond anything I was capable of feeling. I chose to hang close to Tommy and do my best to be there for him.

No one in Milwaukee or any other state in the union was in much of a party mood that week. We played our engagement at the Holiday House to an audience that seemed to have no emotions left. Nevertheless, the show had to go on, and so we did our best to help the audience, and ourselves, forget the nightmare of the previous days, if only for a couple of hours.

Tommy Boyce naturally lit up when the spotlight hit him; he couldn't help himself. He smiled, he danced, he sang, he connected with his audience. But wait, it wasn't *his* audience. This was, after all, the Teddy Randazzo show, not the Tommy Boyce show. It was no secret that Tommy Boyce was a much better dancer than I was, but he had never worked as a backup singer before. Ironically, Tommy's dancing abilities began to work against him.

He would sometimes get carried away as we backed Teddy on one of his lead vocals, and he'd begin emoting to an attractive young girl at a front table. Randazzo might look over and catch Tommy breaking into a Jackie Wilson step and spinning around as the other Dazzlers, taken by surprise, tried to alter our moves to keep from being thrown off balance, or if that wasn't possible to just stumble out of his way. As the week wore on Teddy began to reconsider his decision to have Tommy replace me in the group.

Also, when you're singing intricate four-part harmonies, it's kind of important that each member of the group sing his own particular set of pre-arranged notes. Boyce didn't see the necessity of actually memorizing the parts as long as the notes he sang sounded good to him. By the end of the Milwaukee gig, Teddy and his manager agreed that Tommy was a liability to the group. Teddy reversed himself and announced that for his next engagements, I was back in, and Tommy was back to being a solo act.

Boyce didn't take it too hard. He had never seen himself as a backup singer anyway. After a cold, uncomfortable Greyhound bus ride back to Manhattan, Tommy went home to Susan. The rest of the band checked into the Bristol Hotel. And I settled back into my home base, one step above homelessness, next door at the Chesterfield. I knew I couldn't let myself start thinking about this too much, because I didn't want to have to recognize that after all this time in the music business I was still living at the matronly old Chesterfield on a tenuous weekly paycheck as a hired gun singing backup for someone else, and still relying almost exclusively on my faith in the future.

For the final three weeks of 1963, Teddy Randazzo and the Dazzlers were booked to play what might have been the most famous nightclub in the world, Manhattan's legendary "Copacabana." This was the place that Barry Manilow later sang about, where "music and passion were always in fashion."

The night we were to open, I found the address on East 60th Street near Fifth Avenue and walked through the front door directly into the rock-hard chests of two burly doormen who had materialized from the darkness inside. I said, "Excuse me, but I'm working here tonight." One of the uniformed "soldiers" instructed, "Not through here, you're not!" The two wise guys physically ejected me back out onto the sidewalk and directed me to go into the lobby of the hotel next door, up the elevator to a small dressing room on the fourth floor. From there I could cross back over to the Copa building from the dressing room level, descend the stairs, and re-enter the club through a back hallway.

♥

We soon found out that the crusty old owner, Jules Podell, ran his club like a military Mafia. The maitre d's and doormen were the captains, the waiters were the lieutenants, the busboys were the privates, and Podell was the general. We civilian entertainers were all instructed to approach the stage from the kitchen, walking down one particular aisle to and from the stage. We were not to talk to, or even look at, any patron while entering or leaving. During our shows General Podell would often shout over the music in a gravelly voice from his corner booth, yelling things like "Quiet, Teddy" or "Teddy, you're playing too loud."

But on New Year's Eve, 1963, the band members became increasingly bold, ignoring Podell's tirades, popping balloons that floated by the stage, and turning up the level on the amps. Our bravery was due in part to the New Year's Eve cheer we had imbibed and in part to the fact that New Year's morning we would be taking the seven a.m. flight from the icy streets of Manhattan to the sunshine and sandy beaches of San Juan, Puerto Rico. We were booked for a month in the main showroom of the Americana Hotel.

CHAPTER 14

Doing What Our Egos Wanted and Our Consciences Allowed

Puerto Rico was more than a breath of fresh air for me. The warm sea air seemed to have a calming effect on my mind, and I instantly relaxed into the laid back culture of the island. I enjoyed carefree days of basking in the sun on white sandy beaches; evenings soaking up the spotlight of one of San Juan's premier hotel showrooms; and warm, intoxicating tropical nights exploring the island's music scene. We immersed ourselves in the fascinating and ever-present Afro-Cuban rhythms and the colorful dance moves that they inspired, exploring a form of music that was excitingly new to me.

I can easily recall walking along the seashore one afternoon down an endless strand of white sand with Teddy and Bobby Weinstein, another one of the other Dazzlers. We stopped in front of a beach vendor and watched as he decapitated three green coconuts with quick swings of his machete, inserted straws in each, and presented them to us to quench our thirst.

As we walked along talking, I could feel the old walls that seemed to keep me from ever sharing anything below the surface of my life begin to crumble. It was as though the tropical breezes were blowing away some of the dust of my isolation, and in the process, the loneliness I had carried around for so long. I heard myself confiding to my friends, "This is the first time in more than a year that I finally feel some relief from the clouds of intense sadness and loneliness that have followed me around since the breakup of my family."

That night, just before show time at the Americana, I took a call backstage. With his knack for promotion, it had been no problem for my old twist sidekick, Barry Richards, to have his call put through to the stage extension. "Hey, man, I just called to say 'Hi.' What's going on out there?" When I told him that the show was about to start and I had to get on stage, he said, "Just leave the phone off the hook and I'll listen to the set." As I came offstage an hour later, I picked up the dangling headset, and we continued our conversation well into the morning.

A couple of weeks into the gig, I began to receive a series of notes from someone in the audience, hand written on cocktail napkins. Waitresses would deliver them to me on stage during the shows, and each one was signed at the bottom, simply, "Keely." The notes became increasingly provocative. "Why are you ignoring me?" "What are you afraid of?" "What are you going to do with me?"

Soon I learned that other members of the band were already friends with Keely. Apparently, I was not the first Dazzler to be pursued by this uninhibited and confident lady with the incredible voice. Still, somehow it seemed hard to believe that a big star like Keely Smith would actually be romancing me! Excited by the attention but overwhelmingly intimidated, I plotted my escape, and the first few nights I snuck out the back stage door.

♥

My life over the next year was a study in the black and white contrasts of living, as we all do, in a world of duality. Our casino engagements along the Nevada circuit were twelve weeks long, followed by twelve weeks of unemployment. In the three months we would have off in between, I would work in L.A. clubs with the Cajuns for part of the time, and then catch a plane to New York and write songs with Tommy.

In Manhattan I wrote all day but earned no income. After rent and child support, I sometimes would have to budget myself to a mere twenty-five cents a day for food. That would buy a burger from a street vendor or a plate of rice and beans at the Horn & Hardart Automat. The automat was a uniquely impersonal cafeteria where inserting coins would cause a little glass window to open, revealing access to my chosen entrée, which I would eat in a drab depressing room full of strangers.

For this half of my year, I would spend my evenings in a city where I didn't know anyone, walking the streets alone in the snowy cold before returning to my tiny flophouse room at the Chesterfield. The contrast to Vegas was poetic, and it probably helped me keep my head on straight and my ego somewhat in check. I was alone most of the time, except for my writing sessions with Tommy, and unnervingly disconnected from the earth's sun and soil and maybe my own soul.

Then there was the other half of my year: I lived in a lovely Las Vegas suite at the Savoy across the Strip from the Thunderbird, basking in the warm sun around the pool in the afternoons and performing at the T-Bird Lounge every night from midnight till seven a.m. Invariably, by our second set the lounge would be full of beautiful showgirls from the main showrooms of the hotels that lined the Strip, fresh from their performances, which were over by 1:00. I had spending money, the weather was beautiful, the food was great, and as you might imagine, for an inexperienced Arizona boy the romantic opportunities were unprecedented.

Inhibitions flow freer than water in Las Vegas. In this exciting environment, my somewhat reserved personality seemed to morph naturally into a sense of confidence that I had not known before. All of a sudden I became aware that a kind of magnetic power was available to me, and I experimented with using and misusing it. To an uninterested observer, I would have easily blended in with the multicolored tapestry of young personalities from all over America, collectively immersing ourselves in the culture of 1960s Las Vegas, doing what our egos wanted and our consciences allowed.

My relationship with alcohol in this lifetime would last merely a few short months. When I first joined Teddy's group, the drummer, Billy Lewis, invited me to explore the streets of Reno and grab a beer. When I explained that I didn't drink, Billy decided it was his duty to take me under his wing and educate me in the ways of the experienced road musician. "A cold Coors," he told me, "and a wooden-tipped Hav-A-Tampa cigar" were the hallmarks of "the good life" for sophisticated artists such as ourselves.

Then at the Copa in New York, he introduced me to a sweet, creamy drink called a White Russian and I occasionally indulged, especially on New Year's Eve. By the time we were performing in Puerto Rico, Billy had discovered that a shot of local 151-proof rum in a glass of pineapple juice cost only 75 cents at the hotel bar. Nights after performing, I would join my fellow musicians for a cheap buzz. I quickly learned that this drink shouldn't be taken lightly, regardless of its affordability, once I experienced the super strong punch it delivered. But then, some things are easily forgotten.

Soon after returning to our semi-permanent gig in Las Vegas, Billy and I drove to a liquor store between shows and purchased a bottle of our favorite concoction and some juice. After work we mixed a few in the car before returning to the T-Bird Lounge. There I met an attractive young lady at the bar, and feeling ten feet tall and bullet proof, I began letting my newly found charm run wild. It was only a few minutes before I felt the immediate need to leave quickly—and alone.

As I walked through the casino, the people and sounds began to cross-fade into a blur of color and clanging noise. As I stepped outside the protection of the casino air conditioning, the morning air struck me, heavy and hot. I made it through the thankfully light traffic on the Strip toward my waiting suite at the Savoy, but now I was facing the deep vacant lot that I would need to negotiate to get there. I felt my boots begin to sink into the sand. On the pavement, I was already on shaky ground, but now the desert sand was relieving me of any stability I might have still possessed.

My head began to spin. After a few steps I fell to my knees and then toppled over like a tree after the final strike from a lumberjack's ax. I lay there on my face in the sand for a time, nearly helpless. The morning sun was warming the sand, and I gradually became aware that it was starting to burn my skin. I forced my uncooperative body up on all fours and began to crawl, pulling myself inch by inch across the vacant lot desert.

I had become the French Legionnaire in a long-forgotten movie from my distant past. In a blur, I could see the Kasaba, or was it the Savoy, getting bigger as I wormed my way across the Sahara. Finally, Peter Lorre (or was it the kind doorman who recognized me) spied the spectacle and helped me through to my room. I avoided ever feeling ten feet tall and bullet proof again after that experience. And that was the last time I ever got drunk.

While on the surface the life I was living in Las Vegas may have been every young man's dream, it didn't take long for this lifestyle to begin to wear thin. There was a subtle empty space deep in my heart where the music and romance couldn't reach. I knew that I was far away from developing the capacity to really love, and although I had many girlfriends, I had very little confidence in believing that I was really loved by anyone else.

The sporadic and spontaneous conversations I would have with God, the spiritual enthusiasm that had seemed to come so naturally in my childhood years, had gradually dropped by the wayside of my busy life, obscured by the everyday battles of raising a family and forging a career. So, without a clear map to lead me to my treasure, this twenty-four-year-old walked along with the others, exploring clues and looking for roads into myself.

A young sax player who played in another T-Bird lounge band introduced me to his friend, Warren Stagg. Warren was tall and older than us with deep, knowing eyes. He told me he had lived for months with a Native American tribe in Texas along the Mexican border. After some time, the elders had trusted him enough to make him an honorary brother and had shared with him their mystic rituals that revolved around ingestion of pods from the peyote cactus. Warren claimed to have gained hallucinogenic wisdom and insights from these experiences.

Warren began to suggest reading material that he thought would be helpful in my own spiritual search. The first book was *Meetings with Remarkable Men* by the Greek/Armenian mystic, George Ivanovich Gurdjieff. Gurdjieff postulated that each of us has innate potentialities that are rarely realized because of the self-effort required to bring them into expression.

Much of Alan Watts' *The Wisdom of Insecurity* seemed to make sense. He postulated that life in this ever-changing world is inherently insecure, so we should just relax and embrace it. By tensing and *trying* to float on water, you sink, he reasoned, but when you give up and relax, your body will float naturally. His philosophy seemed to be the polar opposite of Gurdjieff's emphasis on self-effort. I began to ask myself, "When it comes to my spiritual life, am I trying too hard or not hard enough?"

Then, Warren told me to check out *The Life and Teachings of the Masters of the Far East*. The books chronicled the spiritual powers and stature of certain East Indian yogis and opened up my decidedly Western mind to a whole new world of possibilities.

♥

Maybe my renewed spiritual search and the philosophical books I'd been reading had raised my consciousness slightly above the mundane. At any rate, only a little introspection had convinced me that the right thing to do was to try to reunite with my wife and family. One evening, I called Becky in Phoenix and invited her to Las Vegas for the weekend to see the show. She left her job an hour early that Friday night, dropped Bobby and Bret off at her folks, and I picked her up at the Las Vegas airport.

It was so great to see her after all those months. In some ways, it was as if we had never been apart. She was the warm, charming girl that I had known since she was twelve. After she was settled into her room, I took her to a restaurant I knew where we enjoyed a romantic dinner over candlelight at a sidewalk table overlooking the Strip.

"I wasn't sure I should come," she confided, "but my friends at work told me that I deserved a weekend away." Time had given us enough distance from the reality of the breakup that we were finally able to relax around each other. For over an hour we laughed and talked about the old times. Finally, at just the right strategic moment, I swallowed hard and plunged headlong into the subject at hand. "I've been doing a lot of thinking lately," I began, "and I know it isn't right for me to be apart from you and the kids. I've missed you all so much. Is there any chance that we could maybe start over again from where we were before I made such a stupid blunder?"

The reflection of candlelight was sparkling in Becky's eyes. She looked at me for a long time in silence, trying to find the right words. I held my breath and waited. "Bobby, I've been seeing someone in Phoenix. He's a great guy and he's asked me to marry him . . . and I told him 'yes.'"

CHAPTER 15

I Need You to Get This Kid Out of Town

"Hey! Where're you going?" Tommy was asking Susan one spring evening, seeing her dressed for a night out. He had arrived home at their New York apartment as usual after his appointments that day. "Oh, Nancy wants me to go along with her to this music business event she was invited to. You don't mind, do you?"

Back in New York, Tommy Boyce and Susan Hudson had been living together for nearly two years by now. Maybe the hum-drum routine of teaching part time at NYU and playing housewife in between was beginning to feel a little boring for the adventurous Susan. Or, more likely, having higher aspirations for her life, she began to reassess her future with a still struggling pop songwriter. Whatever the cause, a strain in the relationship had been developing for a while now.

Susan and her friend Nancy, who worked at a recording studio, found the address on Manhattan's Upper East Side and the elevator opened directly into a luxurious penthouse apartment. It was an upscale, catered affair, with live music and uniformed servers. The view from the balconies which overlooked the city was spectacular, the fare was first class, and the night seemed magical. An hour in, her friend Nancy confirmed what Susan might already have been thinking "This is the life we were meant to live!" Then, around eleven, someone introduced Susan to the man she would eventually marry.

George Goldner, the legendary rock 'n' roll pioneer, had been one of the most influential early purveyors of East Coast doo-wop. He was responsible for a bunch of the records I grew up with, producing and releasing them on his own labels.

His friend, innovative producer Shadow Morton, has suggested in interviews that Goldner may have even coined the term, rock 'n' roll, usually attributed to disc jockey Alan Freed. According to Morton, it was a time when George was the one pulling many of the famous disc jockey's strings after skillfully developing the concept of payola and using it to build a powerful fiefdom with himself as feudal lord. But by 1964 George had made, and reportedly gambled away, several fortunes.

Years later, Linda Goldner told me that her father once confided to her that the real reason he began calling Susan Hudson was to see if he could get betting tips on the NYU sports teams. But, I guess her sweet southern drawl began to beguile him, and soon Susan became George Goldner's latest game of chance.

An expensive watch arrived at the apartment one morning, a present from George. Her friend Nancy was Tommy's friend too, but she told Susan that if the choice for her future was between the struggling young songwriter or the millionaire music legend, it was a "no brainer." She urged her to "Go for the good life." Susan was not convinced. Even though she was intrigued by George, she was still in love with Tommy and, day by day, she seemed to become more conflicted.

One summer afternoon while Tommy was downtown writing, Susan took a call from Goldner. After a long tug of war she finally agreed to meet him in Manhattan to talk. Seated at a dark corner table of a nearly deserted, upscale mid-town restaurant, she told him that she still could not commit to leaving Tommy. Now, George Goldner had long been accustomed to getting what he wanted and, pretty much, getting it when he wanted it. He excused himself, walked to the pay phone near the men's room and placed a call to another music business legend.

It was Don Kirshner. Known as "the man with the golden ear," Kirshner had built his Aldon Music into the top publishing firm in the country, signing a stable of extraordinarily talented, young songwriters that included Goffin & King, Mann & Weil, and Sedaka & Greenfield. Kirshner picked up George Goldner's call. "Donnie! Congratulations on the

Screen Gems deal. What a killing, you Devil!" Goldner was talking about the multi-million dollar offer Kirshner had just accepted from Columbia Pictures/Screen Gems Television to buy his whole operation, while letting him continue to manage it.

Three thousand miles west, a young Screen Gems Television producer named Bert Schneider was already planning a TV show about a fictional rock group, and he needed to find a source for some top quality song material. Where better to gain access to the top young writers in the music business than to buy the country's top music publisher, Aldon Music. Conveniently, Bert's father Abe Schneider was the president of Columbia Pictures, so it may not have been too big a stretch for Bert to convince his dad to make Donnie Kirshner an offer he couldn't refuse.

Anyway, back in the midtown restaurant, George Goldner continued, "Listen, Donnie, I need to call in a marker. There's a kid named Tommy Boyce. He's written a couple of hits. I want you to offer him a hundred bucks a week and sign him up. I'll pay his advance money myself. There's only one thing, though. I need to get him out of town. You've gotta send him out to your West Coast office."

Of course, neither Tommy (carrying his guitar on the subway into Manhattan every day) nor I (lying by the pool at a Las Vegas luxury hotel) knew anything about Goldner's involvement at the time. I'm not sure Tommy ever knew. But he went along to his meeting with Don Kirshner just the same.

Donnie told him that "Come A Little Bit Closer" was one of his favorite songs. He mentioned that they had just recently opened publishing operations offices in Los Angeles. The offer of an exclusive contract with a top publisher like Screen Gems-Columbia Music was a big break for Tommy. Tommy loved Susan, but his dream had always been a career in music, and music was his life. There were raindrops on the windowpanes of their apartment and in the eyes of the two lovers the morning Tommy finally told Susan that he was accepting the offer.

♥

Boyce had already jetted out to the West Coast by the time I got back to Manhattan for my next hiatus from performing. He had called me on the road to give me the sad and wonderful news. My first week back, I had a call from Susan. It seemed when George Goldner had set up a date to record a young rockabilly singer in Nashville, Susan had convinced him to include a Boyce & Hart song on the session. In a show of continued loyalty to her old friends, she had further persuaded George to invite Teddy Randazzo and me to accompany them to Nashville for the recording.

Goldner was warm and dignified. He was four years younger than my dad, many years older than Susan, and I had mixed feelings at seeing Susan and George together as a couple. But the weekend was much less uncomfortable than you might imagine, due largely to George's sincere friendliness and easy manner.

Since Goldner didn't like to fly, we boarded a train at Grand Central Station and the round trip afforded me ample time to get to know the man who had so quickly replaced my partner in Susan's life. I had heard the rumors so I kept a sharp eye out for any indications of Goldner's mob affiliations, but I witnessed nothing firsthand to confirm them that weekend. At the session, Teddy earned his keep by explaining to the session players in musician's terms, the particular "feel" that George had in mind for one of the songs. I, on the other hand, along for the ride and totally unnecessary, fully enjoyed my first look at the Nashville recording scene.

♥

On the train ride back to New York, Teddy told me that Don Costa had signed Little Anthony and the Imperials to his DCP label and asked Randazzo to write the arrangements and produce the records. He invited me to come around to Bell Sound studios a few weeks later to monitor the first session, and that's where I first got to meet the group. Teddy and Bobby Weinstein had written some great songs for the session, and watching Randazzo conduct the string section, taking the musicians through his beautiful arrangements for the first time, was an inspiration in itself.

But witnessing Anthony Gourdine sing his heart out, as he superimposed his classic falsetto range voice onto the tracks that night, was an experience somewhat akin to what it might have been like for an art major to watch Da Vinci as he painted the Mona Lisa. The combination of Anthony and Teddy was magic, and that first DCP session yielded two standards, the first of nine Little Anthony pop chart hits to be produced by Randazzo. The group's first single release, "I'm On The Outside (Looking In)" peaked at #15, but the follow-up became Anthony's second top ten single, "Goin' Out Of My Head."

In November we all headed back to the Thunderbird for another twelve-week stint, but this time without Gerry McGee, who had decided to take a break from the road. Teddy asked the other two "Cajuns" and me to leave early so we could spend some time in L.A. auditioning guitar players. We chose a somewhat reserved but very likable guitar virtuoso named Vince Megna who became my roommate and, soon, my friend.

Vinnie picked up the phone one afternoon in our room at the Savoy, held his hand over the mouthpiece and said, "It's for you, Bobby. Says his name is Tommy Boyce." Over the next few weeks, Tommy's calls became more and more frequent and more and more compelling. He'd say, "Forget the road, Bobby, there's no future for you out there. You can play clubs for the rest of your life and you'll still be living from paycheck to paycheck. Come on back here to L.A. and sign with Screen Gems. I can get you the same deal they're giving me. We'll write some hits."

Of course, the one hundred bucks a week from Screen Gems would be considerably less than I was making with Teddy in Vegas. But, finally one afternoon after one of Tommy's more persuasive phone calls, I found Teddy and gave him my notice, agreeing to finish out this last three-month commitment. As it turned out, staying on the road for those last few weeks gave me the opportunity to co-write one of the biggest songs of my career.

By the time Little Anthony and the Imperials' second release had become the sixth biggest selling record in the country, Randazzo and the Dazzlers were already including it in our show. One night in December, after the first set, Teddy called a group meeting. "Listen guys, I've gotta fly back to New York to record a new session with Anthony. "Going Out Of My Head" has peaked on the charts and we don't have anything in the can." Since he had to be gone for two nights, he told us that on

Tuesday, after our regular Monday night off, each of the Dazzlers would be expected to take turns replacing him on the lead vocals for the shows.

When the band members had left the meeting, Teddy told his three singers, "Come on, guys, let's go upstairs and use the piano in one of the banquet rooms. We need a new single for Little Anthony. Bobby Weinstein was Randazzo's regular writing partner, and although I had written a few songs with Teddy by this time, I considered myself fortunate to be asked. The third backup singer had a date and begged off. So the three of us headed up to a cold, dimly-lit convention room on our one to two a.m. break.

Weinstein suggested some titles, and when Teddy heard the words *hurts so bad*, he began to sing a melody, crafting an arrangement on the piano as he went. My two co-writers were in perfect sync and began trading lyric line contributions: "I know you—don't know what I'm going through . . . " It was shaping up to be a story of lost love and the pain of running into an old flame again on the street.

By the time the first chorus was ending, "Let me tell you that it hurts so bad to see you again," I was trying desperately to contribute. After "to see you again," I blurted out, "like needles and pins." It was a rhyme where no rhyme was needed. The chorus was already complete, and we were heading back into a new verse. But Teddy liked the tactile description and added a little descending melody line to accommodate the extra words.

Now, with renewed confidence, I jumped into the fray and we finished the lyric with ample time to return to our two a.m. show. Envisioning the emotion in Little Anthony's pleading voice, we had ended the epic by giving him the words, "Please don't go, please don't go."

The next Tuesday night, I sang "Turn On Your Love Light" and "That'll Be the Day" sitting at the T-Bird lounge piano while Randazzo scribbled out orchestral arrangements on the "red-eye" back to New York. The next day Anthony walked to the microphone in Manhattan's Bell Sound Studios and sang "Hurt So Bad" even more heart-wrenchingly than we had imagined. I was thrilled when I finally got to hear the performance. Actually, Teddy recorded three of my songs with Anthony & the Imperials in that session: "Reputation," the song I had written on the

Greyhound bus my very first week back in New York, and "Never Again," co-written with Teddy at the stone country house he owned in the beautiful wooded suburb of Nyack, New York.

"Hurt So Bad" by Little Anthony and the Imperials hit the top ten in February 1965. Happily, the song was back in the top ten again by the Lettermen barely four years later, and once again, Linda Ronstadt's version reached *Billboard's* #8 position in 1980, making it one of the only songs ever to break into the top ten three times by three different artists in three different decades. Sometime back, BMI presented me a Special Citation of Achievement commemorating the fact that "Hurt So Bad" has been played more than three million times on the radio in the U.S. alone.

In April of 1965 I closed my last gig with Teddy, never again to be a Dazzler. I boarded a cab to McCarran Field, took the hour-long flight to LAX, and riding high off of my second top ten song I made my triumphant return to the City of the Angels where I had been invited to sign an exclusive song-writing agreement with Screen Gems-Columbia Music.

CHAPTER 16

"So Long, Chumps.
I'm Getting Out While I Can."

Tommy picked me up at the airport and we drove back in to Hollywood. When he began to pull into the parking garage of his apartment, I turned to Tommy and exclaimed, "Boyce! This is the Beachcomber, the same apartment complex where Becky and I lived when we first got married six years ago!"

It was not surprising that Tommy had made friends with his neighbor in the next apartment. However, it was astounding that his next-door neighbor turned out to be my old buddy, Barry Richards. One day, my name had finally come up in a conversation across their adjoining balconies. When they compared notes Barry and Tommy had each claimed to be my best friend. For me, it was a happy best friend reunion, two for the price of one.

For the first couple of weeks I slept on Tommy's couch. But living at the Beachcomber felt too much like the past for me, and the sad memories overshadowed the good ones. Within a few days I was trying to convince my writing partner of the far superior merits of renting our own house somewhere in the Hollywood Hills. With visions of Sedona dancing in my head, I had woven word tapestries for Tommy of how great it would be to draw from the inspiration of nature and the feeling of country living. But it was my final point that finally sold him. "And we could play our music as loud as we want to!"

We drove around the hills and soon found the perfect rustic two bedroom A-frame, hanging over the side of Woodrow Wilson Drive. It was small but affordable, with a balcony overlooking a deep canyon of green brush and a mountain of stately pines. Tommy and I called it the "Boat House" because of its unique shape and the fact that it had been built by a team of ship builders.

We furnished our new bachelor pad with some couches and chairs from the storeroom at Screen Gems after getting permission from our new boss, Lester Sill, who was now head of the West Coast operation. I guess the office furniture was our first corporate perk. I spent my last hundred dollars at Sears on a symbol of luxury that, until now, I had only fantasized about owning: a king-sized mattress. We put colored bulbs in the chandelier and somebody made us a housewarming gift of a lava lamp, which became the centerpiece of our interior design fashion statement. For Tommy Boyce and Bobby Hart, as well as thousands of other West Coast flower children, this was the dawning of "The Summer of Love."

As I walked into the West Coast offices of Screen Gems-Columbia Music at 7033 Sunset, it felt like the air was filled with the vitality and excitement of an approaching storm. Looking back, it seems that my return to Los Angeles had neatly coincided with a paradigm shift in the entire music industry, its center of gravity having quickly, if unintentionally, followed me from the East Coast to the West.

Lester Sill welcomed me that first day, showing me the offices and introducing me around to the staff. He said he remembered me from the day four years earlier when Phil Spector and I had met in his office. My welcome and my confidence were both enhanced by the fact that "Hurt So Bad" happened to be in the top ten that week. Lester soon became a warm, encouraging father figure to me as he already was to Tommy. He was always in our corner, whether sending us out on assignments or listening to our new songs. He even invited us to join him and his family on their weekend spring break outing to Palm Springs.

Professionally, Boyce and I hit the ground running. My first night back in town we wrote two songs on Tommy's rented piano, "In the Night (Where Your Dreams Are Waiting)" and "Out of the Picture." Lester and his general manager at Screen Gems Music, Chuck Kaye, got them both recorded, the first by Eric Burdon and the Animals, the second by Gary Lewis and the Playboys.

While waiting for me to join him in Los Angeles, Tommy hadn't exactly been sitting around on his hands. He had only landed at Screen Gems a few months ahead of me, but in that time he had already written three important songs. This was the third time that Boyce had tested the waters of success in the field of popular songwriting before I'd had a chance to join him at the pool party. He had had hits on both coasts before I joined him in New York, and now he had beaten me to the punch on the Left Coast.

This time, there was "Peaches and Cream," the infectious hit by Ike and Tina Turner's backup girls, the Ikettes. Plus, there were theme songs for two popular new music television shows, *Shebang!* and the Dick Clark after school dance party, *Where the Action Is*. Its theme song, "Action," had become a top-ten hit by Freddy Cannon.

Boyce had written these hits with another Screen Gems contract writer, a young, good looking Greek-American named Steve Venet. Steve was warm and generous in making me feel welcome as I joined the team. But one morning, Boyce and I arrived at the office to find a note from Venet. It said "So long, chumps. I'm getting out while I can." I never learned the story behind Steve quitting the music business so abruptly. But he never again returned to work at Screen Gems.

After the success of "Action," Dick Clark Productions began calling us to do the music for all their new shows. Not unlike short order cooks, Tommy and I would often write a theme song to the specifications of the producers and deliver it to them, fully mastered, the very next day.

We ended up working with Dick Clark many times throughout our careers, in front of and behind the scenes. Two years later, when we became recording artists, we made numerous appearances on his shows, *American Bandstand* and *Happening*.

♥

One afternoon, Lester sent us over to the Columbia Pictures studio lot for a meeting with producers Ted and Betty Corday about composing music for a daytime television drama. The husband and wife team had been very successful soap opera producers, going back to the days of radio. Now, they had a new one coming out on NBC television called *Days of Our Lives*, starring Macdonald Carey.

The Cordays told us they had recently seen *Fiddler on the Roof* on Broadway and asked if we could compose a theme song that would evoke the emotion of a particular song from that show called "Sunrise, Sunset." In a few days, we were back in their office to play them a demo. We had hand-tailored our new instrumental theme to reflect the mood of their favorite new song. They hated it. A few days later we sent over to the Cordays a new demo of our second melodic stab at their theme.

Tommy and I were working in a small demo studio called *Eldorado* when we got the call from Lester telling us the Cordays had hated our latest effort even more than the first. Tommy erupted, "Hey, we don't have time for this. These people don't know what they want. We need to concentrate on making hits." I said "Okay, Tommy, but . . . before we give up, I've got one last idea. There's a Hammond B-3 sitting over there. Just let the tape roll and I'll lay down a few minutes of music. I'll try to capture the spirit of the organ I remember hearing as a kid as it underscored the drama of my mom's daytime radio soaps." So that's exactly what we did. Ted and Betty loved it.

Arranger Don McGinnis took our organ tape and arranged the song for full orchestra, including a distinctive introduction. Then Screen Gems flew him to England where he recorded the theme with members of the London Philharmonic Orchestra.

When Ken Corday took over the helm of the show after the death of his parents he replaced most of our musical underscore with his own compositions, much more in keeping with the ominous plot lines into which the show had morphed over the years. But, to his credit, thankfully he has allowed our "Theme from Days of Our Lives" to continue tick-tocking behind the hourglass opening of this timeless institution of daytime television well into its fifth decade.

Like probably every other pair of writers, Tommy and I had our disagreements and struggles. I often told him he was too eager to jump into the unknown, and he would sometimes get frustrated that I always needed to pause and think before doing anything. This was a time when we traded places and it paid off for both of us. *Days of Our Lives* would be playing on network television five days a week for the next fifty years, not only becoming a national fixture, but also a major export to other countries around the world.

CHAPTER 17

Soaking Up Our Share of the Peace and Love

The Sunset Strip is a two-mile stretch of Sunset Boulevard beginning at the Beverly Hills city limit and rambling eastward to the vicinity of our offices at Screen Gems. The summer was especially warm in 1965, and already a few contingents of colorfully dressed flower children were beginning to congregate along the Strip. But within a few months, there would be thousands of kids crowding the sidewalks and spilling over into the streets. And ground zero for this emerging phenomenon was a nightclub called the Whisky A Go Go.

Now Tommy and I were spending our sun-filled California days doing what we loved, having a great time writing new songs and learning how to create demos that made them sound commercial enough to get recorded. And we were more than pleased that some of them had already been cut by soft pop artists like Herman's Hermits, Gary Lewis & The Playboys, and Dino, Desi & Billy.

But nighttime would find us at our regular table at the Whiskey, soaking up the counterculture sounds of groups like Arthur Lee & Love or Jim Morrison and the Doors. These were shockingly new sounds to us, worlds apart from the pop of the first half of the sixties, and we were excited and inspired by them. We had long since developed the habit of being vigilant to be able to notice early on any new directions in which the constantly changing stream of pop music might be flowing.

The result was a new assertiveness in our writing and a string of new songs with a little harder edge to them, such as "I'm Not Your Stepping

Stone," "She," and "Words." It wasn't long before we were getting them recorded by some of the new, more rock-influenced groups like The Leaves, the Boston Tea Party, and Paul Revere and the Raiders.

The Boyce & Hart sound would later become lumped by some into a dubious new category called "Bubble Gum Music," meaning productions aimed at teens and pre-teens. It was an allegation memorialized by the 1969 hit record of the same name. The verse started out, "Tommy Boyce and Bobby Hart wonder what she's doin' while The Monkees are singin' 'bout Valleri." But once we started including the sounds of feedback guitar licks, tamburas, and other Indian instruments in our productions, a more apropos description of the music we began making in 1965 might have been "Psychedelic Bubble Gum."

For our harder rock demos we would bring our friend Keith Allison into the studio. "Guitar Keith" was a natural heavy rock player who could lay down some incredible Stones-style riffs when we needed them. The lanky Paul McCartney look-alike had been Ray Peterson's guitar player since his high school days in San Antonio, and that's where Tommy had met him four years earlier. Now Keith, too, had recently relocated to L.A.

We learned how to produce records by analyzing what we liked about our favorite tunes on the radio, and we honed our craft a little more every time we got to go into the studio to produce a demo of one of our new songs. Soon Screen Gems was selling some of our demos to record companies to be released to the public as masters. One of the first was an MGM record featuring Tommy Boyce as the artist. When it came time to promote the record, Tommy was booked to appear on *Where the Action Is*. As it happens, the location for this episode of the popular after-school show was to be the Whisky A Go Go. I went along to watch the taping.

On this very summer afternoon, Keith Allison had stopped by the Screen Gems offices to pick up a check for his guitar work on one of our demos. The check request needed the signature of the producer, so Keith headed on down to the Whisky to find one of us and get a John Hancock on the form. As Tommy performed for the *Action* cameras, Keith and I stood in the crowd along the wall, watching from the sidelines.

Well, it turns out that when the camera panned by to capture the crowd and the dancers, we were included in some of the shots. This "cameo" appearance would have absolutely no impact on my own career. But Keith Allison? Well now, that's another story.

In the next few days, Dick Clark Productions was flooded with thousands of letters from all over the country. The viewers wanted to know "Was that really Paul McCartney in the audience?" or "Who *was* that long-haired dreamboat?" For days, the Dick Clark people searched for the identity of the mysterious stranger in the crowd. Finally, their detective work led them to Tommy and me. After a few phone calls we tracked down our friend in Las Vegas. Keith had taken a gig playing with The Crickets at none other than my old haunt, the Thunderbird Lounge.

We put an incredulous Keith Allison in touch with the Clark office, and they told him that his appearance had sparked the biggest fan response they had ever received. When they learned that he sang and played guitar, they signed him to appear as a regular cast member of *Where the Action Is*, alongside Steve Alamo and Paul Revere and the Raiders.

An overnight sensation, Keith Allison began dominating the pages of the fan magazines and soon signed with Columbia Records. When the TV series ended, Keith toured and recorded for several years as an official member of the Raiders.

♥

Now, more and more, Tommy and I were beginning to immerse ourselves in the newly emerging psychedelic culture. We walked a fine line between our day gig in an intense and competitive business and our evenings when we would blend in with the hippies on the Strip, trying to soak up our share of the peace and love. To us, it seemed the best of both worlds: we were professionals with the security and creative outlet of our careers; but we also felt naturally at ease hanging out with the kids and feeling a part of the gathering storm that was beginning to transform the culture of our country.

Those spontaneous gatherings that they called love-ins or be-ins were beginning to spring up everywhere, first at San Francisco's Golden Gate

Park and then right in our own neighborhood at Griffith Park, and we would go whenever we could. It was a kaleidoscope of clothes, colors, incense, dancers, and laid-back onlookers, and we wanted to be a part of the excitement.

The first time the wonderfully strange sounds of the sitar and tablas came wafting on incense breeze, through the trees and between the free-spirited dancers at one of these events, it felt anciently familiar. In this lifetime, I had never heard anything like this striking music of India, and yet the sound of these exotic instruments and demi-semitonal musical scales seemed to instantly transport me to a distant past and brought the unshakable feeling that I had just come home.

Mind-expanding substances were readily available at these gatherings, and I watched their effects on the many participants. Some sat peacefully observing, their faces radiating a knowing smile, while others gave themselves over to wild kinetic dance or more disturbing gyrations. LSD, still too new to be illegal, was freely offered in many colorful configurations. My spiritual curiosity, largely dormant since leaving home, had begun to re-emerge in Las Vegas. Now I was hearing about ways to speed up the evolution of my consciousness by just popping a pill.

One evening I attended a lecture by Richard Alpert,* one of the professors who had pioneered the study of psychedelics at Harvard, alongside Timothy Leary. I sat captivated as he began to speak about the tremendous amount of sensory input that was relentlessly bombarding each of our human psyches. He explained that our brains have inhibitors on the synapses that let only the most pertinent information filter through. What LSD does, they had found, was to remove some of the inhibitors, letting more of the information through and allowing one to see things from all sides.

I believed that the professor knew what he was talking about, but I also had witnessed firsthand the toll that this powerful agent was taking on

---

* Later, Richard Alpert journeyed to India searching for spiritual guidance. There he met a holy man and was astounded when the yogi remained totally unaffected after ingesting massive amounts of Alpert's LSD. After accepting the yogi as his guru, Alpert took the new name of Baba Ram Das. Upon his return to America, his book *Be Here Now* became a sixties spiritual classic. Through his Love Serve Remember Foundation, Ram Das continues to serve the spiritual community from Hawaii.

the bodies and minds of some of its most loyal enthusiasts. I began to look around for ways of expanding my consciousness without the use of drugs.

One day after a session at Western Recorders, I was talking to our sound engineer, Henry Lewy, who later produced many of Joni Mitchell's hit records. Inevitably, the subject of spiritual philosophy surfaced, and I mentioned my interest in Eastern mysticism. A few weekends later Henry invited me to attend a small gathering with him and his wife to see the Maharishi Mahesh Yogi during one of his early visits from India. It was my first opportunity to hear a real Indian yogi speak about Eastern meditation, and soon after I signed up to learn how to practice his Transcendental Meditation.

That night I lit some incense, sat quietly on my built-in king sized bed, and tried to focus on the single Sanskrit syllable I had been given at my initiation. After trying for a few minutes, I became vividly aware, probably for the first time in my life, of this incessant stream of thoughts—thoughts both trite and profound—that must have been spontaneously chattering on and on in the background of my mind since birth, without my even noticing.

Eventually the repetition of the *mantra* began to distract this obstinately chattering "monkey" mind of mine. My heart rate began to slow down and I soon found myself in a place of positive peace. After a time, memory thoughts began to float back into my consciousness, but this time in a much more relaxed and orderly fashion. I resolved to find a few minutes, morning and evening, to continue my new meditation practice.

Around this time, someone turned me onto a book called, *Psycho-Cybernetics*, which compared the human brain to a computer. I was inspired by author Maxwell Maltz's proposal that the mind is the storehouse of unlimited potentiality, and that the method for shaping our own futures and obtaining the things we want in life was to imagine them in vivid detail.

I explained the concept to Tommy, "Vividly imagining is the best way to program your brain-computer and let it know what it is that you want it to help you achieve. But I also think that a big part of what it does is to help get rid of the negative thoughts and self-images that have been holding us back from realizing our dreams." He and I added an intense regimen of self-programming to our individual morning routine schedules every day, visualizing the super success that we had been craving.

As we hung out one night at the Boat House, I remember over-confidently telling our friend Del Shannon, "Tommy and I are going to make a lot of money this year." I had seen it in my mind every morning, and it was increasingly beginning to feel like reality. Del, who had *already* made a lot of money in the music business, was kind enough to not embarrass me and supportively agreed, "Yeah, those new song demos you guys played me tonight are unbelievable!"

VISUALIZATION

(1) GOALS: TELL THE UNIVERSE WHAT YOU WANT

VIVIDLY IMAGINING WHAT I WANT is one of the most powerful tools I've found to program my mind to help me achieve my goals. OUR HUMAN COMPUTERS (our minds) are incredibly powerful and anxious to help us achieve the things we want. Figure out what you want; then spend a few minutes each day visualizing it in vivid detail and living color.

(2) ZIGZAG YOUR WAY TO SUCCESS

IT'S NOT ENOUGH to form a strong goal, or even to visualize it in clear pictures. Constant vigilance is required to notice when you are straying from the target. In Dr. Maxwell Maltz's groundbreaking book Psycho-Cybernetics, he talks about how guided missiles never shoot straight to their destination, from A to B. After they're launched, environment and circumstances will inevitably cause them to veer off course. But the missile has a mechanism that not only makes it aware that it's straying, but also gives it the exact coordinates it needs to course correct. In other words, it zigzags its way to the goal. It's the same with human beings. Be watchful to know when it's time to correct your course.

(3) DON'T BE AFRAID TO FINE TUNE

IF YOU FOCUS TOO NARROWLY on your original goal, you may fail to recognize brighter opportunities as they materialize along the way. Stay open to fine-tuning and improving your goals as you're provided with more reliable information and more favorable circumstances.

CHAPTER 18

A Grammy or a World Wide Wrestling Federation Award?

T ommy and I recited our names to the guard at the Columbia Pictures gate, where we had driven one afternoon in the summer of 1965 in Tommy's pink and cream colored Cadillac. He had affectionately named his car "Peaches and Cream" in honor of his recent Ikettes hit. We were directed to the offices of Raybert Productions for our first meeting with television producer Bert Schneider. Bert was the *bert* in Raybert and the *Ray* was Bob Rafelson, the future acclaimed director of movies like *Five Easy Pieces, Stay Hungry,* and *The Postman Always Rings Twice.*

Schneider was a relaxed 6'3", soft-spoken and laid-back, dressed in a white knit sweater and jeans with loafers. Wasting no time, he asked us if we had seen *Hard Day's Night* and *Help* and, of course, we told him we had. Then he explained that he and his partner were planning a new show utilizing the same madcap chase romps and filmic techniques that The Beatles had used in their movies. "Basically," he said, it was to be "an American Beatles on television." They were calling it *The Monkees* with two e's.

The concept struck a chord with us right away, and when we learned that the music used in the show would also be released on records, Tommy lead the verbal whirlwind to convince Schneider that we were his guys. Tommy and I were excited about the sales potential of combining phonograph records with weekly television. We remembered what had happened when Ricky Nelson sang his first song on the *Ozzie and Harriet Show.* Bert told us that the pilot episode would require three original songs, a romantic ballad, a dance number called "The Chase," and a theme song called "The Monkees" that would open and close every show.

The next few days were spent enthusiastically planning and coming up with material for our latest assignment. We immediately thought of a song we had recently written called "I Wanna Be Free," perfect for the Davy Jones walking-along-the-beach-after-breaking-up-with-his-girl-friend scene. Then we quickly came up with a song you could dance to for the party scene. Now, we needed to compose a more enduring piece of music that could serve as the theme song for the show. Over the weekend, after reviewing how Schneider had described the new group's image, we plotted the elements that we thought should be incorporated in the lyric.

One ordinary August morning, Tommy grabbed his guitar and we walked the four blocks from our Boat House down the hill to the tiny Paseo de Cahuenga Park, the perfect environment in which to write while still enjoying some relaxation and sunshine. Along the way, Tommy started snapping his fingers to the rhythm of our swinging footsteps. Soon I joined in, making the "choo-choot-cha-choo sound of an opening and closing hi-hat cymbal with my voice. In the back of my mind I was hearing the hi-hat and finger-snapping groove of "Catch Us If You Can," the classic Dave Clark Five single that had been all over the radio that week.

A few cars sped past us on our narrow mountain road, their drivers glaring at us like we were crazy to be out walking in a city thoroughly dominated by motor vehicles. Tommy not only ignored the road hogs, but boldly announced a claim to our space with the music and words that sprang effortlessly from his lips, *"Here we come, walking down the street."* Without missing a beat I sang back, "We get the funniest looks from everyone we meet; Hey, hey, we're The Monkees . . ." By the time we reached the park, most of this anything but ordinary theme song had been created.

I can't say that we consciously tailored every line to accomplish our predetermined list of goals, but intuitively we had captured the elements that we thought were important. In a three minute romp, we'd pointed out the Marx Brothers image of our as-yet-non-existent new band (*People say we monkey around);* we had taken a deeper look by identifying them with a more serious and articulate youth culture (*We're the young generation and we've got something to say);* we reinforced the non-threatening visual image that our long-haired hippie types would be portraying on TV (*We're just tryin' to be friendly* and *We're too busy singing to put anybody down);* and we ended by providing them with a plug for their in-person performances, *(Come and watch us sing and play, Hey, Hey we're The Monkees, You never know where we'll be found, so, you'd better get ready, we may be coming to your town).*

When we played our rough versions of the songs for the television show's producers, Burt and Bob both smiled and told us they were very pleased. We stayed in touch with them, working together for nearly a year as they developed their concept and we fine-tuned our music. In the weeks that followed, we weren't just busy creating the songs that were needed for the pilot show, we confidently plunged ahead with writing new material for a first Monkees album.

We also spent a lot of time preparing ourselves to take full advantage of what we viewed as the biggest opportunity to have yet come our way, producing records for a potential hit group with the power of television behind them. Inspiration is not just the feeling of being uplifted by the sentiment of a sermon or a song. To me, inspiration is when you're so excited about the prospect of creating something new that you just can't wait to get started putting all the puzzle pieces together, exhilarated as much by the challenge as by the anticipation of what you might accomplish. That's the kind of inspiration I was feeling during the late summer months of 1965.

One day in early fall we drove down to the beach and enjoyed a late breakfast while watching the white-capped waves break against the Sunset Beach shoreline through the windows of the Surfrider Café. Moments later we had spread out our blankets on the sand below and were laying on our backs, exposing our chests to the warm rays of a cloudless California sky. On the blanket, next to our relaxing frames, were the three prerequisite tools of our trade: Tommy's Gibson guitar, a yellow legal pad, and a sharp pencil.

But we had not come to write music or lyrics on this particular day at the beach. Today, our mission would be piecing together the myriad scraps of creativity and wisps of inspiration that had been revolving around in our heads for months. We knew we needed to be ready when the studio doors swung open, and today we needed to commit to paper a surefire, cohesive musical concept for this extraordinary project.

On our blank canvas (the top page of the yellow pad) we painted sample colors of the pop acts who we thought could be possible influences for our new group: The Beatles, Stones, Hermits, Rascals, Turtles, Spoonful, Shondells, Raiders, Hollies, Kinks. Then we narrowed the hues down to what we thought were the most complimentary shades. We had been told, "American Beatles on television," but we knew that trying to steer the sound of our new group too close to the biggest ship in the ocean of pop music would be risky and unfulfilling, especially since the TV show would be borrowing heavily from the visual antics of their films.

Still, we had learned what we could from analyzing The Beatles records and trying to identify some of their tricks of the trade: strong lyrical storytelling, great instrumental riffs and intros, and stellar vocals. I wrote down what to us had emerged as a standard formula for the mix of songs in their albums. All their LPs would be heavily loaded with up-tempo numbers, but there was always that one killer ballad and the obligatory novelty song. Beyond that, we would not be thinking of The Beatles as we worked out new material for The Monkees.

On another yellow page, as Tommy and I recapped our thoughts, I made a list of songs we had already written that we thought would be strong for The Monkees. In addition to the new "Theme" and the obvious string quartet ballad, "I Wanna Be Free," there were "I'm Not Your Stepping Stone," "Words," "She," a song that Tommy had written with Steve Venet called "Tomorrow's Gonna Be Another Day," a song we were still working on, called "This Just Doesn't Seem To Be My Day," and our nomination for the novelty slot, "I'm Gonna Buy Me a Dog."

On the next page, in typical Boyce and Hart fashion, we left some "negative space" on our canvas. "There may be elements that might pop up as we get deeper into the project," I wrote, "We need to stay open to that!"

Then, things got exciting the week of September 8th when the producers placed a small ad in each of the industry trade papers, *The Hollywood Reporter* and *Daily Variety*. It simply read:

MADNESS!!
AUDITIONS

FOLK AND ROLL MUSICIANS–SINGERS
FOR **ACTING ROLES IN NEW TV SERIES.**
RUNNING PARTS FOR 4 INSANE BOYS, AGE 17– 21.
WANT SPIRITED BEN FRANK'S TYPES.
HAVE COURAGE TO WORK.
MUST COME DOWN FOR INTERVIEW.
CALL HO 6-5188

Packed into this short cattle-call invitation was a wealth of secret meaning that might not have been obvious to the casual observer. On a visit to the Columbia lot one day, we found out how much thought Bert and Bob had put into their tiny advertisement. We silently listened as Rafelson explained to Tommy and me the strategy behind the message.

"Ben Frank's types" was code for "hippies." Ben Franks' was the name of the popular all-night diner on the Strip where the flower children, and sometimes Tommy and I, would hang out after the clubs closed at 2 a.m. "Running parts" was meant in the most literal sense, considering all the running the boys would be doing during the show's madcap romps. And according to Rafelson, "Must come down for interview" was sending this message: "If you're on drugs, you'll have to come down from your high, before you come in to see us."

During the week of auditions, Tommy and I sat in and watched some of the hundreds of young hopefuls as they did their best to impress the producers. Finally, out of the 437 boys, the lucky four were chosen, two actors and two musicians. Of course, they all thought they had been hired to play one of the four lead roles in a new television series. They might not have realized as they showed up at the studio that first day for work, that within a few months, all four of them would be instant American idols.

Micky Dolenz was an effervescent comic actor with a gift for improvisation. His quick wit and stream-of-consciousness rants reminded me of a young Jonathan Winters. He had been the child star of an early TV series called *Circus Boy*. Now, he was just happy at the prospect of having a steady job again. I instantly liked Micky and appreciated his professionalism and instant willingness to do his best. In some ways, his high energy reminded me of Tommy, but Micky's personality was far more frantic and far less complicated.

David Jones was unquestionably a charmer with a great smile. His personality combined an instantly bright flash of impertinence with a respectful and polite British formality. He was a new breed of cat to me, and I willingly took him at face value. At barely twenty, Davy was already the most accomplished actor of the four. Discovered in his hometown of Manchester, England, he had been cast in the BBC soap opera, *Coronation Street,* at age eleven.

Jones landed the role of Dickens' Artful Dodger in the West End production of *Oliver* and then originated the Broadway role when they brought the show to the United States. For his Broadway performance, Davy garnered a Tony award nomination for himself when he was barely sixteen. I saw endless potential in this young talent and also lots of layers to his personality that I wasn't sure how to interpret or understand.

Peter Tork was very personable, although more reserved with his energy and gestures than the others. It only took a few minutes of conversation with Peter to see how bright and thoughtful he was. As he and I chitchatted, he described how he had come to the show straight from the folk music scene. Peter was proficient on a number of instruments including piano, guitar, bass, and banjo.

I enjoyed talking with Peter about his life in Greenwich Village. We had been living in the city at the same time but were moving in entirely different worlds. Peter finished his story of becoming a Monkee by revealing that his friend from the Village scene, Steven Stills, had suggested Peter for the show after Steven himself had not been a match for the project.

Michael Nesmith strolled through the studio audition room door like a cowboy entering a saloon in a John Wayne western. Mike was wearing ironed jeans with a neat crease, a western shirt and boots. He had a duffel bag full of laundry slung over his shoulder like it was his saddlebags. I had a vision of his horse being tied up in the studio's parking lot. There was a tension in his energy, not hostile, but certainly not relaxed or approachable. He seemed to exude a feigned nonchalance, claiming to not have much time for the meeting since he was on his way to do something important at the laundry-mat.

Almost immediately Nesmith had emerged as the de facto leader of the group. He was an accomplished singer, songwriter, and musician with several records under his belt. During my first attempts to talk with Michael, he seemed to me to be somewhat unapproachable. I didn't push it because I had heard that he was already beginning to feel like he was being taken advantage of and was already looking to find some way to control the musical material and direction for the group. To him, Tommy and I must have appeared to be two of the major establishment figures who were standing in his way.

The pilot show was scheduled to be shot in the middle two weeks of November 1965, so Tommy and I were asked to book the studio and put The Monkees' voices in place of our own on the musical tracks of the three songs they would be lip-syncing in the show. We had sent over lyric sheets and copies of our demos to the studio lot so that our four new TV actors could learn the material. We were excited about our first chance to get to know The Monkees and lay the foundation of our working relationship. They all showed up together and on time.

Tommy and I were conferring with the sound engineer in the control booth at Eldorado Studio, as to how we intended to record the vocal tracks when our new artists arrived. We walked out of the control booth and into the main studio to meet the guys. The four new Monkees were still just getting to know each other, and there was a lot of kinetic energy in the room as they jockeyed to establish their relationships with each other.

We welcomed our four singers and spent several minutes trying to calm them down and make them feel comfortable. After a period of socializing as we attempted to establish a working rapport with our new band, we fitted each singer with headphones and then moved quickly into the control booth. The engineer rolled the tape, I pressed the talk-back mic and slated, "Theme from *The Monkees*, take one." The background instrumental track began to play, but at the end of the introduction, we didn't hear any singing coming from The Monkees' microphone.

Peering out through the soundproof plate glass window, we saw that the guys were continuing to clown around, ignoring the music coming out of their headsets that had been scattered carelessly on the floor. Tommy and I walked back out into the studio and tried to join in on the jokes until we could get their attention and restore order. But it was obvious that neither Tommy nor I had grown up with brothers or played team sports. To us, they seemed to be acting like teenage boys at summer camp and we weren't comfortable with trying to be part of their tug of war. Maybe to them we sounded like dorm monitors as we tried to get the energy focused on making a record.

Back in the booth, we tried it again. "Take two." Still there was no singing coming over the control booth's speakers. We turned up the lights in the studio again, and there were the four future superstars entangled in a dog pile on the floor. After the third try, we realized that although we were sitting in a "control" booth, we had lost all control. We dismissed the session.

We walked down the long studio stairway and out onto Vine Street shaking our heads. At that moment, Boyce and I made a command decision. As we climbed into Tommy's car, I put it into words, "From now on, only one Monkee at a time will be allowed in our recording sessions." It was a vow that we semi-religiously enforced throughout our future work with the group.

In later months I concluded that their antics had probably been prompted by trying to fulfill the image they thought they had been hired to project: off-the-wall, irreverent, and outrageous. But maybe at a subtle level, is was also a show of protest and non-cooperation with two guys who represented the corporate power that would be dictating their musical direction against their will.

As we drove down Hollywood Boulevard, Tommy seemed more relaxed about it all and mused, "Maybe our new recording artists were more interested in winning an award from the World Wide Wrestling Federation than a Grammy." The TV show was sold to the network and sponsors with The Monkees lip-syncing all the songs in the pilot to the pre-recorded voices of Tommy Boyce & Bobby Hart.

CHAPTER 19

Candy Store Prophets
and Disappearing Monkees

It was great to be getting a steady paycheck for the first time since I left my day job at the print shop. Still, my new Hollywood lifestyle would require that I supplement my fat, one hundred dollar a week Screen Gems check with some extra pocket change while we waited for song royalties to come in. I called Vinnie, my guitar player friend from the Randazzo band. After our last three-month stint in Las Vegas, Billy Lewis and Larry Taylor had opted to return to New York with Teddy, while Vince Megna, like me, had come back to L.A.

Vince agreed with my plan to get together a drummer and bass player and look for a local booking agent. Before long Vinnie was picking me up and driving me to gigs in clubs all over the Los Angeles area. Soon I had my own transportation and was able to pick Vinnie up for the jobs. My friend Keith Allison had presented me with a dilapidated 1951 Chevy as a present. The car had no pink slip, no registration, and no insurance. But it did have quite a history. It had been passed on gratis from musician to musician through several generations of philanthropy. Now Keith was able to afford a decent ride and had designated me as next in line to be inducted into the Brotherhood of the Grey Chevrolet.

Halfway through its inaugural voyage, as Vinnie and I were flying down the Santa Ana Freeway, radio blasting and windows open, we were nearly blinded by a snowstorm of Zig Zag cigarette rolling papers that had come flying out of the torn headliner above the windshield, a leftover legacy from a previous rocker who rolled his own. A few weeks later, after a night of playing in Long Beach, the car limped into Hollywood and died a painless death in a gas station parking lot. We took taxis home and never looked back.

One day our agent sent us out for a cattle-call audition being held at the historic nightclub that was originally called *Ciro's*, now the Comedy Store, on Sunset. When we got there we learned that we were competing to be the opening act and backup band for a girl singer named Kathy Kersh. It turned out that Kersh was the girlfriend of actor Vince Edwards, who was very popular at the time as the star of the highly successful television series, *Ben Casey*.

After watching all the out-of-work L.A. bands that went on before and after us, Edwards and Kersh introduced themselves and told us that they liked our performance and that we had the gig. Kathy was a beautiful, statuesque blonde who had been a spokesmodel and actress and now wanted to try her hand at a singing career. After a brief rehearsal, we opened at the *Pink Carousel* in Downey. Kathy would come out near the end of our 45-minute sets and sing three or four numbers and, of course, her name was featured high on the marquee, at the top of the bill.

But after a long engagement the agent booked us back in Hollywood at the Red Velvet, a popular hangout for entertainers and other local revelers. It was next door to our offices at Screen Gems on Sunset Boulevard. This time the club owner wanted to put my name on the top of his marquee to take advantage of the fact that I was better known around the Hollywood club scene. Kathy took the billing downgrade better than Vince Edwards, and she and I remained friends long after our short-lived nightclub collaboration ended.

While I was playing blues clubs around town with Vinnie, Tommy Boyce also had a moonlighting job. On weekends he played and sang behind the piano bar of a little Los Feliz area Mexican food restaurant called *Kiki's* for forty dollars a night plus all the tacos he could eat. He would share the money (and the tacos) with his drummer, who on any given weekend might be Keith Allison or Barry Richards.

Tommy's father would faithfully attend the performances disguised as Sid, the Virginia Kid, an appreciative customer who always primed the tip jar. Tommy was nothing if not a charmer, and by showtime on Friday nights the bar would inevitably be packed with middle-aged ladies. Boyce would look into their eyes and sell his songs with a smile and a wink, performing standards like "I Don't Know Why I love You Like I Do" and "I'm in the Mood for Love" and pumping Jerry Lee Lewis and Fats Domino pieces.

Sometimes he would throw in an original, like the song we had written for Dean Martin. Week after week, Tommy would introduce it by saying that Dino was going to record the song any day now. Well, the weeks dragged into months and Martin never did cut the song. But Tommy was able to save face when, later in the year, Dean Martin released a different Boyce & Hart song called "Little Lovely One."

One day, not long after Vince Megna's departure for Milwaukee and a more secure career, I got a call from Bill Lewis. He and Larry Taylor had reunited with Gerry McGee back where they had started on the West Coast. Gerry McGee and the Cajuns and I picked up right where we had left off. We began an indefinite engagement playing six nights a week at a club on Pico Boulevard called "The Swinger."

Soon we began to toy with the idea of becoming a real band and shopping for a record deal. We incorporated some original Boyce & Hart songs into our repertoire: "She," "Words," and "I'm Not Your Stepping Stone." I guess you could call our music psychedelic blues. When Larry Taylor's stepdad heard about the plan, he offered to be our manager, adding, "I've got the perfect name for the group, The Candy Store Prophets." The Prophets signed with a publicist, and soon members of the Hollywood music scene were coming down to check us out.

♥

Lester Sill told us that the hot stable of New York Screen Gems writers had been pitched early on to submit songs for The Monkees to record, but no one in the East Coast head office, including the big boss himself, Donnie Kirshner, had been very excited about one more unsold pilot show. However, within a few months, the series had been picked up by the NBC television network; Yardley Cosmetics and Kellogg's Cereal had come on board as sponsors; and RCA had agreed to distribute the records under a new imprint, Colgems Records, created especially for the Monkee product. Finally in June of 1966 Kirshner, technically the music supervisor of the television show, flew out to Los Angeles for the first time to supervise the music.

Soon after arriving for work on a morning that up until this moment had been filled with cheerful optimism and promise, from a low flying hovercraft Donnie dropped a bombshell. "Sure, you guys have had hits as *writers*," he told us as we met with him at the Screen Gems offices, "but for a project of this magnitude, we need record producers that have a proven track record." "But, Donnie, this is our project." Tommy protested. "Bert assured us that we would be producing the music for the show *and* the records. We've created a whole sound for the group." "Sorry, guys," ended the discussion and the meeting.

We were devastated. We left the office and didn't return for days. Boyce was quiet as we drove, and I respected his space. But I was thinking "All of our preparation and planning, all of our formulations and analysis, all of our dreams and inspiration, had been for nothing." I could see the disappointment on Tommy's face, but in typical fashion he remained silent. When he did speak on the subject, he said, "Donnie may have golden ears, but he doesn't have the first clue of what to do with this opportunity."

On the following Monday we decided to put it all behind us and ventured back into the office. But when we met Lester in the hall, it wasn't hard for him to see that we were still crestfallen. In a valiant attempt to cheer us up, he reasoned, "Don't worry, guys, we're going to get some of your songs into this project. Donnie likes your writing, and don't forget, you've already got the theme song. That's a big deal!" We nodded and went back to our office, but we felt little consolation from his efforts. Our chance to shape the musical direction and sound of The Monkees had slipped through our hands.

Kirshner sent our theme song to top British producer, Mickie Most, who was hot from his hits with artists like Lulu, the Animals, Herman's

Hermits, and Donovan. A few weeks later, Lester confided to us that the Mickie Most productions had not worked out. Donnie had gotten the production tapes back and was not happy with what he heard.

Next, Donnie gave our songs to top West Coast producer, Snuff Garrett, who had produced a ton of hits for Bobby Vee, Sonny & Cher, Johnny Burnette, and many others. This time when the masters came back, Donnie was even less pleased, saying, "They sound like Gary Lewis and the Playboys tracks." Also, we heard from Lester that The Monkees had not gotten along well in the studio with Garrett.

Finally, Kirshner brought Carole King and Gerry Goffin out from his New York office. Lester told us the next morning that Goffin and King had flown back home in the middle of the night after the "Impertinent Four" had brought Carole to tears in the studio. By now, he was wondering if The Monkees were trying to sabotage all of the established producers that Donnie was bringing their way.

By July of 1966, just weeks before *The Monkees* television show was to go on the air, there were still no releasable Monkees records. Kirshner was beginning to get desperate. Boyce and Hart seized the opportunity and concocted a last ditch plan.

We caught him one morning in the hallway outside our Sunset office and Tommy, always the consummate pitch man, made our plea. "Check this out, Donnie," he emoted. "We'll take Bobby's club band into this little ten-dollar-an-hour rehearsal studio we know and work out the arrangements on two or three of our songs. You come down around noon and listen. If you don't like what you hear, you can forget it. All it'll cost you is fifteen minutes and thirty bucks. If they sound like hits, then you've gotta give us our project back."

When Donnie walked into Rainbow Studios on the corner of Yucca and Vine Street the next day, we were ready for him. Our hot new recording band was primed and standing by: Gerry McGee and the Cajuns (now the Candy Store Prophets) plus two guitarist additions we had met over the past year of making demos, Louie Shelton and Wayne Erwin. We counted off and they unleashed our fresh arrangements of "This

Doesn't Seem to Be My Day," "Let's Dance On," and the "Theme from *The Monkees.*" Right from the first chord, Kirshner was blown away from the songs, the arrangements, and the sounds that filled the room. "These sound like hits!" he said, "Go ahead and book the studio, guys. You're going to be producing *The Monkees!*"

CHAPTER 20

Something About a Train to Somewhere

The Monkees' first single, "Last Train to Clarksville" was born on the floor of our Woodrow Wilson "Boat House." But it was conceived the evening before when I pulled into our carport, still punching through the radio presets in my old '51 Chevy, before its demise. I hit the KHJ button just in time to hear the ending of the brand-new Beatles release. As Paul McCartney droned through the round-like fadeout of their latest single, he sang *"pa-per-back . . . ."* but my straining ears heard, *"take the last . . ."* I figured the rest had to be something about a train to somewhere.

The next day, Boyce and I finally heard the record all the way through while driving home from the office. It was then that I realized that "Paperback Writer" had nothing to do with trains or taking the last anything to anywhere. I told Tommy the title that I had mistakenly "heard," and he suggested that maybe I should consider shopping around for a hearing aid. Then he said, "You know, I think 'The Last Train to something' is a pretty cool title. I know there's a good song idea floating around in there somewhere, and we need one more song for the album."

That night we tossed around destinations to complete the title. We discarded the usual suspects, Detroit, Seattle, and Philadelphia, deciding that our story could be more easily told if we placed it in a rural setting. Finally, Tommy asked, "What are the names of some of the little towns in Northern Arizona where you used to go every summer?" I thought of "Sedona, Jerome, Cottonwood, Clarkdale." He cut me off at "Clarkdale." "Clarkdale," he repeated. "Or better still, how 'bout Clark*sville?*"

Escalation of the Vietnam War had begun in earnest just one year earlier, and with it had come a wave of protest from the hippies and college kids here at home. Their chants of "Hey, hey, LBJ, how many boys did you kill today" could be heard on the evening news shows. Boyce and I knew that we could never get away with recording an overt war protest song with a group like The Monkees, let alone expect to have it played on network television. Still, we were inspired to add our voices, even in a veiled way, to the disapproval of the war that we shared with the youth of America.

We fashioned a story line about a soldier heading off to face combat and an uncertain future. Frantically, he was trying to arrange train transportation for a rendezvous to see the girl he loved for what could very well be the last time. That night, we came up with one of my favorite lines from all the songs I've co-written: "We'll have time for coffee-flavored kisses and a bit of conversation." The next morning, we called the musicians and booked the studio. The studio was the ten-dollar-an-hour dance rehearsal hall where we still worked out our new arrangements with the band ahead of time.

After we showed them the basic tempo and groove and sang the song down a couple of times, I told the guys, "Now we need a great intro, a guitar riff, maybe something like "Day Tripper." Usually our three guitar players would vie to come up with the missing ingredients by playing us their respective ideas, and often we would work all three into the arrangement. But this day Louie Shelton's iconic reply, "How 'bout this one," led immediately into his playing the signature riff that fans around the world for nearly five decades have identified most closely with "Last Train to Clarksville." Then we booked the *real* studio.

In 1966 RCA Studios, on the corner of Ivar Street and Sunset Boulevard, was a world-class recording facility and a hotbed of pop culture. While we were producing Monkee tracks in Studio A, Andrew Loog Oldham was making Rolling Stones records in Studio B with Mick, Keith, and the boys. Outside, in two lines, two distinctly different types of fans waited for a chance to catch a glimpse of their respective musical idols. The fans in The Monkees line were decidedly younger, more suburban, and more innocent looking. Stones fans were "hippie" types who looked like they belonged right where they were, on the Sunset Strip.

RCA Studios A and B were each bigger than some people's houses. And the staff engineers were all top flight. But when Tommy and I walked into RCA to do our first big studio production, we were extremely fortunate to find that an experienced and creative studio engineer by the name of David Hassinger had been assigned to us. We hit it off with David right away and soon discovered that his confidence, skill, and personality would be the safety net we needed to allow us to relax and have fun in the studio. We gave him our trust, and he helped to create an atmosphere of confidence for two young producers on their first big studio assignment.

The Musicians Union allowed music producers to record four songs in a three-hour union scale session, and that's what the record companies expected us to do. This means we had forty-five minutes to record a final basic track of the bass, drums, guitars, keyboards, and sometimes percussion instruments. As the producers, in our heads, Tommy and I already knew the way we wanted the record to sound. But in just two or three run-throughs, the engineer would have to quickly bring himself up to speed, becoming familiar with a song he'd never heard before and then make it all gel, balancing the level of each instrument with the others and hopefully adding some creativity of his own.

That's exactly what Hassinger did on "Last Train to Clarksville." With one finger on the pot that controlled the microphone on the drummer's high-hat cymbal, he raised the sound of it nearly to capacity for a split second on the "one-and" beat of every other bar, creating a sharp percussive "shooop" effect reminiscent of a train's steam brake and adding something extra to what became The Monkees' first hit record.

Gerry McGee, Larry Taylor, Billy Lewis, Louie Shelton, and Wayne Erwin became the core band of studio musicians on all the Monkee records that Tommy and I would produce.* Tommy and I settled into

---

* The following year, in various configurations, they became the Boyce & Hart touring band. After that, Larry (the Mole) Taylor went on to become a founding member of the premier blues group, Canned Heat; Bill Lewis continued as an L.A. studio musician until his untimely death in 2005; and Gerry McGee toured with Kris Kristofferson and more recently has performed for many years as a member of the Ventures. Louie Shelton became a sought after L.A. session player after our Monkee sessions and produced a dozen chart records for the duo, Seals & Crofts, including the classics, "Summer Breeze" and "Diamond Girl."

a straight-ahead formula for producing our records with The Monkees. During the day we would record and fine-tune the instrumental tracks featuring Gerry, Billy, Larry, Louie, Wayne, and sometimes Tommy Boyce on acoustic guitar and me on organ. For percussion Lester had suggested a veteran musician named Gene Estes, and he ended up being a permanent fixture on most of the sessions. For particular keyboard parts we usually called in our friend Michel Rubini.

Next, Tommy, Wayne, and I (and sometimes studio singer Ron Hicklin) would sing the background vocal parts. Then the recording would be finished, except for one very important element: the lead vocal.

So, enforcing the "one-at-a-time" policy that we had set after our first failed experience with Monkee vocals, we would send for Micky or Davy to join us at the recording studio. Boyce and I considered ourselves fortunate that The Monkees auditions had provided us with two very commercial lead voices. The Manchester sound of David Jones could not have been more timely, and Micky Dolenz gave us what turned out to be one of the definitive pop voices of the 1960s. The group's hectic filming schedule on the set of the television show would often go on for twelve hours or more, so we'd be lucky to get them over to RCA by ten or eleven at night.

Around 10 p.m. on Monday evening, July 25, 1966, Micky Dolenz arrived at the studio, and we taught him the words and melody to "Last Train to Clarksville." As in most of our sessions together, Micky listened as we went over the song while singing along with the backing tracks. After timidly following along for a couple of run-throughs, an already exhausted Dolenz looked up and said, "I don't know, guys. I don't think I can sing this song."

Tommy seemed to size up the situation instantly. He put his arm around Micky's shoulder and asked, "You hungry, Mick? Let's go across the street to Norm's and get some soup." Hassinger and I waited patiently in the studio, knowing that this down time was an equally important part of the recording process. We knew within half an hour or so, Micky and Tommy would be back in Studio A, and Dolenz would confidently walk into the vocal booth and nail the song and give us his fabulous performance in just one or two takes.

Tommy and I had written an unusual machine gun-paced bridge for "Clarksville" with a million words to spit out in just eight bars. This, regardless of Tommy's pep talk, had Micky's head spinning and his tongue twisting. He pleaded, "How about if I just sing deh deh deh deh deh deh deh dehs?" We gave it a try and it seemed to work for the record.

I think that by now, after working with all the well-known producers that Kirshner had tried before us, perhaps The Monkees were starting to see Tommy and me as the new kids in town, maybe the lesser of all the big corporate evils. With every vocal session we began to form closer working relationships with Micky and David as they gradually came to trust us and respect our creativity as much as we respected theirs. Several weeks after working together, Micky excitedly walked into the studio one day and told us, "I just found out you guys have written all these big hit songs before you even knew The Monkees." He was belatedly impressed.

When it came time to pick the song that would be released as The Monkees' first single, Donnie rented out a restaurant on Vine Street and held a lunch-time listening party for the executives and promotion team of RCA Records. He had narrowed it down to four Boyce & Hart productions: "Theme from *The Monkees*," "Tomorrow's Gonna' Be Another Day," "Last Train to Clarksville," and the Goffin & King song, "Take a Giant Step."

I was silently rooting for the theme song, reasoning that the exposure it would receive appearing each week over the TV show credits would give it the greatest edge. Intently, I watched the faces of the executives. As they silently listened, I could see grins break out across their faces. When the music stopped, the head of the RCA promotion department shook his head and said, "Give us any one of these songs and we'll make the record top ten." The next day, Donnie revealed his choice for first single.

"Last Train to Clarksville" had already been zooming up the *Billboard* charts for weeks before the first episode of *The Monkees* hit the airwaves on September 12th, 1966. A short time later, it reached the number one position, and our pictures were on the covers of the music trade magazines. For me, "Last Train to Clarksville" had become a metaphor for the high-speed freight train that had become our careers, and that was the week it would begin barreling down the tracks.

Exhilarated after a late night recording session with The Monkees, Tommy and I stopped by Tiny Naylor's drive-in on the way home to celebrate with a nightcap of coffee and pie. As the cool air filtered through the open windows of Tommy's Cadillac, our conversation turned introspective and we began to relax. Tommy reflected, "Some of the hottest record producers ever had been in studios around the world cutting Monkee records before we had even gotten our chance back. Mickey Most, Snuff Garrett, Carole King, even Michael Nesmith had been in the studio before us." "Yeah," I responded, "why had *we* been the ones who finally got the green light to produce the first Monkees album?" In the car that night, the two of us decided that there were at least three reasons.

First, to the busy veteran record producers, this was just another in a long line of run-of-the-mill projects and sessions. To us, it was the chance of a lifetime! In the eleven months between our first meeting with the show's producers and our first recording sessions with the group, Boyce and I had been just short of obsessed with thinking about and planning ahead for our big break. Having created in our minds a clear-cut image and musical sound for the group, we were easily able to actualize it when Kirshner finally gave us our project back. Boyce summed it up succinctly, "We had done our homework and we were ready."

The second reason was Gerry McGee, Larry Taylor, Billy Lewis, Louie Shelton, and Wayne Irwin, the great recording band that we were lucky enough to bring together. We could have used the outstanding click of studio musicians who worked around the clock playing on most of the records being produced in L.A., and for many other projects we did. These studio stalwarts were the musicians who played on the sessions turned out by the record producers that we had competed against for The Monkees project, and by most of those who produced their later cuts.

But instead, during our time in the trenches recording demos, we had assembled a real band. And, in a very real way, this was a band that Tommy and I were a part of. We shared their culture and their lifestyle.

We worked with them on the arrangements that would become the foundation of the records we made, and we had actually performed with them in person and now in the studio. In some configuration or another, this band had been already together for three years. Ultimately, Louie, Wayne, Tommy, the Prophets, and I brought a fresh, authentic instrumental sound to The Monkees' first records that could only have been provided by a "garage band" of young musician-friends, and one that just may not have been possible with the regular studio guys.

And, last but not least, was the fact that we had been able to work well with our two terrific young song stylists, Micky Dolenz and David Jones. Tommy and I loved their voices. When we first heard and got to work with the sounds of our new lead singers, I told Boyce, "I think we just hit the jackpot!" Maybe, the previous potential producers had not been able to foster a sense of camaraderie with their novice lead singers or create a studio environment that was comfortable enough to bring out the best of their performances.

Having the records completely finished and sounding like hits when we proudly and loudly played them for Davy or Micky in the studio, lent a certain excitement to the process and a bit of inspiration to the vocal sessions. And having the background vocals already on the tracks gave an instant support to the leads. Maybe all the producers had done that. But, on a song like "I'm Not Your Stepping Stone," for instance, it's easy to notice the symbiotic relationship between our voices and Micky's. It's not just the blending of our voices on the three part harmony of the chorus and the call and response background parts—Tommy's adlibs of "NO!" and "Oh, no not me" and my scream of "NOOOO!" fit seamlessly into the breaks between Dolenz's impeccable performance.

Picking the two voices that we wanted to interpret our songs was critical. It wasn't that Peter and Michael didn't sing well; they both had good voices and were gifted at musical expression. But every member of the band can't be its lead singer. And with Micky and Davy we had a wealth of talent and everything we needed to work with in the studio.

David Jones' voice plunged his young, worldwide audience into a subliminal familiarity that the British invasion had created over the previous two years, but without sounding like one of The Beatles. And, Micky Dolenz, blessed with an exceptional vocal range and natural soul qualities beyond his years, would turn out to be of one of the most memorable and enduring classic pop voices of the decade.

CHAPTER 21

Seventeen Songs in the Top Thirty

One morning a few weeks before The Monkees' first album was scheduled to be released, Lester Sill came into our office a little panicked, and informed us that no one had thought to shoot a photo session for the cover of the LP. Lester called a young photographer he knew named Bernard Yeszin, and Tommy and I picked Bernie up at his house and escorted him through the guard gate of the Columbia Pictures lot. Once on *The Monkees* set, we waited patiently for a break in the filming and then informed the guys that we needed a few minutes of their time to shoot their record cover photo.

Michael Nesmith lined the guys up in a little alley outside the soundstage and told us categorically, "Okay, guys, you've got ten shots." Bernie expertly snapped them off in as many seconds, as Michael counted them down. If you check out the cover of *The Monkees*, their self-titled first LP, you can clearly see Micky, Davy, and Peter are smiling. But Michael Nesmith is mouthing the word "Seven."

As soon as we were back in the car, I unleashed my concern, asking Bernie, "Do you think you were able to get anything we can use?" Tommy chimed in, "I mean we've gotta have that one magic shot for the cover of the album, man." "Don't worry about it," Bernie retorted and then continued to grumble all the way back to his house about how he had never been treated so unprofessionally. We tried to calm him down by agreeing with him and then pointing out that the guys were under a lot of pressure for four young kids. Tommy helped restore a semblance of tranquility in the car with his closing remark, "The only thing that matters now is that we got the photo."

At the end of our many visits to the Columbia Pictures lot to arrange some business with The Monkees, or to just watch the filming of their television series, we would always stop in to see the newly successful television producers, Bert Schneider and Bob Rafelson. On one such visit, we were talking with Bert and Bob when a buddy of theirs came into the office. They introduced him to us as Jack Nicholson. Jack, we were told, was an aspiring actor. He had just come from the set of *Funny Girl*, where he had a walk-on, or in this case, a dance-on part in the movie. He flashed an exceptionally wide and energetic grin and emoted, "I got to dance with Barbra Streisand!"

Tommy and I ran into Jack from time to time at the Raybert offices, but we got to know him at the weekend gatherings around Bob Rafelson's pool. When I walked into Bob's house I could usually hear Jack's distinctive speech patterns and vocal timbre. There always seemed to be girls around him, listening to his every word as his ambidextrous eyebrows and his captivating thousand-watt smile made everyone think he was about to say something dirty.

♥

For Tommy Boyce and Bobby Hart, The Monkees had changed everything! Now we could easily get in to see the top record company brass who were eager to hear our new songs. Our peers in the music business would address us with new respect when we would meet. The wrench that could open the floodgates to the money stream had finally been handed to us. We no longer had to make demos of our songs. Now we were hit producers; we had a golden ticket to go straight into an expensive recording studio and make master recordings for release to the public.

By the end of May 1967, seven of the top thirty-two albums on the *Cashbox* chart contained songs written and/or produced by Boyce & Hart. (There were 17 songs in all.) The #1 LP was *More of The Monkees* and featured "She" and "I'm Not Your Stepping Stone"; three albums: Andy Williams' which came in at #11, Ed Ames at #15, and Roger Williams, slipping to #32, all contained covers of our song "I Wanna Be Free";

Paul Revere & the Raiders Greatest Hits at #12 included their version of "Stepping Stone"; Herman's Hermits' #22 LP contained "If You're Thinkin' What I'm Thinkin'"; and *The Monkees* self-titled first album, featuring ten songs that Boyce & Hart had produced and seven that we had written, was still going strong at #23.

Quick success can make you start to feel invincible. The first instance I can recall where Tommy and I started to go over the edge in thinking that we could have anything we wanted has been logged in my memory as the "Nipper Caper." Nipper was the name of the trademark mascot dog of RCA Victor Records. Every RCA record featured in its logo a picture of Nipper listening attentively in front of an old fashioned horn-shaped Victrola speaker, and underneath were these words of explanation: "his master's voice."

In the lobby of the RCA Victor building stood a larger-than-life-size plastic statue of Nipper, the dog. As Tommy and I exited the studio through the deserted lobby at about two a.m. after a long night of mixing, we became inexplicably overcome by the desire to see Nipper gracing the living room of our Boat House. Throwing caution to the wind, we spontaneously scooped her up and walked the five-foot high pooch to the car.

She looked great from our couch, her smooth, white coat with black and brown spots accented by our ocher shag carpet. But no sooner had we set her in place to admire her than our inflated vision of reality had returned to relatively normal size and the gravity of our actions had set in. "What have we done?" we asked ourselves. "We're not thieves." Getting Nipper out of the RCA lobby had been a piece of cake. But smuggling her back in would require the most creative stretch of our young criminal minds.

The dog statue we had kidnapped would be ours for the day. There was no chance of returning her, undetected, during office hours. The following night we dressed in dark clothes and returned to the scene of the crime. Circling the block, we meticulously timed the rounds of the night watchman. At precisely the opportune moment, Boyce eased the Cadillac to a halt in front of the Ivar entrance and ran to open the double glass doors to the lobby. In a flash, I swept through the room and deposited the missing mascot in her familiar spot near the receptionist's desk. As the night watchman strolled back into the lobby, we offered him our customary two-finger salute and walked casually to our getaway car.

♥

After the success of "Clarksville," radio stations around the country, unwilling to wait for a second Monkees single to be released, began playing another song from their first album as if it were a top ten single. But, ultimately, the record company decided not to release "I Wanna Be Free" as a single so that the fans would have to buy the entire LP in order to own the song.

Tommy and I usually wrote songs to order on-demand and almost always under the threat of a deadline. But a quiet evening in 1965 had found us both home early with some free time on our hands. I emerged from the cocoon of my downstairs room to find Boyce in the living room, guitar in hand, lost in his musings over the kernel of a song idea.

Tommy was haunted by a piece that Roger Miller had written called "One Dyin' and a Buryin'." The subject was suicide, and the song ended with the words "I wanna be free." The thought was that all it would take to accomplish this freedom would be "one dying and one burying." Tommy had been playing the record over and over again. He had already put some chords together and was trying to construct a new idea using the last line of the song for inspiration. I stood quietly, letting Tommy take his time to acknowledge my presence in the room. I knew the song was special to him, but I wouldn't find out how special and personal until many years later.

Tommy looked up at me and sang me his first lines with an original melody, "*I wanna be free, don't say you love me say you like me.*" He said "I don't know where to go next." "It's cool," I said, but it sounds more like a second verse to me. Maybe we should try to paint some pictures first like: *I wanna be free like the bluebird flying by me, like the waves out on the blue sea . . .*" Together we hammered out, "*If your love has to tie me, don't try me, say goodbye.*" Looking back, "I want to be your friend, but don't tie me down" was the somewhat unromantic philosophy expressed in many of the Boyce & Hart songs and also in the personal choices we made during our bachelor days and nights in the middle sixties.

We even managed to maintain a feeling of independence and freedom from *each other*, in spite of the fact that we were together so much of the time. Tommy was my closest friend, the brother I never had. I admired his talent, energy, and confidence. I emulated his social graces and innate people skills. But there was something deep inside my soul that constantly kept me striving to assert my own independence, and oftentimes it would demand that I retreat into seclusion.

Sometimes I would find myself driving by my first apartment on Whitley Avenue, and each time I relived a piece of the feeling of loneliness and uncertainty about my future that I experienced there. And while unspoken, I could sometimes sense that Tommy would be lost in his own feelings of how fragile success and happiness can be.

But there seemed to be something in the air that night as we wrote this song together, and I think both of us were feeling it. "I Wanna Be Free" was one of the few songs that we wrote with no assignment or specific artist in mind, just because we felt like writing a song together, and once we started working on it together, it couldn't have taken us more than half an hour.

Conveniently, the song was already in our drawer when we went looking for a romantic song for Davy's beach scene in *The Monkees* pilot show. And once again, it served us well when we needed a "yesterday-type" string quartet ballad for their first album. It has probably been recorded by more artists than any other Boyce & Hart song. One of my favorites is the stripped down and unplugged YouTube performance by Richard Marx.

One day in early 1967, Lester Sill gave us the good news that Andy Williams would be recording his own version of "I Wanna Be Free" for his forthcoming *Born Free* album. When Andy's *Born Free* sessions were set, he invited Tommy and me to stop by the studio to meet him and sit in as he recorded our song. On the appointed day, we arrived at the Columbia Records studios on Sunset and were shown into the control booth where, through the glass window, we watched as the legendary standard/pop singer breezed through a beautiful and effortless performance.

CHAPTER 22

More Records Than The Beatles and Rolling Stones Combined

Tommy's heart was pounding as he flew through the door of my dressing room, backstage at San Francisco's famed Cow Palace stadium. His breathing was coming hard and he was more excited that I had ever seen him. Before I had time to unbutton my Gene Autry-style Candy Store Prophets suit, he was in front of me, yelling over the muffled din of screaming Monkees fans that was still coming from out front despite the show having ended several minutes before. "Bobby!" he gasped, "That should be *us* up there!"

At the end of 1966, on the heels of their first number one record and hit TV show, *The Monkees*, had been booked for their first in-person concerts. We ran into Michael Nesmith at Western Studios a couple of days after they had returned from their dress rehearsal concert in Honolulu. When we asked him how it had gone, Michael said "Unbelievable! We're bigger than The Beatles, and I can't even play the guitar." It was classic Nesmith, superiority and modesty in the same sentence. In fact, he played the guitar very well, and over the next two years The Monkees *would* sell more records than The Beatles and the Rolling Stones combined.

The January to April hiatus from television filming was peppered with bookings for personal appearances by The Monkees. Ward Sylvester from Raybert Productions called me at home one morning to ask if the Candy Store Prophets and I would go along. "You guys would do a twenty-minute set to open the show. And then I need you to play behind the four singers when they each do their solo performances."

Playing to their strengths, Davy had worked up a show tune, "Gonna Build Me A Mountain"; Michael would shake his maracas and belt the Bo Diddly standard, "You Can't Judge A Book By Its Cover"; Peter would play the classic bluegrass banjo solo "Cripple Creek"; and Micky would perform the Ray Charles classic, "I Got A Woman," complete with credible James Brown dance steps and cape.

For the rest of the show The Monkees would play their own instruments, a counter move to the growing hullabaloo in the press where the "Pre-fab four" were beginning to be accused of being actors who were just posing as musicians. I could only marvel at the irony! During that first Monkees' tour, an increasingly confrontational Michael Nesmith stoked the media fire in a *Saturday Evening Post* interview: "Tell the world we're synthetic because, damn it, we are. Tell them The Monkees are wholly man-made overnight, and that millions of dollars have been poured into this thing. Tell the world we don't record our own music." It was the opening salvo in a well-planned battle to wrestle control away from Don Kirshner and be able to write and produce future Monkee records themselves.

On December 26, 1966, Gerry, Billy, Larry, and I flew to Denver and checked into the Hotel Cosmopolitan. About an hour before The Monkees' first concert, I walked through the snow flurries, the four blocks to Denver's Auditorium Arena and greeted the ticket taker. "Hi. I'm with The Monkees band and I need to get in." He was unimpressed. "Look, we're the opening act and if you don't let me in, the show won't be able to start." He said he didn't know anything about it and shut the giant double doors, leaving me outside in the seventeen degree weather. Finally, about twenty minutes later, Ward Sylvester noticed me through the lobby windows and hustled me in, much to the chagrin of the "ticket master."

After the show I called Tommy from my hotel room and caught him watching television at home in L.A. Exhausted, yet with my mind still racing, I tried to tell him about the surreal other world that the unsuspecting Prophets and I had been thrown into that evening. I did my best to describe the never-ending tidal wave of adrenaline that had been packed into those three hours of Monkeemania. But it was really impossible for me to fully convey the feeling of what I had just witnessed because I still had not been able to fully comprehend it myself.

I told Tommy how the Candy Store Prophets had come out and done our opening set to polite applause seasoned with plaintive cries of "Micky!" and screams for "Davy." And how as I ended our warm-up show with my best impression of Eric Burdon's "See See Rider," a rumbling thunder had begun to arise across the arena. "You know, Tommy, remember all the hysteria we saw on television when The Beatles played the *Ed Sullivan Show* or Madison Square Garden? It's like that. Except, I'm in the middle of it!"

The memory of those black and white film clips had failed to prepare me for the incredible shock to my nervous system from the ear-piercing, high pitched roar that began the moment The Monkees were introduced. It was coming from thousands of young girls, wild with uncontrolled anticipation.

Hysteria is a medical term characterized by "emotional stimulation and outbreaks of wild, uncontrolled excitement." But this moment was more than just an explosion of adolescent frenzy and energy. Time seemed to stand still when I looked into the massive crowd of excited faces and began to realize that this unique phenomenon was erupting from their feelings of love. It came from the fans en masse, in waves so powerful it almost knocked me down as I stood there motionless, face-on from the stage.

I tried to describe how the heat of the lights hit me full in the face as I heard the introduction, "Here they are, straight from Hollywood, The Monkees!" And then like a huge asteroid speeding from the sky, a crash of light, sound, and energy had exploded around them as they played the first notes of our song, "Last Train to Clarksville," and I explained how that was just about the last of their music that was audible over the screaming shrieks of these irrepressible teens.

Tommy listened politely, but I knew that hearing me tell it just wasn't the same as being there, even when I described how after the show we had been forced to retreat time after time as we tried to find an exit. Finally,

Billy Lewis and I had been caught in a stairwell and crushed against the handrails by a sea of hyper teenage humanity. We felt our excitement turn to fear for our lives as the blood drained from our faces while our breath was squeezed from our bodies.

The numbers and intensity of the audience only grew as we made our way across the South, through the Midwest, and on up into Canada. I made a point to continually call Tommy with reports from the road, trying in vain to paint the word pictures that would convey some of the feeling of what we were experiencing.

April in Canada enjoys a blending of the long, hard winter and a hint of the warm, soft evenings to come. I remember watching the bare tree limbs catching the last rays of sunlight as the black 1967 Cadillac limousine sped us to the sprawling 18,200-seat Maple Leaf Stadium. Six motorcycle officers had escorted us, sirens screaming, from the Toronto airport tarmac and onto the freeways, directing all other motorists to pull over and let us pass. Once we reached the inner city, we sat silent as the humming sound of the tires created a peaceful moment of reflection. Just a few blocks ahead an experience of a magnitude I could never have imagined only months before was waiting to explode into my reality.

There were already crowds of fans waiting in front as we checked into Toronto's matronly old King Edward Hotel. As I waited for room service before the show, a strange, echoing sound of familiar chanting reverberated into my room and compelled me to the window. As I slid it open, I could feel something in my heart also began to open. I was struck silent by a sense of awe as I looked down and witnessed literally thousands of young people holding a vigil eight floors below. Oblivious to the drizzling rain, they were looking up and singing to their idols, the songs that Tommy and I had written for them.

As we opened the show that evening, I looked back to see Micky grabbing his drum sticks with his effervescent smile highlighting his unique gift for improvisation. His quick wit and stream-of-consciousness rants were flashing like a hot 4th of July fireworks show. His joy with his new seat of royalty in the pop music world helped me enjoy even more my own position in the king's court.

Davy was smiling and shouting back at the frantic girls in the audience. His natural sex appeal and boyish charm was like adding gasoline to an already white-hot fire on stage. His thoughtfulness and generosity to the band on this tour made a lasting impression on me. In the hotel coffee shops Davy would often stop by our table and pick up our checks, knowing that we didn't get a per diem for our food. Remembering Davy's poise and confidence on the tour had helped me feel more comfortable as we did our opening song that night.

Peter seemed to me to be a little overwhelmed with all the wild energy focused on the stage. I glanced in his direction to see him carefully and deliberately plugging in his bass and checking his marks. I had a passing feeling of empathy for him because I knew this electric life was not his preferred world of music, but his desire to please his fans was exhibited by the smile that rarely left his face.

Michael was busy giving orders to a stagehand and double-checking his guitar and amp. Even in this extreme energy, Mike looked rather nonchalant and ready to play music.

I looked out from the stage, dodging the stream of missiles that were being lovingly hurled onto the stage. Like all the shows before, I saw the desperately emotional faces of twelve-year-old girls, eye makeup running down their faces, throwing stuffed animals, love beads, and sometimes harder products like combs and compacts onto the stage. But there in the audience that night, I spotted something that I had not seen before, Canadian crowd control at its most creative.

Stationed at the junctions of each isle, were hundreds of watchfully patrolling attendants in nurses' uniforms, each holding trays that had been stacked high with wet towels. Whenever one of the nurses spotted a young girl who, in her judgment, was becoming too overwrought as she expressed her devotion to the newly minted teen idols, a wet towel would be summarily plopped smack dab onto her face. Already, there were hundreds of kids around the arena who had been duly "cooled down"; some were now standing on their seats and waving their wet towel souvenirs high in the air.

And an extra treat was waiting for me that night. Since there was an available seat, I was invited to join The Monkees for the flight out of Toronto. I sunk into the luxurious leather armchair next to David Jones. Overwhelmed by the once-in-a-lifetime view, I silently watched the peaceful and inspiring panorama unfold before me, as the lights of Canada seamlessly transformed into the lights of the United States of America through the pilot's windshield of their leased Learjet.

The Prophets and I had experienced all of this and a whole lot more, first hand, during our months of Monkees' personal appearances. This time, San Francisco's Cow Palace was the last concert on a tour of major North American cities where we had played the largest venues available. For us, this was the end of the tour.

But for Tommy Boyce, this was his *first* Monkee concert, and he was still reeling from the experience. "We know how to write the songs," he yelled at me backstage. "And you know the guys want to produce their own records now. It's the perfect time for us to launch our own singing careers. Next year, that'll be you and me up there on stage."

CHAPTER 23

They Got What They Wanted, but They Lost What They Had

Tommy was right about The Monkees wanting to produce their own music. Almost from the beginning, Michael Nesmith, the oldest and most music-business savvy member of the group, had positioned himself as their ringleader. He knew the value of songwriting royalties, and he had been led to believe that he'd have a say in the music the group would make.

Lester Sill had told us that Nesmith had argued long and hard against the theme song we had written for the show. He told his boss, Bert Schneider, "The Beatles would never sing about themselves like that. 'Hey, hey, we're The Beatles?' Come on, give me a break!" Of course, Michael didn't know that it was Schneider who had designated in our first meeting that the theme song for the pilot should be called "The Monkees."

Building on the groundwork that he had laid, Nesmith was soon joined by his fellow musician, Peter Tork, in an open revolt to wrestle away from Kirshner at least a measure of control of the group's music. The two musicians who had become actors now had to convince the two actors who had become musicians to get on board with the plan.

As The Monkees became the single largest money-making project for the giant Screen Gems organization, the four actor/musicians found themselves with more and more political capital. By early 1967, in just four months, their first single, "Clarksville," their double-sided second hit, "I'm a Believer" backed with "I'm Not Your Stepping Stone," and their two LPs, had already sold nearly twelve million copies.

Of course, Screen Gems was keeping the lion's share of the royalties, allotting a small agreed-on percentage to the group. According to their contracts, when they toured, even when they were selling out large arenas, each Monkee still received only his regular weekly salary of $400. Adding insult to injury, when the second album was released, most of the group had never heard most of the music on it.

Contractually, Don Kirshner retained total creative control of the group's music. Sure, he had placated The Monkees by letting them go into the studio and record whatever they liked, but he didn't expect them to produce anything releasable. And, since their studio expenses were recoupable, they were really just spending their own money. Rather than addressing their discontent at being left out of the process, Kirshner flew into town and arranged a celebratory meeting at his Beverly Hills Hotel suite. There he hoped to brighten their collective mood by handing each member of the group a royalty check for nearly a quarter of a million dollars. Their reaction was not what Kirshner had expected.

Lester Sill, who witnessed the scene, told us the news the next morning at the office. When Michael, speaking for the group, voiced his discontentment with the recording process, he was reminded that contractually he had no say in the matter. Making a point with his arm instead, Nesmith put his fist through the wall of Kirshner's hotel room, punctuating his physical blow with a verbal explosion aimed at Donnie, "That could've been your face, @#%!"

Now, the group was able to convince their TV producer, Bert Schneider, that they should at least be represented on the B sides of their singles with a group-produced recording. Schneider assured the four singers that he would see to it. After all, his dad was still president of Screen Gems-Columbia.

But the man with the golden ear turned a blind eye to Bert Schneider's official request. Kirshner released a Jeff Barry-produced side written by Neil Diamond as the Monkee's third single, "A Little Bit Me and A Little Bit You." The group had already leaked it to the press that they would hereafter be producing their own records. Embarrassed and angry, they went to see Bert Schneider.

On a cold New York morning at the end of February 1967, Don Kirshner was unceremoniously relieved of his duties as head of Colgems Records and music supervisor of The Monkees and all other Screen Gems shows. Lester Sill was named as his replacement. It has long been my personal feeling that this was the beginning of the end for The Monkees.

♥

A few weeks earlier, I had been rudely awakened at the ungodly hour of nine-thirty a.m. I had probably gotten to bed around four after a night of performing with the Prophets at the Swinger Club. Tommy was thrusting a steaming cup of tea toward my groggy face as he tried to make me understand the crisis at hand. It seems that while I slept, Donnie Kirshner had called the house that morning, and a very interesting conversation had ensued between the publisher and his writer.

Over the years, Kirshner had reduced the music business to a series of formulas. He liked to make lists, and often when we were with him I observed him scribbling and erasing notes as he juggled creative ideas in his head. During the course of their conversation this particular morning, Donnie confided to Tommy, "I think that for the next Monkee album, we should include a song that has a girl's name in the title. Maybe it should be the next single."

Tommy never needed a second knock from Mr. Opportunity. Without missing a beat, he retorted, "Unbelievable! I can't believe you just said that, Donnie. The song that Bobby and I wrote just last night is a girl's name song." "Really!" Donnie was interested. "Why don't you guys come on over to the house right now and play it for me? I can't wait to hear it." "Well, Bobby got in pretty late last night," Tommy hedged, "but we could probably make it there by eleven." "Great, Tommy, see you then."

Tommy already had the shower running, and as I forced myself in, the water revived me enough to begin to realize the gravity of the situation. We had *not* just written a new song with a girl's name in the title. Kirshner and his wife Sheila were renting a house in the Trousdale Estates section of Beverly Hills. As I pulled on my clothes, I glanced at the clock. It was after ten, and Kirshner's house was at least a twenty-minute drive across the hills. Still, I wanted the next Monkee single as badly as Boyce did.

At 10:45 I climbed behind the wheel of my white 1954 Jaguar Mark VII sedan while Tommy and his guitar piled into the white tuck and roll leather upholstered back seat. As we wound around the curves of Mulholland Drive, Tommy began to play with a catchy little chord progression. For Boyce & Hart, deadlines had always prompted creativity rather than panic. "Throw out some girls names," he yelled over the sound of the old car's engine, confidence beginning to replace the desperation in his voice. "Sally . . . Virginia . . . Susan . . . Linda . . ." By now, we were only blocks away from Donnie's address. "Valerie," I said. "Valerie!" Tommy shouted. "Let's work with that."

As we pulled up in front of the house, all we had were some chords, a song title and a couple of words to go with them. Donnie welcomed us into his living room and Sheila came in to listen. I had seen Boyce make song presentations before. He was good. He could combine the salesmanship of a Fortune 500 executive with the charisma of a rock star. But this day I gained a new respect for his chutzpah and his sheer nerve.

As he strapped on his guitar, Tommy sized up the coffee table, judging that it could hold his weight. "Wait'll you hear this, Donnie. I think we came up with a smash last night." He jumped up on the table and began to play, sing, and sell the song. Standing to the side, I tried to look supportive as I joined in with the harmonies. "Va-ah-ah-ah-al-er-ee, I love her, Va-ah-ah-ah-al-er-ee," we sang. Then he quickly explained, "There's a little verse that goes in here, and then . . ." We continued the melody, "Her name is Va-ah-ah-ah-al-er-ee". We finished the song with a flourish of chords on the guitar and the room went silent. Donnie was beaming. "It's a smash!" he exploded, "It's gotta be the next single." He nodded to Sheila, who was smiling her approval.

Within days, we had rehearsed the band and booked the studio. The band locked in the arrangement and laid down a track that gelled like gummy bears. The dependably versatile, yet often surprising, Louie Shelton, played some unbelievable flamenco guitar licks. Davy Jones gave us the consummate vocal performance like only he could have done. We left the studio knowing in our hearts that we had created another classic pop hit.

Then, of course, the bomb dropped. Kirshner was out, and the new edict stated that in the future, "Only self-produced records by The Monkees would be released." Nesmith and his cohorts had won! Their self-produced third album, *Headquarters*, contained three Boyce & Hart songs that the boys had re-recorded, but "Valleri" continued to sit on the shelf for over a year and a half.

During this period, sometimes together under the leadership of their appointed producer, Chip Douglas, and later, each one working separately, The Monkees logged hundreds of hours of studio time. Their fourth single, "Pleasant Valley Sunday" written by Carole King & Gerry Goffin, and the fifth, "Daydream Believer" written by John Stewart, charted into the top three. But by the end of 1966 Lester told Tommy and me that he couldn't find a record in the bunch that was good enough to be released as a single.

Sill shut the door to his office and, in hushed tones, he told us the plan. He said, "We all know that "Valleri" is a smash, and I need a hit single bad. But I can't release it because the union contract lists your names as the producers. So, here's the deal: you've gotta go back into the studio and re-make the record, note for note. But this time, you don't take producer's credit." Tommy and I waited for the rest of the plan, but that was it. Tommy and I shook our heads at Lester and he gave us back a happy smile.

In the car I waited for Tommy to give me his take on what had just happened and what we should do about it. Tommy drove effortlessly through the Sunset Boulevard traffic without saying a word as the AM radio played the hits. Finally, I softly ventured, "It's pretty weird, man, to cut a hit record and not get credit for it." Tommy looked over at me and calmly said, "Yeah, but we still get the writers' credit, you know . . . and the royalties!" Then he turned his eyes back to the road and lifted my spirits with his trademark smile and positive thumbs up gesture.

Tommy and I and the band did our best in the studio to duplicate the magic of the record we had made sixteen months earlier. We came close. Louie always felt that his flamenco riffs didn't quite measure up to his original performance. David Jones' vocal was pretty much a ringer for the first one he had done. Fans who have time on their hands can judge for themselves; the original may be heard on Rhino Record's *Missing Links 2* while the hit single version is available on most any Monkees greatest hits collection.

On March 9, 1968, the new and unimproved "Valleri" captured the number three spot in *Billboard* magazine. All of the records that we recorded with the group were eventually released. But after "Valleri" The Monkees never again cracked the top ten. They got what they wanted, but they had lost what they had.

CHAPTER 24

Paisley Painted VWs and Limos All Headed for Monterey

"The Monkees are the hottest thing out there right now. And there are millions of kids who love their music," our attorney was expounding. Our first week back in L.A. from The Monkees tour, I was in Abe Somer's office, listening to him and Tommy explain to me their view of the economic realities of the music business. He and Tommy had pre-arranged this opportunity to double-team me on their vision for the future of our careers. Tommy said, "You saw those unbelievable Monkee fans out there on the road. You know, you were there! This is a once in a lifetime opportunity." Abe pointed out that both Tommy and I had been pursuing solo careers for years with little to show for it.

Tommy and I were almost brothers in many ways, and as partners we were having great success in the fields of songwriting and record producing. But each time the idea of the two of us teaming up to sing together had been raised (and it was coming up more and more frequently lately), I had resisted the plan. Our musical tastes and styles were so disparate. We both had come from country music roots, but Tommy's singing style had evolved into pure AM radio pop. I loved gospel and blues, and after my rockabilly beginnings, my live performances had morphed into more of a black sound, singing mostly R & B material.

Tommy taught me the value of in-your-face commercialism; give the people what they want. I was always a student of subtlety. Although I'm a big fan of intuition, there's something to be said for the surprise of the counter-intuitive. I'm reminded of a video clip I've seen where Sam Cooke performs his hit, "Twistin' the Night Away." It's full of cool dance moves, but he never once succumbs to doing the Twist.

It was true that we had tried in vain for solo careers for nearly a decade. Since leaving Era Records in 1961, I had recorded over a dozen records under my own name and under pseudonyms like the Pendeltons, the Ascots, and the Bluehills. If the releases hadn't been such a secret, I might have been arrested for singing under the influence of James Brown, Bobby Vee, the Fleetwoods, Bobby Blue Bland, or Wilson Pickett. And Tommy's track record was no better than mine.

"Your faces are all over the teen mags, *Tiger Beat, Sixteen,* and all the rest, as the guys who wrote and produced all this music they love," Abe continued, "Let me talk to Jerry and Herb at A & M. I think they just might jump at the chance to sign you two, if you record as a team." We already knew that Abe Somer's position as general counsel for A & M Records was a huge plus. "Bobby Hart & Tommy Boyce?" I questioningly conceded. Spontaneously, Tommy established the inevitable, "No, Tommy Boyce & Bobby Hart! It just sounds hipper that way."

A & M Records had an interesting and impressive history and reputation. It was an independent label formed in 1962 by Herb Alpert, a local record producer who also happened to play the trumpet, and Jerry Moss, a local record promoter. By 1965, Alpert & Moss' A & M had grown so successful that were able to buy the Charlie Chaplin Studios movie lot at La Brea and Sunset in Hollywood to house their growing empire.

On a Monday morning Abe drove Tommy and me past the guard shack and on to the lot. We parked in a visitor's spot and walked up the stairs to the second story executive offices of A & M Records. We were there to sign the papers. We met first in Jerry Moss's office to take care of the business. Then Abe walked us next door to meet Herb Alpert. He welcomed us to A & M Records and told us that he had been following our careers and admired our work. Before we left his office Herb promised that he'd always be available if we needed to talk, and then he suggested that we walk around and meet the staff.

Tommy and I wasted no time in composing an album's worth of songs. Within weeks, we were ensconced in the recording studio with our ready-made band of hit recording musicians: the Prophets plus Louie and Wayne. We decided to call our first album *Test Patterns* because we were still experimenting with who we were and what we should sound like musically.

♥

"Tommy, Bobby, this is Derek Taylor." In his office at A & M, Jerry Moss was introducing us to the iconic journalist/publicist who had heralded The Beatles' career since their meteoric rise in 1963. "Derek will be doing your publicity and writing the liner notes for your first LP." We clasped hands with the Englishman of slight build whose kind face was smiling back at us. We were well aware of the legend of Derek Taylor and his contribution to The Beatles' career and were overjoyed at the prospect of having him working on ours.

From our first meeting, Derek, Tommy, and I became fast friends. He would come over to the house to hang out and we would often have dinner together. I soon found out that Derek had the most creatively offbeat style of writing. The liner notes that accompanied our album were a series of made-up stories that, although they had nothing to do with reality, were very entertaining. He described us in one press release as "millionaires who are younger than The Beatles and older than The Monkees."

For some time now, Tommy, along with many other self-appointed advisors who had popped up since the start of our new careers, had been trying in vain to convince me to stop combing my hair back and let it grow long enough to fall loosely down the sides of my head. I had sported many hairstyles in my lifetime, ranging from the full blown "ducktail" in my teens to the long ducktail on the sides with a flat crew cut on top that they called a "boogie" during my rockabilly days. But, even though I wouldn't be caught dead without my black Beatle boots, somehow I couldn't picture myself sporting a Beatle haircut.

But when Derek Taylor asked me, I didn't hesitate. "Look, Mate," he said, "you don't have to do the full-out Beatles thing. Pick up some teen mags at the newsstand and check out this French actor named Alain Delon. He's wearing a real short version, but it's combed forward instead of back." The respect that I held for Derek had automatically pushed me over the edge. Soon Tommy and I had joined Sonny Bono, Keith Allison, and The Byrds as some of the first musicians in L.A. to sport the new coiffure fashion statement from across the pond.

♥

Derek stopped by the studio one afternoon and told us, "I'm helping to organize this big music festival in Monterey next month. You guys should really be there." We told our friend that we had already made arrangements to drive up with our attorney who represented the producers of the event, John Phillips of The Mamas & the Papas and their record producer, Lou Adler. In June 1967 Tommy and I took a break from recording and drove with Abe Somer up to the beautiful seaside village of Monterey, California, to attend the happening they were calling The First Annual International Monterey Pop Festival.

It was to be a three-day event, captured on 16mm film, that would bring the top established pop acts of the day together with the best of the rising young stars. It turned out to be the first, last, and *only* Monterey Pop Festival ever held, but it was the granddaddy of all rock festivals, forming the blueprint for all those others that followed throughout the rest of the sixties.

Two hundred thousand people converged on the county fairgrounds of Monterey where jazz festivals had been held for years. They came in paisley painted VW busses, in limousines, and in everything in-between. Overnight, a village of flower children and hippies wearing backpacks, beads, feathers, and flowers sprang up in and around the fairgrounds. Hundreds slept on the ground after all the motel rooms had filled to capacity.

Arriving on the grounds, I was taken aback by the aura of peace and goodwill that I felt coming from the assembled masses. Somewhere in the blue haze of psychedelic smoke you could hear the transporting sound of gentle voices and flutes. And twenty-four hours a day, all around us, youth of a new age were dancing to the changing rhythms and sounds of an endless variety of hand drums.

For an entire afternoon, Ravi Shankar and his group of kirtan musicians improvised on traditional Indian ragas with their sitar, tambura, and tablas. I had never been to India, but I had read and seen pictures of the famous spiritual gatherings called Kumbha Melas. On this day, instead of holy men, these young Americans had come to worship at the feet of stoned idols of rock music, but found Shankar, instead, taking the stage. In the beginning I noticed a striking contrast between the rolling sea of consciousness that was the audience and the calm energy that surrounded Shankar. Then, along with the others, I watched myself getting lost in the sounds that poured from his heart and out though his fingers. It was as though I were feeling centuries of sacred tradition vibrating from his music to me.

I could not have felt more comfortable and relaxed as I sat on the grass of the natural amphitheater that framed a large stage. Stars walked unmolested among the throngs of fans. I saw Paul Simon sharing conversation with what looked like a band of gypsies. Micky Dolenz, who would have been mobbed on the streets of many American cities, was just one of the crowd of spectators. Steven Stills and David Crosby, as yet still musicians from different bands, were strumming their guitars and singing harmonies that the rest of the world would have to wait two more years to hear.

Thirty-two acts had been booked to perform, mostly the established top artists of the day. They included Simon & Garfunkel, Jefferson Airplane, The Who, the Steve Miller Band, Johnny Rivers, the Paul Butterfield Blues Band, The Byrds, Otis Redding, Buffalo Springfield, Eric Burdon & the Animals, Canned Heat, the Grateful Dead, Booker T. & the MGs, The Association and, of course, The Mamas & the Papas.

From the Haight-Ashbury district of San Francisco, Janis Joplin and her band, Big Brother & the Holding Company, were next on the performance schedule. John Phillips said that she was very nervous backstage. But when Janis Joplin took the stage I marveled at her look of super-confidence. She unleashed her version of "Ball and Chain" that personified her loneliness and longing. Janis paced, ran, howled, screamed, growled, and sang her way through her performance that left her electrified crowd an emotional wreck. There was no doubt as to what her future in music would achieve.

When Jimi Hendrix came on stage that cool summer evening, we were confronted with a musical and performance style that none of us had heard or seen before: the on-purpose feedback, the blues and jazz-tinged psychedelic style of both his vocals and his guitar work, and the fact that this wall of sound was coming from just Jimi plus a bass player and a drummer. Even his look was subversive. His English Renaissance-style outfit was topped with a light red feather boa around his neck, and his unruly hair could not be contained by the matching headband.

Hendrix's rabble-rousing renditions of "Foxy Lady" and "Purple Haze" were nothing short of sedition. He seemed to be deliberately agitating and provoking the crowd. After an hour of psychedelic insanity, he brought out the lighter fluid, poured it on his Fender Stratocaster and set it ablaze. Grabbing it by the neck, he then began repeatedly beating it against the stage floor until the beautiful instrument collapsed into small pieces and gave up the ghost! Then, leaving the small smoldering bon fire behind, he turned and exited the stage. I was unsure of what to make of the performance. Like much of the audience I was in shock by the time Jimi Hendrix had left the stage.

My time at the Monterey Festival was nothing if not inspiring. I sat in the back seat as we drove home and tried not to participate in the conversations of the others in the car. I needed time to silently reflect on the many powerful ways I had been drawn into the music, colors, energy, youthful abandon, and the screaming need of so many to feel fully alive. Somehow, I was feeling a personal obligation to do my part to try to fulfill all these needs by expressing them in my own music.

CHAPTER 25

Purple Haze

In less than a month, we emerged from the studio with our first LP in hand. When we played the album for Herbie, he suggested that one of the cuts, a song called "Sometimes She's A Little Girl," should be our first single. At the last minute Don Graham, the award winning head of national promotion at A & M, convinced him to go with another side for our first release. Fresh from a Canadian Monkees tour, I had commented to Boyce on the colloquial way words like "out" and "about" were pronounced north of the border. From this observation, we had fashioned a song called "Out & About," and Graham said, "It has 'hit record' stamped all over it."

Don Graham was the consummate record promoter and lived life large. He seemed to shout everything he said, a habit no doubt acquired over years of conversing on the phone with the top disc jockeys in the country. We started meeting Graham at his office at six a.m. and spending our mornings on the telephone kibitzing with disc jockeys. Don's energy was astounding and infectious as he projected his quips to the jocks with a voice and authority that met them on their own level. Don would shout things like, "We need to get this Boyce & Hart single on your play list by Christmas—THIS Christmas!"

To kick off the release of "Out and About" Don Graham set up and guided us through a first class tour of the top ten U.S. radio markets to meet and greet the jocks. He arranged for a popular San Francisco deejay named Johnny Holliday to accompany us on the trip and send back recorded running reports of the tour to be played on his top forty station. Tommy and I decided we should ask our buddy, Barry Richards, to come

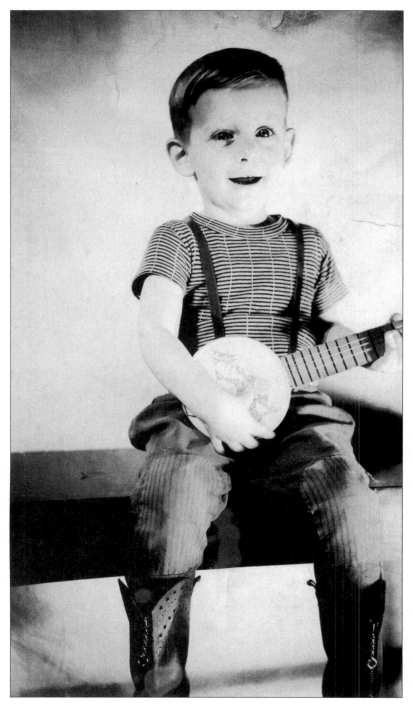

A foreshadowing, at five years old, of me learning to play my dad's real banjo ten years later.
(Bobby Hart private collection)

Our first home that Mom and Dad purchased for $1,200.00

My folks (the Harshmans) with my surrogate summer family (the Kidds). Above: My Dad, my Aunt Pearl, Leota and Bob Kidd, and my mom holding my baby sister, Rebecca. Below: Me and Chris and Clyde Kidd. *(Bobby Hart private collection)*

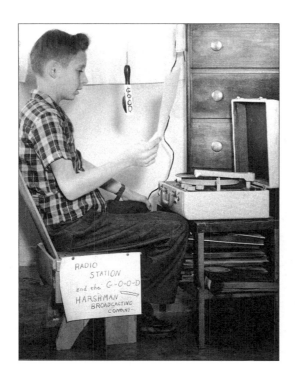

The practice radio station in my room in 1950. It had grown in sophistication by 1956.
(Bobby Hart private collection)

Leaving Phoenix the day after high school graduation for Ft. Ord, California,
and basic training in the U. S. Army, 1957 *(Bobby Hart private collection)*

Rockabilly recording artist, Robert Luke Harshman, 1959
(Bobby Hart private collection)

Our young family in 1960: me, Becky, and Bobby, Jr. *(Bobby Hart private collection)*

ONE WEEK ONLY   Saturday September 22   Sunday September 30
FIRST TIME IN SOUTHERN CALIFORNIA - DIRECT FROM LAS VEGAS
THE SENSATIONAL **BARRY RICHARDS & BOBBY HART**

with the wildest - loudest twist band anywhere

BARRY   featuring the "TWISTING DOLL" MARY ANN   BOBBY

CLUB PRELUDE 4923 LANKERSHIM BOULEVARD
BETWEEN RIVERSIDE DRIVE & MAGNOLIA   NORTH HOLLYWOOD

Barry, Becky, and I slapped these on hundreds of windshields, and by Wednesday night,
the Prelude was packed (1962). *(Bobby Hart private collection)*

My palatial NYC digs—the Crumbling Chesterfield Hotel, 1963 *(Bobby Hart private collection)*

Karmic Fate in Nebraska on our Bootleg Band tour *(Bobby Hart private collection)*

Del Shannon jammin' with Tommy Boyce and me during a weekend visit
from NYC to his Detroit home, 1963 *(Bobby Hart private collection)*

We visit Brian Hyland at his New York hotel (photo by PoPsie, *courtesy of Michael Randolph*)

Back in L. A. to sign with Screen Gems Music in 1965,
Boyce & Hart would keep the Boat House rockin' right on through the "Summer of Love."
(Bobby Hart private collection)

With *The Monkees* on a break from filming, 1966 *(courtesy of Andrew Sandoval)*

Ten days into our A & M Promo Tour Tommy, DJ Johnny Holiday, Barry, and I are surprised to see our first Boyce & Hart single, "Out & About," already climbing the charts, 1967 (photo by PoPsie, *courtesy of Michael Randolph*)

Tommy knocks himself out on the Motown Revue stage in Detroit, 1967 (*photo by Herman Jaffree*)

An overcrowded record store signing with a concerned Don Graham in the lower right corner *(photographer unknown)*

Tommy and I hang with Jerry Lee Lewis at the Palomino Club *(photo by Jasper Dailey)*

Boyce & Hart with our friend and champion Joey Bishop on his top-rated TV Show, 1968
(photo promo shot for the show)

Arriving at our new offices on the Columbia Pictures lot
(Bobby Hart private collection)

Misters Boyce & Hart Go to Washington. Successfully lobbying Congress to lower the U. S. voting age to 18, we meet with Senator Alan Cranston. *(photographer unknown)*

. . . and with some grateful future voters *(photographer unknown)*

Performing on the Grand Ole Opry stage, a childhood dream for both Tommy and me
(Bobby Hart private collection)

The Boyce & Hart Band with Barbara Eden on the set of *I Dream of Jeannie* *(promo shot for the show)*

Serena casts a spell on Boyce & Hart on the set of *Bewitched* with
Elizabeth Montgomery and Art Metrano *(promo shot ABC TV)*

Friends and hit song writers Carole Bayer Sager, me, Toni Wine, Tommy, and Wes Farrell at Tommy's Surprise 30th birthday party in New York, 1969 *(Photo by PoPsie courtesy of Michael Randolph)*

Me, Tommy, and our lifelong friend "Guitar Keith" Allison (Paul Revere and the Raiders) *(Bobby Hart private collection)*

A photographer finds us during a moment of relaxation.
(Photo by PoPsie, courtesy of Michael Randolph)

Our view, sitting at the Source Café on the Sunset Strip *(Bobby Hart private collection)*

Our big "Hat and Cane" number with Zsa Zsa *(Bobby Hart private collection)*

The Integratron Time Machine at Giant Rock Airport, 1970
(Bobby Hart private collection)

My two sons, Bobby and Bret, 1971 *(Bobby Hart private collection)*

Claudia and me with Hugh Hefner at the Playboy Mansion West *(photo by Peter C. Borsari)*

Four generations: Bobby Jr., me, my grandmother Osea, my Dad, and Bret
at Ohio Harshman family reunion, 1973 *(Bobby Hart private collection)*

My 70s writing partner, Danny Janssen (Partridge Family), with Tommy and me in Las Vegas *(photographer unknown)*

With Claudia at our new Hollywood Hills home, 1974 *(Bobby Hart private collection)*

A crowd of 23,000 showed up for our first Dolenz, Jones, and Boyce & Hart concert
in St. Louis, 1976 *(photographer unknown)*

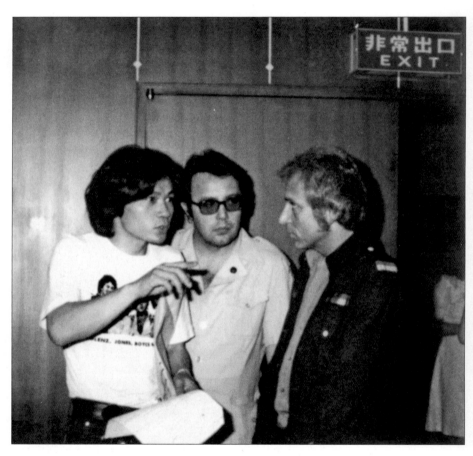

With the Japanese promoter and my friend Christian Dewalden
(Bobby Hart private collection)

In the studio recording my first solo album, 1978 *(photographer unknown)*

My wife, MaryAnn, and I celebrate the European success of her new record with a kiss in Monte Carlo, 1981 *(photo by Barry Richard in private collection of Bobby Hart)*

Barry, MaryAnn, and me on vacation in Manzanello, Mexico, 1982
(Bobby Hart private collection)

Our wedding at the SRF Hollywood Temple, February 14, 1983
(Bobby Hart private collection)

Our pilgrimage in India with Rose & Gary Wright, 1988
(Bobby Hart private collection)

With my sisters, Deborah and Rebecca, warming our hands during construction of the beautiful chateau Deborah's husband, Mark, built for his family in Oak Creek Canyon, Arizona, 1997 *(Bobby Hart private collection)*

Harvesting lemons from our orchard for our morning green drinks *(Bobby Hart private collection)*

Dad and me trying out our new meditation garden on a break from building it
(Bobby Hart private collection)

along just to keep things fun, and he accepted. In the hotels and on the planes Holliday and Richards, both talented impressionists, would keep Don, Tommy, and me and the other passengers in stitches with improvised comic dialogue between say, Bobby and Teddy Kennedy or Donald Duck and Bugs Bunny.

At our first stop in Miami we were thrown into the deep end of a crash course in dealing with the media: Pop Star Touring 101. On our first morning there, we attended a scheduled press reception in the hotel ballroom. As we conversed with the reporters and deejays, Tommy and I noticed that an attractive young brunette had set up a portable record player on a table in the corner. Not surprisingly, her smiles had attracted a number of disc jockeys that were supposed to be focusing on us and our new record, and she was playing them her own recording. When we walked over and introduced ourselves, we were just as captivated as the others by Bobbie Gentry's outgoing southern personality and the sounds emanating from the new record she was promoting, "Ode to Billy Joe."

Since the top station in Miami had immediately added our single to their playlist, Don Graham decided, on the spur of the moment, that it would be nice to invite their deejay staff up to our private suite at the Eden Roc for drinks. Boyce hurriedly called down and placed an order with a surprised room service staff for forty orange smoothies, a frozen concoction that we had sampled the prior evening. Not being drinkers, we assumed that the jocks would share our enthusiasm for these non-alcoholic delights.

The eight radio men poured into the large sitting area that separated my room from Tommy's. We didn't know it at the time, but right away they were quite disappointed in the drink selection we were offering. The orange smoothies sat melting on the bar. To make matters worse, one of the disc jockeys had brought along his very pretty, but very troubled young girlfriend to meet us. Apparently, she had already been imbibing heavily from her own supply before they arrived.

While we tried to chat up the jocks, she slipped, unnoticed, into my room and went shopping in my closet. Discarding her dress, she slipped into an outfit of her choosing, a man's dress shirt and a pair of my blue jeans. As the reception drew to a close, her DJ boyfriend found that she had locked herself in my bathroom and was refusing to come out. He pleaded futilely through the door, but since he was due on the air for his drive time shift in a few minutes, he finally was forced to warily leave her behind in the suite of two budding pop stars.

Thirty minutes later, Tommy and I were scheduled for interviews at that same radio station and with that same disc jockey. Before throwing the switch and welcoming us in that typical, over-the-top, energetic deejay voice, the poor fellow quietly and gravely informed us that he would take it very badly if anything unseemly were to transpire between us and his girlfriend. Don's face went ashen. As he saw it, there was a major record market on the line.

In Tommy's sincere and direct way, he leaned over the studio desk, looked squarely in the eyes of the unsettled young radio personality and said, "Look, Man, Bobby and I are just as concerned about your girlfriend as you are. We could see that she's probably a really great girl who's just had a couple drinks too many. I know you don't know Bobby or me very well yet, but you know Don Graham. I promise you that as soon as the interview is over, Don will go back to the hotel and chaperone her until you get off the air and she's safely in your care." Then, a moment later, we were live on air being given one of the warmest and most complimentary interviews of the tour.

That night, Sunday, July 9th, our limo drove us to Miami Beach and into the artist's entrance of the Miami Convention Hall. There we were escorted backstage where The Monkees were mid-way through their concert. As the intro to *I Wanna Be Free* began, David Jones looked over and spotted us as we watched from the wings. He immediately invited us on stage where he introduced us to thunderous applause from their 12,000-seat audience. The instrumental intro continued to loop on and on, until we waved goodbye and finally Davy went into the opening lines of his signature song.

By the time we reached Detroit, "Out and About" was being played in heavy rotation there (once an hour). The local radio station had arranged for Tommy and me to appear at a big Motown Revue, which happened to be running the next day. When we reached the large old downtown theater we found that all the great Motown Records acts were there, including Little Stevie Wonder, the Four Tops, and the Temptations. We watched from the wings as Martha and the Vandellas finished their classic "Dancing In the Streets" for an appreciative audience who were dancing in their seats.

We were supposed to just go out on stage, greet the fans, and say a quick "hello." As we were introduced, the fantastic Motown band went into an instrumental vamp, horns blaring and rhythm section grooving. All went well as we ran out smiling and waving to the enthusiastic crowd who seemed to already know who we were. We entered stage left, smiled and waved, waved and smiled, and then I began my exit, stage right.

As I turned and looked back from the wings, I saw that Tommy had gotten carried away, as he was sometimes known to do, and was apparently unable to bring himself to walk away from the love and adoration he was receiving. As he danced to the Motown groove, he went into his version of a Jackie Wilson shuffle and spin. As he spun, his feet left the slick stage, he flew straight up in the air and landed flat on his back, where he remained motionless. The band continued the vamp; Tommy appeared to be out cold. For me, time seemed to stand still.

After an excruciating minute or so, almost imperceptibly at first, Boyce began to thrust his pelvis in the air to the Motown beat. As his hips went higher, his head came up off the stage floor to greet his audience with a wink and a grin. They went wild as Tommy got to his feet and danced off the stage and over to me in the wings, where he nearly collapsed. After the show our limousine made an unscheduled stop at a medical supply store and Boyce wore a neck brace for the remainder of the weekend.

The next morning Don Graham got a call from Jerry Moss at A & M Records. "Who's Barry Richards, and what's he doing on the Boyce and Hart tour?" he demanded. It seemed that Barry had been adding on fifty-dollar tips to his massage tabs in the hotel health club. And now the Pontchartrain manager had called the record label to complain that Mr. Richards had walked across the lobby to the hotel elevator attired only in his bath towel.

Don knew exactly why Barry had been asked by Tommy and me to join us on the tour. Don enjoyed Barry's energy as much as we did. Don also knew that Barry helped keep Tommy and me loose and at the top of our game for media interviews. Tommy was appointed to take Barry aside and ask him if he could be a little more careful about his behavior in public and try to keep his tips down to ten percent. I wasn't there, but I'm sure he would have opened with his favorite preamble, "Do yourself a favor, my friend . . ."

We visited Chicago, Detroit, Cleveland, Boston, and Philadelphia, and on July 16th we finally reached New York. It was the second city where our itinerary would cross paths with The Monkees tour. Jimi Hendrix had replaced the Candy Store Prophets as their opening act, and that evening at the Manhattan hotel where The Monkees were staying, Micky introduced Barry, Tommy, and me to this soon-to-be legend. Although he was friendly to us, it wasn't hard to see that Jimi was going through some dark emotions after the show that night.

"America just ain't happenin' for me, man," Jimi finally said between sips of his drink and long, slow drags on his cigarette. He told us he was tired of being booed by the largely pre-teen Monkees' audiences and was obviously depressed by the negative reactions he'd been receiving from their parents. "You know, I've gotta do what I feel, and I'm thinking of maybe blowing this tour off!" Everybody involved must have known that The Monkees and Hendrix would not be an ideal pairing of musical acts. But I had seen and heard the power of Hendrix's music, and it was easy for me to be honest with him.

"You know, Jimi, these kids just don't understand your music yet. It's so different from what they've been hearing on pop radio, and it may take people a little time to understand where you're coming from. We caught you at Monterey, and you're an amazing talent. Someday the world will be celebrating you for your powerful vision and innovation."

Jimi silently looked me straight in the eyes for a long time without any expression. Then the tension seemed to relax from his face as he shrugged his shoulders and said "Thanks man, I know you mean it, and I guess you should know what you're talking about." Jimi looked down to light another smoke and I slowly stood up. Barry, Tommy, and I looked at each other, silently communicating that it was time to go. We said we had another engagement and had to split. Jimi didn't argue and when he reached out his hand, I left him with a friendly shake.

This pivotal week in the careers of Boyce & Hart may also have been the week that changed everything for Jimi Hendrix. It was the week he left The Monkees tour, the week his first hit "Purple Haze" entered the Billboard Hot 100 Bound charts, and the springboard moment that would launch the explosive rise of this musical game-changer.

The Boyce & Hart tour ended in San Francisco where our touring companion, Johnny Holliday, welcomed us to his top-rated radio show. Before the tour had ended "Out & About" was climbing up the national charts. After ten years of trying to be recording artists separately, we finally had our first hit as recording artists, *together*!

CHAPTER 26

Cornering the Sock Market

"Dig this, Hart. You won't believe it! Susan is leaving George!" Tommy had come into my room late one evening beaming as he made the announcement. "We have to pick her up at LAX tomorrow night at nine. She's coming back to move in with me." Of course, "me" meant us.

Tommy Boyce and Susan Hudson had been apart for almost two years now, but I knew she had never been far from his mind. From time to time, he would tell me how much he wished that he could share with her something that he was going through, some fun new experience or a sweet moment of career success.

I drove Tommy to the airport to pick her up. For the happy lovebirds, it seemed as though they had never been apart. Over the next few weeks, Tommy reveled in introducing Susan to our new Hollywood lifestyle and sharing with her our newfound success. The reignited relationship had a distinct advantage over the original version. Susan no longer had to make a choice between a financially secure partner and her feelings for Tommy.

Three being a crowd, one of the first things on Susan's agenda was to take Tommy real-estate shopping for a place of their own. Within a few weeks the lovers had picked out a comfortable four-bedroom house off Laurel Canyon in Studio City, just two miles away from the Boat House, and Tommy signed on the dotted line. But even before escrow had time to close, George Goldner had ferreted out the secret location of his runaway bride-to-be.

The tension in the air was palpable the night she took his call. We never knew exactly what he said to her on the phone that evening at the house, but the next day, two of George's henchmen arrived in a black limousine to escort Susan back to New York. She was packed and ready and went along passively.

Once again, Tommy was heartsick. What should have been one of the happiest days of his life, moving into his beautiful new house with the girl he loved, was anything but. That night, still reeling from losing Susan for a second time, he found himself rambling around in a big empty house as the reality of living alone for maybe the first time in his life set in. I hated to see him in pain and tried to be there for him as much as I could. But he and I both knew there wasn't much I could do to take away his gloom.

In fact, it was a melancholy time for both of us. The quiet was deafening that first evening alone as I walked around the empty Boat House picking up Tommy's discarded leftovers, surprised by the loneliness I was feeling for the first time in years. The energy in the house had been cut in half, just as surely as if breakers had been tripped in the electrical panel.

In typical fashion, Tommy threw himself fully into "career mode," the therapy that always seemed to work best for him. When we weren't working Tommy spent his time converting his new digs into an entertainment Mecca. He installed a state of the art sound system for dancing, complete with mirror ball and flashing strobe lights. Secret panels were bored through the walls that would allow him to mysteriously enter or disappear from the media room unnoticed.

Boyce christened his new estate *Sunshine Park,* and lavishly landscaped the grounds around his pool. Under his weeping willow tree, he installed a moat. The bridge that was suspended over it connected to brick walkways that he had painted yellow and redubbed his *Yellow Brick Road.*

Tommy began to distract himself from his sorrow with an unending parade of houseguests and revelers. A large sauna was erected which he kept heated day and night in case someone was in the mood. On more than one occasion, I stopped by for a steam only to find that the sauna was filled to capacity.

The parties soon became fodder for legend. We had met a lot of California girls over the last three years and they would all be invited. There were old friends like Abe, Barry, Derek, Del and Lester's son, Joel Sill, and there were people he had met at the carwash only the day before.

As I walked into the media room one night, I stopped for a moment to survey the eclectic panorama. Dressed in jeans and a tank top, a beautiful *Playboy* Playmate, who was also a singer/songwriter, was performing her latest as she strummed her guitar. A statuesque starlet in her white mini skirt and white boots was listening attentively while Tommy, at his most charming, leaned in to tell his story. In the center of the floor, unknown flower children in paisley and fringed leather danced to Creedence Clearwater.

In the years ahead the pressures we both felt from the rapid ascent of our careers would take its toll on our relationship. Although our partnership would take a couple more years to zenith, I don't think we were ever as close again as we were before the week when Susan moved to New York and Tommy moved to Studio City.

I remember standing in the corner one evening amidst a room full of partiers. Unnoticed, as I watched Tommy scanning the room, I knew he was searching for that one pair of eyes that could only be found three thousand miles away in some highly decorated Manhattan penthouse. Susan and George were married soon after and became parents of a little girl the following year. George Goldner died three years later at the age of 52.

♥

For Tommy Boyce & Bobby Hart, life had begun to take an upward spiral a year earlier with the advent of The Monkees. Our pictures had appeared in *Time* magazine, on the cover of the music trade magazines and in constant "what's your favorite color" stories in all the teen mags telling about "the young men behind The Monkees." Fan mail began to arrive. And often, as Tommy and I prepared to leave the Boat House in the mornings, we would find that flowers had been left at our front door during the night by admiring young ladies. Now, for the first time, we were beginning to reap meaningful financial rewards for our ten years of working and dreaming.

One summer morning in 1967 I found myself walking down Hollywood Boulevard with the realization that for the first time since 1958 my bank account still had money left in it at the end of the month. My first leap into luxury was a trip to the Broadway department store at the corner of Hollywood and Vine where I purchased thirty pairs of black socks. Now the anticipated freedom from all those trips to the laundry seemed exhilaratingly opulent!

Not long after cornering the sock market, I walked confidently into Mayberry Lincoln-Mercury one Monday morning and signed a lease for the car I had been dreaming about for years. Teddy Randazzo's girlfriend, Shirley, had owned a black Lincoln Continental and I always admired the look and feel of it the few times she had dropped me back at the Savoy. I also noticed the respect that her car inspired when she cruised in from the Strip and handed her keys to the Thunderbird valet.

Kathy Kersh had let me drive her Continental one night coming back from the Downey nightclub where we performed together the following year. I couldn't believe how smooth the ride felt as we negotiated the steep curve into the underpass which connected the 5 freeway with the 101. At the time I was still limping along in my gray hand-me-down '51 Chevy, but I remembered thinking in Kathy's car that night, "This is something I could get used to."

Returning home from the dealership, the burl wood steering wheel slipped easily through my hands as I turned onto Woodrow Wilson Drive. As if on cue, the radio was blasting "Groovin'" by the Young Rascals. The leather seat felt like a living-room arm chair, and as I turned down the radio, I felt like I was silently floating through the clouds.

One morning a few weeks later, Tommy called me and asked, "You wanna go shopping with me? I feel like buying a car today. " I hadn't realized it, but apparently he also had had his eye on a particular car for a long time. Twenty minutes later I picked him up at Sunshine Park. We drove to the Jaguar dealer on Sunset, and Tommy wasted no time in zeroing in on the metallic sky blue 1968 XK-E sports car that was calling to him from the showroom floor. At first the salesman was reluctant to waste much time waiting on two hippies in jeans and sweatshirts, but he performed his minimum duty. It was fun to watch the salesman's demeanor spin 180 degrees and his obvious surprise when Tommy pulled out his checkbook and filled in the entire sticker price.

We outfitted each of our new rides with radio telephones like the limousines used, an expensive proposition years before the advent of cell technology. We told ourselves that they were a legitimate business expense because we needed to stay in touch with each other. But we used them mainly to make dinner reservations on our way to our favorite restaurants. Shortly after this, Tommy spotted an antique 1929 Cadillac sedan on a corner car lot, pulled in, and added it to his fleet. Soon I noticed him telling all his friends that his new car had formerly belonged to the 1930s comedian, W. C. Fields, whom we both loved.

In December I realized that this was the first time I could go shopping for Bobby and Bret's Christmas presents without the normal restriction of a tight budget. Instead of patronizing the local drug stores as I'd done in previous years, I ventured into Beverly Hills and got lost in the wonderland of an entire two-story store that was devoted to delighting and fulfilling the sophisticated tastes of the children of upper income Westside residents.

I didn't really know my sons very well, so I had to rely on a wish list from Becky. But I surmised that they were both rowdier and more uninhibited than I had been in my youth and I tried to choose accordingly. As I picked out box after box of some of the most outrageously entertaining toys I could find, my exuberance was tempered by feelings of sorrow that ours was not a traditional family and that I would not be there to see their faces when they opened them on Christmas morning.

CHAPTER 27

Dear God, See You in Nine Days

The financial changes were great, but I had not anticipated and was little prepared for the powerful and intense lifestyle transformation that awaited me. Before The Monkees we wrote our songs at home, at the beach, or at the park. We stored them up and doled them out to our boss, Lester, in calculated intervals, forming a well-spaced parade of music, so that when we didn't feel like writing we had plenty of time to coast and pursue our other diversions. Little did we know that our lazy afternoons and active nightlife would soon be a thing of the past.

With the advent of our recording artist careers, it was like we had been given two first-class seats on a runaway train, and now it was beginning to pick up speed. In 1967 Boyce and I would begin a three-year grueling, non-stop schedule of recording, TV, promotion, press interviews, and personal appearance tours.

The Candy Store Prophets had become the Boyce & Hart recording and touring band. When Gerry McGee left to tour with Kris Kristofferson, Louie Shelton came on board. When Larry Taylor left to become a founding member of Canned Heat, our friend Leon Russell recommended one of his stable of musicians, John Gallie. John played great keyboard bass with his left hand and incredibly handled all the piano parts with his right.

We signed with the William Morris Agency and played clubs, stadiums, and amusement parks all over the country. I remember dingy back rooms where club owners would count out our money. Later there were large venues, where looking out into a sea of adoring faces I could feel every wave of emotion and affection they were projecting as I watched them screaming with delight and singing along to every word.

It probably wasn't more than a year into my new career as an artist that, exhausted and alone in my room one midnight, I admitted to myself that I was struggling to keep up. We had been up since six in order to make our flight to Cleveland where we arrived around eleven that morning. We were driven to the hotel, checked in, changed, and headed directly out to the sound check at the auditorium where we would be performing that evening.

At one p.m. a reporter and photographer from the *Cleveland Plain Dealer* met us back at the hotel for an hour-long interview, which we had to cut short in order to arrive on time at the top local radio station, *WIXY*, for a live on-air interview. From there we headed to a downtown TV studio where we would be taping the popular syndicated music show, *Upbeat*. While waiting to perform our record, I realized that the title of the show was an apropos code name for what we were expected to be: never-endingly exuberant, entertainingly personable, and eternally *upbeat*.

After choking down a room-service sandwich, we changed again and headed for the show. After our performance, we toweled off, signed autographs, greeted backstage guests, and then headed out to a local lounge where we were hosted by Allan Rider, the promotion man from Main Line, the company that distributed our records in Cleveland. The question of whether I had the energy for this line of work came not from this exhausting day alone, but from the realization that I'd be starting it all over again in the morning and that there was no end in sight to these endless days.

Tommy's natural high-energy temperament and his love of the spotlight made him much better suited to our new lifestyle. But over the years I came to realize that the stresses of this high-pressure business were also taking their toll on him. It's just that he dealt with it in totally different ways. To say that he was always "on" would be misleading. Tommy's personality did not fit the old line, "The refrigerator light comes on and he does a twenty minute show." His personality was the same when the spotlight was on him as it was before he opened the refrigerator door. But that personality was always spontaneous, energetic, and flamboyant.

Although we both loved people, Tommy would seem to be energized by his interaction with others while I could be easily worn down by a constant barrage of sensory stimulation. Whereas Tommy's exuberance was always spontaneous, more often than not, I would have to use sheer will power in order to exhibit the upbeat disposition that was expected of me. This constant pushing myself to perform would contribute to the sense of exhaustion I came to experience. And my exhaustion would become a source of derision from Boyce who sometimes saw me as unmotivated or lethargic.

Common in this high-energy entertainment industry were the props purported to help people like me feel like they were getting the greatest highs of celebrity stature and lifestyle. And the larger the audiences, the more frequent the interviews, the faster the travel pace and the higher the expectations, the more freely these offers flowed. Although it became quite easy to see the downsides of this chemically induced lifestyle on those around me, one early Chicago morning I succumbed to the promise of instant vitality in a pill.

It was my first and only experiment with a pharmaceutical energy booster as I faced a particularly busy schedule during an uncommonly frantic tour. As we climbed from the hotel curb into the local promotion man's car for our ride to a seven a. m. radio interview, he could easily discern my less than buoyant demeanor. "Here, try one of these," he offered. Ten minutes later, the "upper" had made me wonderfully awake, wide-eyed, and full of artificial energy. However, my exuberance gradually began a slow cross-fade into painful fatigue and depression as the afternoon wore on. Laying on my hotel bed around nine that evening, caught in the exasperating twilight between exhaustion and wakefulness, I vowed that for me, this magic bean would never be worth the agonizing experience of sliding back down the bean stock.

Although my physical exuberance was limited, I never gave up my mentally upbeat attitude that allowed me to avoid adding to my physical fatigue by taxing my mind with needless worries and anxieties. I clung to the blessing that I had always possessed a positive mind, and somehow I was able to keep my mental equilibrium by rejecting any thoughts of fear that might have otherwise overwhelmed me.

My morning meditations continued to be a source of grounding even though they weren't as regular as they once had been. At home, in my little meditation room, I had hung a beautiful greeting card recently sent to me by my friend, Victoria. She had written in calligraphy a quote from the Indian guru, Paramahansa Yogananda: "Everything else can wait, but the search for God cannot wait."

But on the road, this little reminder would so often get pushed aside by the avalanche of expectations on my time. I remember offering a silent prayer as I sat in my window seat waiting for our plane to taxi for takeoff. "Dear God, I know I should be meditating this week, but we're starting this grueling tour this morning, so I'll see you in nine days. Amen."

"Out and About" had charted well, but when Don Graham heard the title song from our second album, "I Wonder What She's Doing Tonight," he told us he'd stake his reputation on this being the record we'd been waiting for. Tommy had laid down a killer, energetic rhythm guitar track in one take, with only the bass and drums accompanying him. I added the keyboards later that night, and we flew arranger Artie Butler out from New York on the weekend for the horn overdubs.

Always looking for that little something extra to grab the listener's attention, Tommy came up with the signature "All right, Bobby, let's get' 'em," line as we headed into the second verse, just as he had done for Micky Dolenz' when he suggested the breathy "ahhhs" for "Clarksville."

♥

A year before, Boyce & Hart had been commissioned to perform the theme song for a new Columbia movie, *Where Angels Go, Trouble Follows*. As it happened, we were in Philadelphia on our first A & M promotion tour at the same time they were shooting some scenes for the movie. After a day of visiting radio stations we had stopped by the set to watch the filming, and they ended up filming us for one of the scenes. When the film was scheduled for release in 1968, Tommy and I were invited to fly out to Houston to attend the premiere.

A black tie gala was set up in a large ballroom after the movie premiere and the cream of Houston society was in attendance to get a glimpse of the great film legend, Rosalind Russell, best known for her classic roles in *Auntie Mame* and *Gypsy*. Since we were seated at her table, we enjoyed a running conversation with the charismatic and sophisticated Miss Russell that lasted throughout the evening. Although always dignified, we found her to be very down to earth, and our exchange was laced with laughter and fun.

Rosalind Russell told us that she was a music lover and very much liked the theme song we had done for the film. When we complimented her on how beautifully she was dressed, she confided that having come from the modeling world she had always been cast as a "clothes horse" in her movie roles, a stereotype which she resented. Then she repeated one of the most famous lines of her career, "I always felt like a hot house orchid in a field of wildflowers." After that night, we stayed in touch and became lifelong friends.

CHAPTER 28

In Cities Across America, She'd Find Her Way Backstage

Bob Kidd's brown 1943 Chevrolet was cruising along effortlessly as I rode in the back seat, sandwiched in between Clyde and Christina. We were in a seedy area of South Phoenix, a part of town I had never seen before, at least not after dark. I raised my ten-year-old head up to peek at the unfamiliar figures who stood in front of liquor stores and honky-tonks, casting long eerie shadows as they moved.

Mildly apprehensive, I would have been downright frightened had I not been with my summer surrogate family, the Kidds. I wasn't sure why Uncle Bob had asked me along on this nighttime adventure. Maybe he knew that I was way past due an opportunity to be exposed to other races and cultures. Uncle Bob slowed the car to a crawl for a couple of blocks, and we came to a stop directly in front of the peeling whitewashed door of a store-front church marked only by a crude sign that read True Rock House of Prayer.

The service was already in progress when we turned the knob and entered the small, coarse room. A spirited gospel song was being sung by the faithful, who numbered only seven or eight, accompanied only by tambourine. Our party found five of the twenty or so seats, settled in near the rear, and tried to sing along. It was a song we had never heard, and the singers sounded somewhat amateurish, but there was an exuberance and lyrical commitment that I had never experienced before.

I became a big fan of "Race" music in my teens, just as it was being renamed, "Rhythm & Blues." Then I had reshaped my vocal style when

I played clubs in my early twenties to sound as "black" as I could. Later Donnie Brooks had helped me form a gospel group called Bobby Hart and the Hearts of Joy with former members of the famous Clara Ward Singers. We received rave reviews from the agents who attended our showcase, but, alas, in 1963 there were few places to book a black gospel group fronted by a white lead singer.

But my experience in that humble house of worship that night in 1949 was the beginning of my romance with a musical style that had evolved from the depths of sorrow and injustice in a world where one human being could be the property of another. Over time I developed a deep fascination with the black history of the sixties and the incredible moral bravery of the nonviolent movement of Martin Luther King, Jr., the Freedom Riders, and hundreds of men, women, and children who stood willing to die for the cause of justice.

♥

Tommy and I had been so engrossed in building our careers that there was little time left for the world of politics. Of course, we were not blind to the injustices that swirled around us, and we would often express to each other our frustration or sorrow at the deplorable treatment of blacks, the poor, and even those choosing unconventional lifestyles.

Then, on March 16, 1968, Senator Robert F. Kennedy declared his candidacy for president of the United States, promising to end the long, bloody war in Vietnam. The admiration that Tommy and I had held for his older brother immediately rushed to the surface when we heard the news. A new feeling of hope found its way into our psyches, a hope that the direction of our country could be reversed from war to peace and turned back toward a commitment to equality and justice.

Around this time Tommy and I noticed that a very attractive young lady had been showing up again and again at our concerts. She was hard not to notice. Diane had large sparkling eyes and a very sweet demeanor. In cities around the country, she would find her way backstage after our shows and separately lead Boyce and me to believe that she would like to get to know us better. But the conversations would ultimately get around to her real passion—her glowing enthusiasm and support of the Robert Kennedy campaign.

Diane told us that RFK had traveled to South Africa in 1966 and been one of the first American statesmen to speak out against apartheid. She said that he was building his presidential campaign on his continued commitment to racial equality as well as an end to the war. "And it's the youth of the country," she told us, "that Kennedy sees as key to an invigorated America."

It turns out we weren't the only rock group whose dressing rooms Diane had been visiting that month. What she really wanted was for us to commit to perform at a superstar concert to be held in Indianapolis the following month, with the proceeds going to benefit the Kennedy campaign. Of course, we separately both said yes right away. Later that night I accosted Boyce as we shared a late night supper. "Hey, Tommy! This friend of mine wants us to appear at a show for Robert Kennedy, and I think we should do it." "I'm way ahead of you, my friend," he replied. "I checked with William Morris and we have the date free."

Diane put us in touch with the Kennedy people, and in a few days they got back to us. They thanked us for agreeing to do the show and then asked if we would head up a new committee they were forming. Without hesitation, we became co-chairmen of the *First Time Voters for Robert Kennedy.* Tommy and I went at the campaign for Bobby Kennedy with no reservations. We gave our money, our time, our names, and our energy to the effort. We appeared at Kennedy rallies, carried placards, wore straw hats, and made calls.

One day as I was volunteering to stuff envelopes, I flashed back to when I was a school boy in my parent's garage, printing and then mailing out my own newsletter touting what my teenage mind considered to be important and timely religious issues. I silently laughed at how much and how dramatically my world had changed around me. Even though the day before I had sung for thousands of adoring fans, here I was in a room where nobody recognized me, once again playing the role of passionate communicator, and still trying to avoid the spotlight.

For a while now, I had been paying more attention to the newspapers and the evening news. It was as if someone had pulled the curtain back and let me see for the first time all the deception that was going on in Washington. I felt like a champion for the better America we all wanted. I believed that we are all children of God and, as such, each of us deserves to be treated with respect and fairness.

One afternoon at the volunteer center, I overheard three campaign leaders speaking in loud and upset voices. Apparently a well-connected member of the campaign staff had been describing what he had been hearing on the street about the Nixon campaign. The word was that he had been sending goons around to infiltrate, disrupt, and harass the Kennedy and Humphrey campaigns. I didn't think much about it since my attention was being split between the discussion and the cute female volunteer next to me.

But on my drive home that night I seriously caught myself constantly checking my rearview mirror for suspicious black sedans with two men wearing hats. For the first time, this didn't feel like the America I had been seeing in our audiences' hopeful and happy faces. Still, I remained optimistic that most Americans wanted the war to end, the environment to be treated as sacred, and for all people to give and receive respect and freedom.

But now the political upheaval and unrest sweeping our country had grown too explosive not to notice. It was the most turbulent year in recent American history! The counterculture that had started with peace and love the year before had been joined by voices of opposition to racial inequality and to the war, and now violence was spilling into the streets.

Young black men and women, tired of feeling trapped in the filth and poverty of our nation's inner-city ghettos were setting their neighborhoods ablaze. College students and factory workers, in danger of being drafted to die in a war they didn't believe in and weren't old enough to vote against, were staging emotional and sometimes violent protests.

And yet, the leadership class claimed to not even understand the unrest. In a radio speech I actually heard Spiro Agnew, Nixon's choice for vice president say, "America's silent majority is bewildered by this irrational protest." I knew there were peaceful and positive alternatives out there to racial discrimination, to poisoning our environment, and to war. I had read and heard them outlined by so many intelligent and compassionate young people. How could the old guard be so blind to all the new ideas?

Nixon was trying to portray himself in the press as the man who could bring stability and safety during this period of national unrest and upheaval. But I had a hard time trusting his motives or even making it through any of his campaign speeches. I knew from the media that he had been openly attacking the hippie counterculture and the anti-war demonstrators by using tactics that were both vicious and illegal.

On April 4th, nineteen days after Kennedy had announced his presidential bid, the Reverend Martin Luther King, Jr. was assassinated in Memphis. Once again, it seemed as if the world had stopped turning. We had a song in the top three that week, but now no *new* Boyce and Hart music would be created for many days. We stayed in our homes and let the weight of the loss sink in on us.

When I hung up from talking with Bobby, Jr. and Bret that week, I said a prayer that our world would find some healing justice before they were old enough to notice the cruelty. Standing at the kitchen sink one morning, looking out the window and drinking a glass of water, I realized that for some unknown amount of time, in the back of my mind I had been silently singing "I Wanna Be Free."

Robert Kennedy, who had been campaigning in Indianapolis at the time of the tragedy, stood on a platform in front of a volatile crowd in the inner city and gave a heartfelt speech calling for reconciliation between the races. Dr. King's assassination provoked violent riots in 125 cities across America that week.

But there was no rioting in Indianapolis. It was one of the reasons we loved our candidate so much and had decided to work for his election. Robert Kennedy was able to touch and move people with his passion, even in this remarkable time when violence had somehow come to be seen as the norm.

That same month and in that same American city, Boyce & Hart performed with our band in a giant rock show at a large downtown Indianapolis auditorium. Sonny and Cher, The Moody Blues, the Ohio Express, and our friend, Tiny Tim, were among the many performers who had agreed to appear with us that day in a concert to benefit the Robert Kennedy campaign.

On June 4th, exactly two months after Dr. King had been murdered in Memphis, Robert Kennedy won the California Democratic primary election. Slightly after midnight at a celebration rally in Los Angeles, like Abraham, Martin and John before him, Robert F. Kennedy was also tragically and senselessly assassinated.

In the summer of 1968 Tommy and I were booked for another *Joey Bishop Show* appearance. Regis Philbin was his sidekick on the late night talk show, and this night Joey had taken the evening off and Regis filled in as the host of the show. That night on the show, Regis presented Tommy and me with a plaque from the campaign thanking us for our efforts in trying to help Robert Kennedy become our next president.

As I mounted the award in its prominent place on the entrance wall of the "Boat House," I was struck by a profound feeling of sadness—sadness for all the injustice and unrest, sadness for the tragic losses, sadness that the nation never got to experience what a difference it might have made to have had Robert Kennedy, instead of Richard Nixon, as the thirty-seventh president of the United States of America.

CHAPTER 29

I Was Never More Proud
of Tommy Boyce

I t was May 16, 1968, forty-two days after the death of Martin Luther King, Jr., and two and a half weeks before the death of Robert Kennedy. Tommy and I had been invited to a private reception for Dr. King's Southern Christian Leadership Conference. We found the Bel Air address, and at about eight p.m. we were admitted to the home of veteran movie producer, Edward Lewis.

We were led into a large living room/parlor that had been stripped of its furniture, but where Picassos, Rouaults, and Pascins still hung over white wooden folding chairs that had been set up for the guests. There must have been forty to fifty people sitting there, and as we walked to our seats trying not to stare, I seemed to recognize nearly every one of them.

The next morning the *Los Angeles Times* printed the names of some notable attendees. To give an idea of the star power in the room that night, here are just a few names from that list: "Marlon Brando, Patty Duke, Barbara Streisand, Natalie Wood, Candice Bergen, Eartha Kitt, Carl Reiner, James Garner, Judy Collins, Leonard Nimoy, Ben Gazzara, Rod Serling, Martin Landau, Lorne Greene, Walter Matthau, and James Baldwin . . ."

At the front of the room, an impromptu podium and microphone had been set up. And seated nearby were the guests of honor, Coretta Scott King, the Rev. Andrew Young, and Dr. King's successor as head of the SCLC, Dr. Ralph Abernathy.

Harry Belafonte, chairman for the evening, came to the microphone and laid out the reason for the event before introducing the three guests of honor. Near the end of his life Martin Luther King had announced the launching of the *Poor People's Campaign*. "Someone has said that Dr. King had come to see poverty as the root of inner city violence and to believe that 'gaining a seat at the lunch counter wouldn't count for much, if you couldn't afford the meal once you got there.'"

Rev. Ralph Abernathy, speaking in sincere and relaxed tones told the stellar crowd, "You cannot be safe in Beverly Hills if your brothers are slaves anywhere. Injustice anywhere is a threat to justice everywhere."

Bravely, barely six weeks after her husband's death, Coretta Scott King stood before us, visibly moved as she looked out at the faces of what Army Archerd in his *Daily Variety* column called, "more Hollywood celebs than we've ever seen in one house." With tears streaming down her face, she welcomed her extraordinary audience and thanked them for their presence and their caring. She said that she had always known that assassination was a possibility for her husband because of his role as an "extremist for good."

Andrew Young, SCLC's executive vice president, said that it was his contention that it was "artists like the ones gathered here tonight, who shape and mold the hearts and minds of the people, more than all the preachers in all the churches in America." All three guests of honor spoke about Dr. King, his vision, and their resolve to carry on his work in his absence. They were there to rally support in the Hollywood community for a "Poor People's March on Washington" as a tribute to the fallen leader. The crowd, of course, was sympathetic to their cause and when the three had finished speaking, it seemed the evening would end there.

Then, after a few moments, civil rights writer and journalist, Louis Lomax, sprang up from his seat and came to the microphone. I knew him from his programs on local television. He said,

> *I'm sure that everyone in the room this evening passionately supports Dr. King's vision for a better and more just America and for this great campaign. But it's been my experience that in meetings like this, unless tangible commitments are given while we're here in the room thinking about it, often the cause can be*

easily forgotten when we leave and go off to our homes. Before we
end this memorable evening, I'd like to see some pledges of support
for these folks who have come all the way from Atlanta to be with
us tonight.

An uncomfortable silence began to creep over the room. Lomax
stood his ground. The sound of the wind-up grandfather's clock coming
from somewhere in the back of the room grew louder and louder. *Tick-
tock, tick-tock; Ta-lick-Ta-lock, Ta-lick-Ta-lock; Ka-BLICK, Ka-BlOCK,
Ka-BLICK, Ka-BLOCK!* Two or three minutes must have gone by.
Nobody moved and nobody said a word.

I knew Tommy Boyce pretty well, and sitting next to me inches away,
I could feel the wheels starting to spin in his head. I could hear his breathing speeding up, and glancing over, I could see beads of perspiration forming on his brow and that his knuckles were turning white as he held on
to his knees. I knew that if he exploded, he would be speaking for both of
us, and I was afraid of what he might say in the heat of the moment. I half
turned to him in the darkened room and gave a slight shake of my head,
but before I could whisper a word, Tommy had sprung to his feet.

"My name is Tommy Boyce," he started slowly. "My first success in
this business was from a song I wrote for Fats Domino, a black man. Now
my partner and I are doing very well in the music business and I just think
it's time for us to give something back. So, I'd like to pledge five thousand
dollars tonight from Tommy Boyce and Bobby Hart."

Another few moments went by as the guests digested what had just
happened, but now the ice had been broken. Two rows ahead and to the
right of us, singer Johnny Rivers stood up, and in his New Orleans drawl
pledged to match Tommy's contribution. Next, our new friend, Rosalind
Russell, too shy to stand, leaned over and asked Tommy to announce
her commitment. The dam had broken. The pledges were coming closer
together and the figures being mentioned were growing larger.

In a fittingly dramatic climax, actor Jack Lemmon stood up. I'll never
forget his words, "Let's face it," he said, "I'm hot right now!" After some
scattered laughter, he continued. "Not the picture I'm working on right

now, and not the next one, *April Fools*, but the one after that. I'm going to give fifty per cent of my salary from that movie to support the Southern Christian Leadership Conference and the Poor People's March on Washington." The room erupted with applause.

After the meeting, we stood around with a number of the others, feeling pretty good about what had just happened and not wanting it to be over just yet. Miss Russell asked us if we would mind stopping by her Beverly Hills home the next morning to pick up her check and turn it in together with our own. We left, knowing that we had been allowed to witness something very special and that this would be an evening we would not forget.

Driving home, words didn't seem appropriate, so we turned up the AM radio, rolled down all the windows, and let the music help us celebrate our exhilaration. When I glanced over, Tommy was smiling and singing along to the radio. I knew he must have been feeling some of the same emotions that were cascading over me: feelings of pride for having been a part of something bigger than myself. But for me, there were also feelings of gratitude that I had a partner and friend whose caring, compassion, and courage had made it possible. Looking back over all the years I knew him, I was never more proud of Tommy Boyce than I was that night.

CHAPTER 30

Between Hollywood
and Sandalwood

In 1968 I made a heart-felt commitment to myself to find a way to get to know my young boys. I was delighted when Becky agreed that Bret and Bobby, Jr. could spend part of their summer with me in California, and also a little apprehensive. I picked them up at LAX, and during the forty-minute drive back to my house they were unexpectedly quiet. They sat stone-faced in the back seat and responded only when prodded. I reasoned that they didn't know what to expect from me, and it was only natural for them to be a little shy at first. I told myself that it was going to be a long cold summer as we tried to get to know each other.

But within an hour of moving into their room at the Boat House, their true personalities proved to be just the opposite of my first impression. At ages seven and eight respectively, they were smart, fast, curious, and full of energy, bordering on wild. As they ran up and down the stairs, exploring everything within their range of sight, I smiled to myself, wondering what I was in for.

Their first full day in town, I took the boys with me to The Sound Factory West where Boyce and I were recording horn overdubs for what turned out to be our fourth hit, "(You're Still My Favorite Girlfriend) Alice Long." There were the usual delays before recording while the engineer got the musicians matched with their microphones and their audio levels set. It took us a good deal of time, working with the engineer, to figure out and adjust the headphone levels to each musician's unique and separate listening needs so that they could hear well enough to play along with the already recorded instruments. Out of the corner of my eye I watched the boys flow back and forth between interest and frustration with the time-consuming process.

Hours later, after rewriting some of the arrangements and sending someone out to purchase emergency replacement reeds for the saxophones, the recording session was finished for the day, and I told the boys it was time to go home. Bret had fallen asleep on the control room couch and Bobby was looking at pictures in a *Billboard* magazine left on the floor.

The next morning Becky called to check on her boys and to ask how they were enjoying Hollywood. From the other room, I could hear Bobby Jr. tell her "Everything's okay, but it's a little boring. Then, I broke into a smile when I heard him tell his Mom, "He *does* have a job, Mom, and it's really hard work, too."

This little epiphany may have something to do with the great work ethic that both Bobby and Bret have both exhibited throughout all of their adult years. Currently Bobby is on the management team of a thriving landscape business; Bret is the banquet chef of a major hotel, and I couldn't be more proud of both of them.

♥

By the time we were due to go into the studio to record our third album for A & M, the Boyce & Hart dream had transformed in ways I could not have imagined back in the days when Tommy and I would take a leisurely drive to the beach, hang out, have lunch, and write a couple of songs. We now found ourselves faced with continual creative and business decisions on which we frequently disagreed. And those infrequent breaks when we could have just hung out together as friends, would more often than not, find me exhausted and retreating to the quiet of my room and the solace of solitude, while Boyce was out seeking the stimulation that more suited his temperament.

There were other reasons why we had been growing apart. Although we were both committed to our careers, Tommy was more driven than ever to reach the pinnacle of success, while I was beginning to rethink my priorities. I had just finished reading the remarkable spiritual classic,

Autobiography of a Yogi by Paramahansa Yogananda, a Christmas gift from Barry. Although his Indian yoga culture was a world away from my Pentecostal upbringing, I found their core values to be in perfect harmony.

Of course I'd already read a number of books on Eastern mysticism, but this one treatise had convinced me that here was a man whose life was demonstrating what he taught, and I was captivated by the undreamed of possibilities that he introduced. Every word seemed to resonate the truth within my own intuitive core. So I became aware of an inner conflict as I drifted back and forth between my Hollywood and my sandalwood states of mind. I now saw myself as a very different person from the one who had set out with his partner on this career journey a mere two years earlier.

Now, I found myself writing on my own at the Boat House when I had free time. And I knew that when inspiration struck, Tommy was two miles away, over at Sunshine Park, working on his own songs. The words and music that I had been writing privately were not pop love songs, and so I was understandably apprehensive when late in 1968 we got together to plan our third LP.

Timidly, I played Tommy my vision for an album based on my budding new awareness of the spiritual verities. To my surprise, he said, "Hey, man, this could be a great idea for a concept album." Apparently our "bubble gum" musical direction was also beginning to wear thin with Tommy. He had brought along to the meeting his new compositions: "Strawberry Girl," "We're All Going to the Same Place," and other songs that contained a deeper awareness and a harder rock vibe.

I had begun to see it as my responsibility to use my art and celebrity as a platform to pass along to others what to me were liberating new concepts. I was not so deluded, however, as to believe that just because my mind had apparently shifted to this exciting new paradigm, that the collective minds of our audience had changed all that much. The trick, I imagined, was to weave some of my essential philosophy so subtly into entertaining musical pieces as to not make waves with our loyal teen fans.

The lyrics, I surmised, would soar above the interests of most. But for the few who might listen closely enough, whether in 1968 or a hundred years later, maybe one line could spark an interest that would start them on their own search for ideas deeper than "You're Still My Favorite Girl-friend Alice Long," the one typical Boyce & Hart song that made it onto our third album, and the only one that had been written when both of us were in the same room.

The linchpin of my concept was a double meaning for an old side-show tent barker's pitch that I had heard at carnivals in my youth, "Step right up, ladies and gentlemen. It's all happening on the inside." The first half of the phrase, "It's all happening!" was how Rodney Bingenheimer, the unofficial mayor of the Sunset Strip, always responded whenever we met, and the greeting was now being used as a common retort when other flower children greeted one another up and down the strip. The point that I hoped to slip in was: the world that we perceive around us is a prod-uct of what we create in our own minds, so we can change what we don't like, if not in the world, than certainly within ourselves.

♥

The National Association of Recording Arts and Sciences asked Tommy and me to perform some of the nominated songs at the eleventh annual Grammy Awards. A short time later we found out that we had been nominated for our own Grammy in the category of Best New Con-temporary Pop Artist of 1968—Duo or Group.

At the afternoon rehearsal in a large ballroom of the Beverly Hilton, I ran through my version of "Little Green Apples," which had been nomi-nated for Song of the Year. Perhaps the style of my rendition borrowed slightly from the trademark "blue-eyed soul" vocal quality of the Righ-teous Brothers' Bill Medley. As I descended from the stage after my sound check, I was surprised to look up and see the man himself coming toward me. Bill turned to me as he passed with a mischievous smile on his face and said, loud enough for me and others to hear, "Stop singing so good!"

Boyce and I had fun that evening, rubbing shoulders with music business luminaries in the relaxed ballroom atmosphere. "Little Green Apples" won the Song of the Year award that night, but the Best New Artist of 1968 turned out to be Jose Feliciano. I leaned over to Tommy and whispered, "Who needs a statue. We've had three hits this year!"

THOUGHTS

(1) YOUR THOUGHTS CREATE YOUR REALITY

MY LIFE IMPROVED TREMENDOUSLY when the truth finally dawned on me that those ethereal thoughts that constantly flash through my head actually can create the objects of my physical universe and the conditions of my life. Being careful of what I think has proven to be important to my happiness and well-being. Dwelling on thoughts of lack, disease, unworthiness, and fear would manifest those realities in my life. So, how do we get rid of the thousands of negative thoughts that course through our consciousness every minute of the day?

(2) THESE ARE NOT <u>YOUR</u> THOUGHTS

FIRST, DON'T TAKE OWNERSHIP OF YOUR THOUGHTS. Technically, you did not create them and you need not take responsibility for them. What we <u>are</u> responsible for, is how long we entertain them. Evict an unwanted thought right away; don't let it stick around until it starts to feel like an old friend. So, how do we evict these unwanted thoughts?

(3) BRING IN THE LIGHT

Telling ourselves over and over "I will not think this crazy fearful thought" is like trying to use a vacuum cleaner to remove the darkness from a room. Instead, we turn on the light by systematically replacing a negative thought with its positive opposite. It's not just positive thinking—this is the secret scientific technique of letting your mind know what it is you want it to help you manifest in your world.

(4) WATCH YOUR HEAD!

STAYING CONSCIOUS, CONSENTRATED, AND VIGILANT is the primary imperative of any important endeavor, and this is the hardest part of the work. But constantly watching for, and replacing, negative thoughts with positive ones, will produce wondrous improvements in the quality of your life.

If You Hire This Guy,
I Can't Represent You Anymore

Television was now firmly established as the preferred medium for record promotion, and Tommy Boyce & Bobby Hart were booked to appear on all the music shows of the era. We were guests on *Hollywood Palace*, *American Bandstand*, *Upbeat*, *Happening '68*, and all the talk shows, including the *Tonight Show* with Johnny Carson, the *Merv Griffin Show*, and the *Steve Allen Show*.

One of the most popular late night talk shows, second only to Carson's *Tonight Show*, was hosted by another great American comedian, Joey Bishop. Bishop had begun in vaudeville in the tradition of a long line of New York Jewish comedians. In the fifties he began a friendship with Frank Sinatra while opening club dates for him. Sinatra made him the fifth member of his Rat Pack along with Dean Martin, Sammy Davis, Jr., and Peter Lawford. Joey emceed their notorious Las Vegas shows and reportedly wrote most of the outrageous comedy material for the act. He also co-starred with them in their movies, such as the original *Ocean's Eleven*.

From our very first appearance on the *Joey Bishop Show*, both Tommy and I felt a genuine affinity for the down to earth host with the deadpan delivery. Joey clearly took a liking to us, too, and started booking us to appear on his show every few weeks. After a couple of appearances, we felt like we had made a friend.

One day Joey Bishop reached Tommy and me by phone at our Screen Gems offices. He said, "Listen, guys, there's this group of students at the University of the Pacific in Stockton, California, and they've started a new grass roots movement to get Congress to lower the voting age in this country from twenty-one to eighteen. They're calling the campaign, 'L.U.V.' It stands for Let Us Vote."

He told us that he was trying to support the students and had been talking up their cause on his show. "I'm flying up to Stockton this Friday to appear at one of their rallies. I thought you guys might like to write a L.U.V. campaign song and come along with me and sing it at the rally." As Tommy and I listened to Joey's invitation on the speakerphone we gave each other simultaneous nods, using the almost undetectable visual short-hand we had developed over the years, as we spoke in unison, "we're in!"

We met Joey Bishop at the Van Nuys Airport where the university had arranged for a Learjet to pick us up. We were met at the Stockton airport by one of the school's professors and a large crowd of screaming coeds. It had not been unusual for Tommy and me to be met at airports in various parts of the country by screaming girls. But as we jostled our way through the crowd, it became very apparent that these screams, as well as the signs and banners, were not meant for us, but for our pal Joey. We followed behind Bishop, who was quickly loaded into a black limousine by the professor. We did a double take as the door was closed before we could jump in.

The professor shepherded Tommy and me into a waiting taxicab and piled in behind us. He wore a pinstriped business suit, looked to be only a couple of years older than us and maybe a few pounds overweight. He had a booming voice and a compelling presence, and he wasted no time in establishing a rapport. "Hi. I'm Dr. Kevin Mathews, from the Political Science Department here at the university," he opened the conversation, reaching out his hand. But instead of pausing there, he launched straight-way into one of the most fascinating stories I had ever heard in my life.

It was all happening so fast, and Tommy and I were both so mesmer-ized by what we were hearing, that we never thought to ask ourselves why the professor would be disclosing such revealing personal details to two complete strangers.

Kevin Mathews told us had learned his way around the Washington Beltway in the early sixties as an aide, providing public relations duties for some high-ranking political figures including Senator George Smathers of Florida. By the time he received his bachelor of arts degree, he said, he had already been named "Outstanding Young Man of the Year" by the Miami Junior Chamber of Commerce. Then he described how, after being admitted to the Florida State Bar at age 24, he had set up a thriving law practice in Miami and established an exceptional reputation in local society circles and in Democratic politics. No surprises here. He *was*, after all, in the Political Science Department. But the Doctor was just getting started.

In Miami, he had pulled off some astonishing successes, many revolving around anti-Castro clients. One, he said, was so impressive that it had been immortalized by Jack Webb on an episode of his True Adventure TV series. In our minds, we imagined the scenes as the professor unfolded his plot.

First, the young Mathews had sued Fidel Castro on behalf of some American companies that had been nationalized after the Cuban Revolution and won a large monetary judgment in federal court for his clients. Then, when Castro came to New York City to speak before the United Nations assembly, Mathews went to the airport with forty armed marshals, confiscated Castro's cadre of jet airplanes, and had them sold to satisfy his client's judgment.

But, he told us, he had gotten into some difficulty in Miami, something to do with over spending and passing bad checks, which resulted in him withdrawing from the bar. To avoid jail time, he pleaded insanity and entered a state mental hospital for treatment.

It may have been at this point that Mathews first began what was to be a long career of morphing himself, like the antihero in *Catch Me If You Can,* into one larger than life persona after another. Clearly, by now, he had begun to realize that he had the talent and charm to be anything he wanted to be, simply by changing his hat and claiming the necessary credentials.

His next hat was military by design, and had a full bird eagle on either side for decoration. By simply donning an officer's cap, and without any military experience, he became *Colonel* Mathews at the Florida Air Academy.

By the time we were pulling onto the university campus, we had heard the details of these and other amazing stories, and Mathews was heading into the "capper." While teaching at the University of the Pacific, Mathews told us he had conceived the idea for the student campaign to get Congress to change the Constitution and lower the voting age in America. He said, "The political climate is right and I know we can actually get this thing done now. I appreciate you guys coming up for the rally. It'll be a big help."

The trip from the airport to the university campus couldn't have taken more than twenty minutes, but Dr. Mathews had spoken fast and eloquently, leaving us marveling at his energy and incredibly smooth personal presentation. He had given us only a thumbnail sketch of his background, but it was impressive to say the least. Then, he hinted that he might be forced to leave the school shortly for "political" reasons. Perhaps the attention that the national campaign was now receiving was bringing with it a scrutiny of Mathews' personal past.

As the cab pulled to a stop, Tommy and I looked at each other, thinking, as we often did, in tandem. Dr. Kevin Mathews had impressed us as much with his commanding voice and articulate demeanor as he had with the stories of his fantastic accomplishments. Just before we exited the cab, we said, "Listen, Kevin. When it hits the fan, give us a call. We might have a job for you."

There was a very different vibe in the air when Tommy and I stepped onto the rally stage a few minutes later. The faces we saw in this packed auditorium of college-age kids held expressions of hope, unity, and strength. The response was thunderous when we introduced ourselves and expressed our solidarity with their cause. We sang our new song, "L.U.V. (Let Us Vote)," and by the second chorus the audience was enthusiastically singing along.

> *It's been a long time getting here. A change is coming and it's very near. A way to change things peacefully, and live together in harmony. Let us vote! It's time that we all made a contribution. Let us vote! It's the solution.*

For the first time, I felt a deep connection to an audience that was based on something bigger than the just the music.

Tommy and I had not been activists like Joan Baez or Phil Ochs. We had not written "We Shall Overcome" like Pete Seeger or sang "Walking to D.C." like the Staples Singers. Perhaps we had been too busy writing commercial pop songs for pre-teen consumption to develop a grown-up attitude towards our place in the world. But this week we had been given the chance to write music that could actually be an influence for change. In my heart, the feeling that I was serving my country was stronger than it had been since my army days and it felt good. Soon after, Dennis Warren, the University of the Pacific student leader of the L.U.V. movement, appointed our "Let Us Vote" as the official campaign song.

Back home in Hollywood I talked about lowering the voting age to everyone who would listen. I had become convinced that giving a say to the youth of our country, who were so articulate, involved, and passionate for peace, could make a dent in the Washington good ole' boy network and the industrial/military establishment. I had never felt knowledgeable enough to be very open about my political and social beliefs, but now I had a cause I could champion. Even the waitresses at Schawb's Drugstore on Sunset heard me declare that if we could give young people a voice, we could change America.

A few weeks later, we got the call from Kevin Mathews. "Hey Bobby, get Tommy on the line, too. Listen, guys, I'm taking a sabbatical from teaching." The voice on the phone was as flamboyantly strong and confident as the one we remembered from Stockton. Tommy and I had often discussed the fact that we could be our own "George Martin" in the studio, but we needed a "Colonel Tom Parker" in the office if we wanted to take our careers to the next level.

In a five-minute phone conversation, we struck a deal with the man whom we envisioned might be one of the only people in the world who could fill that role. Well aware of the fact that Matthews had told us about the dark side of his past, and had no previous experience in the entertainment business, that day we accepted Mathews' proposal to provide us with his personal management services. "Give me $1,200 for the first month. At the end of 30 days, either we'll shake hands and part friends or you'll increase my salary to $5,000 a month." We reasoned that with his gift for creative thinking and his dynamic personality, just by putting on this new hat, he could become our "Colonel Tom."

Like two high school boys who had just been selected for the football team, Tommy and I arranged a meeting in Abe Somer's office to blurt out the "good" news and introduce him to our new manager. Abe had become a top music business lawyer in a relatively short time. For years, he had been our close friend and we had never made a business decision without him. From the moment we entered the meeting, the air between Abe and Kevin was vibrating with tension.

Mathews laid all his cards on the table and remained calm as Abe cross-examined him mercilessly for over and hour. He defended himself brilliantly against Abe's attacks and at one point, I thought he had won him over. Then, Abe asked Kevin to wait outside. "It's a big mistake," he told us. "The man obviously has a personality flaw. No matter how bright and dynamic he may be, he can't stay straight. Why, he's admitted to being a crook." Tommy interrupted Abe to re-pitch the benefits of our new high-powered manager, but Abe held up his hand and took his position to the edge. Softly, but firmly Abe intoned, "If you insist on hiring this guy, then I can't represent you anymore."

We were stunned to think that the attorney who had been a long and close friend would even consider dropping us, two of his first clients. When it came to career advice, his had always been the last word. Was Abe intimidated—thinking that he might have to share this position with another strong personality? After a long night of deliberation, we concluded that, to the contrary, he was genuinely concerned for our safety.

Of course, the dangers involved in having Kevin represent us were obvious, but from our perspective, on balance, the opportunities loomed so much higher than the risks. We re-doubled our resolve that when it came to finances, we would keep a keen eye trained on, and a short rope tethered to, our new manager. We had put our money on Mathews, and we would go ahead and spin the wheel.

CHAPTER 32

Changing the US Constitution? How Hard Can That Be?

My initial glimpse into the workings of Kevin Mathews' mind came on his first day in town. Tommy and I were scheduled to perform at the Grammy Awards that night, and while we rehearsed in the afternoon, he had our secretary Barbara drive him around to his appointments. Barbara told us that evening "Mr. Mathews was pumping me for information all day and saying terrible things about you and Tommy." That night after the performance, Kevin told us that Barbara was disloyal and that his first act of office was the decision that she must be fired immediately. Barbara had been with us for years and was like a part of our family. Nevertheless, we decided to honor his decision and I was elected to do the dirty work.

But, when it came to business, right from the beginning, Kevin Mathews did not disappoint our expectations. We had never seen anything to match the creativity, energy, and demeanor that he exuded! Wasting not a minute of time, he immediately surpassed our wildest expectations.

Kevin suggested a weekend in Palm Springs to get acquainted. We took a suite of rooms at the Ocotillo Lodge where, in between sun and sauna, Mathews interviewed us and dictated his ideas for our career planning, goal setting and mission statement to his executive secretary who had flown in from northern California. Then Monday morning, Kevin rolled up his sleeves and launched into his offensive from the Brentwood apartment we had rented for him.

Fortuitously, our three-year agreement with Screen Gems-Columbia Music was just about to expire. Instead of renegotiating with Lester Sill in the music publishing division, Kevin took meetings with the top brass at Columbia Pictures and threw himself into days of negotiations with the giant entertainment corporation. By the time we re-signed on the dotted line, we were no longer just songwriters; we were record company owners and stars of our own upcoming television show.

Columbia would set up our own record label, B&H Aquarian Records, which their existing record division would distribute. We would release all our future records on Aquarian, and the company would make available funds to sign new recording talent that we might want to develop. They would provide us with a suite of offices on the Columbia Pictures lot to use as our new base of operations. And they would green-light the immediate development of a new television sitcom, which would star Tommy Boyce & Bobby Hart.

Then, on the strength of our exploding record careers and the prospect of our forthcoming television show, Mathews renegotiated our agreements with BMI, the society that collects and pays performance royalties when music is played on radio and television. BMI agreed to a previously unheard of, non-recoupable, high six-figure advance.

Well capitalized, and with the foundation of our first-phase goals well in place, Kevin now turned his attention to the next plateau on our career agenda. "You can't play to teenyboppers forever," he said. "Las Vegas is calling and you two are going to be headliners." Without the benefit of an appointment, Mathews walked into the offices of Bill Miller, the Director of Entertainment at the Flamingo Hilton on the Strip.

Back in L. A., he told us that while waiting to be admitted, he had overheard Miller on the phone with Tom Jones' manager. The two were in a tussle as they negotiated Tom Jones return engagement to the Flamingo. When the secretary showed him in, he introduced himself: "Mathews from Columbia Pictures. I represent two pop stars who are getting ready to explode with their own TV series. And I guarantee that once you've built them into a top cabaret draw, they won't hold you up for their return engagements." One hour later, he walked out with a deal memo in his pocket for Boyce & Hart to headline the main showroom at the Flamingo Hotel for three weeks, beginning in January of 1970.

Established in his new suite of offices on the Columbia lot, Kevin launched an extensive advertising campaign. He ran a series of full-page ads in the *Hollywood Reporter* and *Variety* that featured an illustration of the "Boyce & Hart Music Machine" depicting the components of our conglomerate ventures into stage, small screen, songwriting, and recording. In the picture all of the elements were working together so smoothly, and the mechanism seemed to be so well controlled. But when I looked at the graphic, I was struck by the realization of just how complicated our lives had suddenly become.

Boyce and I were ecstatic at how much Kevin had been able to create in only a few short months. His vision for our careers had gone far beyond our own, and he always seemed able to quickly turn his dreams into reality. During the years when I had worked in Vegas as a backup singer, it never even occurred to me that I would ever play one of the main rooms as a headliner. If I had underestimated my abilities in the past, I was now more than eager to embrace a future of unlimited promise, and it seemed that now all doors were open.

♥

A short time after Mathews had come aboard, we received a mysterious call from Joey Bishop. He said, "Look guys, I've gotta talk to you about a matter of grave concern. I'm really upset about it, but I don't want to talk on the phone. Can you come over to the television studio this afternoon and meet with me while I get ready for the show?"

Joey followed us into his office, closed the door and spoke in hushed tones. "I've been getting all this mail from the university students up North. You remember all those girls screaming for me when we arrived in Stockton that night? Well, a lot of these girls have written letters claiming that Dr. Mathews had forced them to do that. Basically, he told them that I wouldn't continue to support the movement if they didn't scream and fawn all over me. I'm telling you, this guy's bad news. If he tries to contact you, don't take his calls. I want you guys to steer way clear of him."

We had never seen Joey upset before. I knew that his ego had been bruised a bit, and I felt really bad for the embarrassment I saw on his face.

We tried to let Joey know that we were taking the matter seriously while keeping our replies as noncommittal as we could. We let him do most of the talking, thanked him for letting us know the situation, and left.

Of course, Kevin Mathews did not accompany us to the television studio when we made our next *Joey Bishop Show* appearance a few weeks later. The audience gave us a warm reception as we entered from the back of the studio audience and made our way up the aisles and onto the stage, singing to the marching band beat of our new "L.U.V." record. After the taping, Joey invited us, along with some others who had been his guests on the show, to join him at his home and watch the program when it aired that evening.

♥

Kevin had not only settled comfortably into our executive suite of offices on the Columbia lot to run our companies, while Tommy and I were relegated to token trailer offices like the ones they used for star's dressing rooms, he had also relaxed into his new role. I'd like to say that he got right into playing the part of the movie studio executive, but in reality, he wasn't playing. As he had done so many times throughout his life, he instantly *became* the role.

On an overcast morning as I arrived at my office, a secretary from Kevin's executive suite called me over and spoke in low tones. She said that Kevin had sometimes been verbally abusive to the staff and didn't always treat them with respect. We had cautionary talks with him, pointing out that it had always been important to us to treat everyone with respect and kindness. And besides, we had reputations to preserve. He responded that he had no patience for incompetence. A few weeks later, one of the daily Hollywood tip sheets for actors intimated that Mathews had been holding casting-couch auditions in his offices after business hours. When we pointed it out, he dismissed the warning as ridiculous tabloid rag gossip.

♥

Mathews arranged with Dennis Warren and the students in Stockton for Boyce & Hart to become the national celebrity spokesmen for the

L.U.V. campaign. We promoted the cause in media interviews everywhere we traveled on our personal appearance tours around the country. "The Vietnam War has already been raging for much too long," we told the press whenever they would listen, "If you're old enough to die for your country, you should be old enough to vote."

In the early spring Mathews made travel arrangements, set up an itinerary, and the three of us flew to Washington, DC. With Kevin leading the way, we walked the halls of Congress, lobbying our elected officials face-to-face for a bill to lower the voting age. We were overjoyed to find that Mathews had been right. Nearly everyone we talked to was sympathetic to the idea of granting our eighteen-year-olds the right to vote. I remember two congressmen, in particular, who wholeheartedly supported our cause right from the beginning.

Representative Henry Gonzales welcomed us to his offices for a chat and a photo op. The Democrat from San Antonio, Texas, was elected in 1961 and carried much influence in Washington. My consciousness hovered above my head, watching me talking politics with a member of the U.S. House of Representatives. Henry Gonzales had ridden in the Dallas motorcade on that fateful day, five years earlier, when President John F. Kennedy was assassinated. Tommy and I both expressed the admiration we held for J.F.K. and mentioned that we had supported Robert Kennedy's campaign and were still grieving from his loss.

Later, after a long day that included posing for pictures in front of the Lincoln Memorial, joining Winston Churchill in flashing the peace sign in front of his bronze statue, and signing autographs for crowds of field trip students on the steps of the Capitol building, we met with the legendary Democrat from California, Senator Alan Cranston. Cranston expressed his resolute support of our cause in full view of a group of students.

As the three of us walked away from the crowd, Cranston shook our hands and left us with a curious comment. "You guys are really brave!" he said. Letting his remark slide, we thanked him and left the senator with what I'm sure must have been blank, questioning stares on our faces. When we were out of conversation range, I turned to Tommy and asked,

"What do you think he meant by that?" Boyce shrugged it off with a tilt of his head and changed the subject.

It wasn't until three years later, when *The Washington Post* began publishing the work of their investigative reporters, Bob Woodward and Carl Bernstein, that I began to speculate about our roles in the 1969 Let Us Vote campaign. Could Tommy and I have unknowingly placed ourselves in danger as we went up against Nixon's "law and order" political machine? Probably not, I told myself. I've never been a big believer in conspiracy theories. Still, a little research revealed some intriguing information.

The week that Boyce and Hart released our last single on A & M Records, *L.U.V. (Let Us Vote),* was the same week that Nixon was inaugurated in January of 1969. Almost immediately after taking office, Nixon began his paranoid crusade against anyone suspected of disloyalty to his political agenda by hiring his first agents to conduct political intelligence operations and wiretaps. Quotes later revealed his vitriol, "Get them on the floor, and step on them, crush them, show no mercy." These were the same months that Tommy and I had been working to lower the voting age as national spokesmen for the L.U.V. movement.

Although Nixon pretended to support the movement to lower the voting age in his 1968 campaign, it is generally believed that he secretly feared giving the vote to this younger demographic whom he believed were overwhelmingly against the Vietnamese war. Number seven on his 1971 "enemies list" was a liberal politician named Allard Lowenstein, and next to his name, he was noted to be a "guiding force behind the 18-year-old 'Dump Nixon' vote drive."

Near the end of Nixon's first term, Woodward and Bernstein learned from an FBI official and others that at least fifty undercover Nixon operatives hired by his Committee to Re-elect the President had been working to undermine, disrupt, and spy on Democratic campaigns around the country. When the reporters connected this new information to other Nixon "dirty tricks" they had already been aware of, it lead them to speculate that the Nixon campaign had undertaken political sabotage long before the Watergate break in.

There had been a lot of press coverage of our work to lower the voting age, and for years it had been common knowledge that we were against the war in Vietnam. Did Senator Cranston know something that we didn't know on that blustery day on the steps of the Capitol building when he had complimented us on our bravery?

What we do know, of course, is the happy ending to this chapter. On the wall of my study, hangs a framed copy of the Twenty-Sixth Amendment to the United States Constitution. When it was ratified by the states in 1971, it permanently lowered the voting age requirement in United States elections from twenty-one to eighteen.

CHAPTER 33

Pulling the Hair Out of My Head

My dad knew that I was a singer and a songwriter, but it wasn't until he witnessed it firsthand one weekend in the summer of 1969 that he ever *really* knew what I did for a living. For the past ten years my connection with my parents had been limited to infrequent visits and random phone calls. I think Mom and Dad had seen me as a starving singer/songwriter for so long that they might not have realized how much my life had changed in recent years. One July morning as we sat in our Columbia offices planning an upcoming tour to Alabama, I suggested to Tommy the idea of taking our dads along with us on the road, and he lit up when he heard the idea.

I couldn't wait to get home and call my folks, and I was glad that it was Dad who picked up the phone.

Hey, Dad! We've been booked to play a couple of concerts in Montgomery and Birmingham the weekend after next, and the governor has proclaimed it Boyce & Hart Day in Alabama. Tommy and I were talking and we thought it would be nice to bring our dads along. It should be a lot of fun and a good chance to show you what it's like in my world these days.

I told him I'd send a ticket for him to fly over and meet us in L.A. two weeks from Friday.

"Oh no," he protested, "I couldn't take any time off from work right now." But the next morning, Dad called me back. "Your mother thinks I should take you up on your offer if you still want me," he acquiesced, "and my boss said it would be a good experience for me. He reminded me that I haven't taken a day off in years."

Dad and I, Tommy and his dad, Sid the Virginia Kid, along with our band, our roadies, and Kevin all boarded the Delta Airlines flight at LAX, a few steps ahead of the film crew that had been sent along to document the weekend. Midway through the flight, as dad napped, I moved into the vacant seat next to Tommy, and for a few minutes, we slipped into that familiar camaraderie of the old days.

As he strummed his Gibson, we sang in harmony the Bee Gees' "New York Mining Disaster 1941," "Have you seen my wife Mr. Jones? Do you know what it's like on the outside?" As Tommy kept the same tempo and strum groove, we morphed effortlessly into our original, "Girl, You Make My Day." These feelings of close friendship that had come so naturally before the stress of success had taken its insidious toll were far too infrequent these days.

As our plane taxied to a halt in Montgomery, we could see from our small windows, the celebration that had been set up right out on the tarmac. There was a marching band in colorful, uniformed regalia, a crowd of hundreds of welcoming teenagers, and a podium that had been erected on the flat roof of one of the airport buildings.

The sounds of screaming fans hit us the moment our small party deplaned, nearly drowning out the John Philip Sousa arrangement of "I Wonder What She's Doing Tonight" being lovingly played by a local high school band, and wafting toward us across the runway. We were all herded up to the rooftop stage where representatives of the governor, the mayor, and other dignitaries of Montgomery, Alabama, were waiting for us. Cameras were rolling as Tommy and I were welcomed and then presented with keys to their city. I lost contact with Dad when we went down on the tarmac to sign autographs where we were instantly absorbed into a crowding sea of admirers.

Forty-five minutes later Dad, Tommy, and Sid were waiting for me as I jumped into the car and we pulled through the waving and screaming crowd and on to the highway toward the hotel. When I looked over at him, I could see that Dad was almost in a state of shock from what he had just witnessed. Still, at the same time, it was evident that he was energized and excited by his first ride on this strange roller coaster.

When he had been introduced at the airport roof ceremony and pressed to the microphone, dad had managed a shy but gracious, "Hello, everybody. Thanks for being so nice to our kids." With a broad smile on my face, I was thinking, "We haven't been around each other for more than two days at a time since I was eighteen. Does he still think of me as a kid? Now, he was definitely seeing me with new eyes and overflowing with astonishment and questions about what lay ahead on our little trip.

At the concert that evening, he got to chat with many of our enthusiastic young Southern fans and their mothers. As I looked down from the stage I could see that Dad had obviously made friends with some of our admirers, and that they had crowded together to make a place for him in the front row to observe our performance. He was beaming and loving every minute of it. After the show I changed in the dressing room and went looking for him. As I came around the corner of the auditorium lobby, there was Dad standing in the middle of a pool of Southern belles, junior and senior, talking, smiling, and signing autographs.

Before turning in that night, we shared a few moments, just he and I, on the veranda of our motel. I was a little shocked when he told me how astounded he was at our popularity. It wasn't like I hadn't told him about the success we were having as recording artists. But, as I had surmised when I first invited him along, a thousand words couldn't match being there. He said, "I had no idea how much adoration my son was used to receiving. However, what impressed me and made me the proudest," he told me, "was that of all those kids and their moms that I talked to, almost every one of them commented about how nice you and Tommy always are to everybody."

My relationship with my dad had always been very traditional, and I had just thought of it as typical for the 1950s. I loved him and I knew he loved me. But the way we communicated it to each other was not with words or hugs, just by the comfortable vibe that we always felt between us. A strict disciplinarian, I rarely challenged his authority growing up, and I also remember very few times when I did anything to cause him to come to my aid or give me fatherly advice. Before turning in for the night, I put my arm around my dad and gave him a gentle hug, glad to be sharing this moment, even though I knew we probably wouldn't talk about it much in the future.

On the two-hour drive to Birmingham the next morning, my dad and Sid enjoyed some good-natured sparring as they sat next to each other in the back seat of the limo. As Sid finished a long discourse on what a successful ladies man he had always been, he asked, "What about you, Arizona Bob?" Arizona Bob smiled and replied, "Well, Sid, I believe I read somewhere that the real experts, don't usually talk too much about it."

The hotel was surrounded by eager fans as our driver pulled the black Buick sedan up to the entrance. As usual, Tommy and I hung out with them in the parking lot and lobby, smiling, talking, accepting flirtatious but innocent kisses on the cheek, and signing autographs until being called away for our next event. At three p.m. Kevin had scheduled a public walk-through of Birmingham's historic Woodrow Wilson Park. We walked over from the hotel with Kevin and our two dads in tow. The media was already lined up and ready to get to work when we arrived. The afternoon was perfect for a walk in the park with clear skies, a gentle breeze, and a moderate temperature for Alabama in the summertime.

Through the laughing and excited voices of our fans, I strained to hear as Danny, the Birmingham native assigned to be my helper for the day, explained how the park had been renamed for Woodrow Wilson, then in his second term as president. He said that at the end of World War I President Wilson had been the chief negotiator of the terms of peace. I observed to myself that today the park was not at war, and yet with the youthful energy erupting everywhere, it felt anything but peaceful.

Although I tried not to let it show, my mood became decidedly more sober when Danny hurriedly explained that the other motivation for honoring Wilson was because of his support of Southern Democrats who were becoming concerned that the federal government might interfere with their Jim Crow segregation laws.

It had been less than six years since the television sets of America were filled with shocking images of the violence that was raging in West

Park and on the streets that bordered it. The Rev. Martin Luther King, Jr. had come to Birmingham to lead a major protest campaign after the first mass beatings of Freedom Riders had happened here. Kelley Ingram Park, historically known as West Park, was the assembly area for the marches, sit-ins, and boycotts to end segregation in Birmingham.

My mind was a movie reel of Dr. King being arrested and thrown into solitary confinement, where he wrote his celebrated manifesto on non-violent resistance, "Letter from Birmingham Jail." I had watched as thousands of peaceful demonstrators, including children, were blasted with high-pressure fire hoses, beaten with nightsticks, attacked by police dogs, and jailed. The media spotlight on America's most segregated city unleashed a nationwide public outrage. President Kennedy ordered 3,000 army troops to the outskirts of the city. I took a deep breath, grateful that most of the "Whites Only" signs had been removed from the rest rooms and drinking fountains of the city before our visit on this day.

I was jolted back into the present moment when city councilman, Alan Drennen, stepped to the microphone and began his presentation of a key to the city of Birmingham "on behalf the kids, who I believe are the best behaved, best looking, and grooviest anywhere." The kids gave a loud cheer, reacting not so much to the councilman and his key, as to our response: my naturally heartfelt smile and wave and Tommy's trademark thumbs-up.

Tommy and I began our leisurely stroll across the park. We were followed by my dad, Sid, Kevin, our camera crew, some members of the press, city officials, bodyguards, and a few fans. By the time we reached the mid-point of the crossing, the crowd had swollen to a throng of thousands!

Suddenly, I felt a tremendous force as a burly cameraman came crashing into me from behind, propelled by the boys and girls behind him rushing to get an autograph, a photo, or simply a touch of their hero's attire. I felt fevered young hands trying to tear off pieces of my red, satin shirt, and then became aware that strands of my hair were actually being plucked from my head by hysterical fingers as the crowd became more excited.

As I tried to focus on signing the black and white publicity photos, sheet music, and scraps of paper being thrust in front of me, I looked up and realized that neither of our two six-foot-plus State Patrol personal escorts were able to protect us from this mauling. Over the sound system, I could hear one of them yelling his totally futile pleas, "Line up! Line up, we'll get to you faster if you line up."

Then, suddenly, I heard the tranquil voice of Tommy Boyce on the microphone. I raised up on my toes and caught a glimpse of a cornered Tommy, twenty yards away, calmly singing to the unruly fans. "Alabama is a gas," he chanted to the tune of "Here We Go Round the Mulberry Bush." "Everybody keep it cool," he sang, reasoning with the fans. "No pushing. Just a lot of sharing." Tommy's composed attention on them brought a temporary calm to the raging sea of pandemonium, and Boyce's white patent leather shoes lead the huge group on past the center of the park.

I felt like the Pied Piper as I led my contingent of the crowd onward while constantly signing autographs. Like a stop-motion camera, I tried to focus on the constantly changing stream of young faces that were working to get my attention. A sixteen-year-old girl must have said my name twenty times, louder and more desperately each time, until I looked directly in her eyes. I offered a smile and a wink, which caused her to grab her girlfriend and caused both of them to scream and jump up and down repeatedly.

The whirlwind that was our hour-long "walk in the park" continued that night at the show, except that the energy and love of the thousands of fans was contained within in the boundaries of an auditorium. Tommy was full of "Boyce-magic," the band was grooving, and I was flowing with energy and enthusiasm. The audience sang along with every word and the applause never stopped. Catching a glance of Sid, the Virginia Kid, and my dad standing together, smiling and clapping as they watched the show from the wings, brought a little wave of warmth to my heart.

After that weekend in Alabama, throughout the rest of his life, Dad always seemed to look up to me. He became my biggest fan and my number one public relations man. Throughout his remaining thirty-six years with us, he would wax on to friends and strangers alike about his famous son. And he loved recounting his memories of our once-in-a-lifetime weekend in Alabama.

A few weeks after the film crew had documented Boyce & Hart Day in Alabama, Tommy announced to me one day that he thought it would be a good idea if the cameras were to follow him around every day for the rest of his life. I tried to reason with him, saying "Tommy, if your whole life was recorded on film, there wouldn't be any time left for you to watch the play-backs."

Somehow this logic was lost on my charismatic and whimsical friend. Shooting me a look of distain, he changed the subject, resigned to the knowledge that his partner was incapable of grasping the genius behind this brilliant self-promotional concept.

CHAPTER 34

Phantoms of the Opry

We were ecstatic when Kevin told us the news. As we prepared for our latest tour of the South, he had surprised us by calling the management of the *Grand Ole Opry*. When he let them know that we would be coming through Nashville, they invited us to perform on their stage for the Saturday evening show.

Tommy and I had both grown up listening to the *Grand Ole Opry* on the radio. About as far back as I can remember, I looked forward every Saturday night to tuning in my little radio to catch the show that was synonymous with country music. So you can imagine how we felt on a summer Saturday in 1969 as Tommy and I, our band, road managers, Kevin Mathews, and Barry Richards arrived at 116 Fifth Avenue North, Nashville, Tennessee, the revered birthplace of country music, the Ryman Auditorium. We found the stage door, and someone showed us to our dressing rooms.

Almost as if in a dream, we wandered through the long, hollowed halls, taking in every light and shadow of this venerable backstage panorama. We traced the footsteps of a long lineage of kings and queens of country, past brightly lit dressing room doors where, decades later, new royalty were preparing to grant an audience to the commoners. Phantoms of the Opry took possession of my memories as I stood in the wings where Hank Williams and Patsy Cline had waited to greet their devotees. I peered onto the aging wooden stage where the Coal Miner's Daughter had curtseyed and where George Jones had recited the heart-rending fifth verse of the greatest country song ever written, "He Stopped Loving Her Today."

As we walked, the sounds of guitars morphed from one song to another as here and there along the drab, pedestrian walls, small groupings of singers did their last minute cramming. Soon, a stage manager came for us and it was our time to go on.

I remember the surreal, slow motion experience of hearing our band began to play the intro to "I Wonder What She's Doin' Tonight" and the rich tones of the announcer as he said our names. Then I walked toward the light and onto the stage of the Grand Ole Opry to the cheers of a thousand country music fans. The salt of the earth had come with their families from all over the United States on a pilgrimage to the "Mother Church of Country Music." And their kids knew who we were and loved our music. To me, it was more glamorous than my evening at the Academy Awards, more gratifying than meeting the senators in Washington, more memorable than one hundred other stages where we faced throngs of screaming fans.

After a heartwarming reception to the performance of our hits, we turned to a song we had written especially for the occasion, "Let's All Take a Trip to Nashville." We had spent the past couple of days working up a medley of impressions, and we hoped we could pull them off to an audience who knew and loved these people. Tommy broke into a mean imitation of Johnny Cash, singing "Walk the Line," and the crowd loved it when he segued into Kitty Wells, simulating her trademark tremolo by wiggling his Adam's apple with his thumb and forefinger.

One of my favorite artists growing up was the Singing Ranger, Hank Snow. Back in high school I couldn't get enough of his many hits. As the medley continued and the spotlight turned on me, I broke into my best Hank Snow imitation, singing his classic hit, "I Don't Hurt Anymore."

It was going well until, in the middle of my performance, as I scanned the audience, I noticed a face that almost brought my little tribute to a screeching halt. There, sitting in the front row, was the legendary gentleman himself. Hank Snow, in his sparkling sequined white suit and bird's nest hair piece, was watching me do him, and I couldn't tell if he was pleased or not. Somehow I made it through the medley, and Tommy and I were rewarded with a typical Opry thunderous ovation at the end.

♥

Under the terms of our new agreement, Screen Gems Television had been developing a situation comedy for the 1970 fall season that would star Tommy Boyce & Bobby Hart. Of course, Mathews was coordinating the production of this project with the television division. One afternoon he called us over to his office for a surprising update.

"Here's the deal, guys. We're not that far away from pilot season now, and the studio brass want to get you into some acting classes. They're bringing in a private coach and they've set you up on one of the empty sound stages here on the lot. They want you over there at 3:30 every afternoon when you're not on the road." Of course, we were excited about the TV show, but hadn't thought far enough ahead to anticipate what might be required of us in this new venture.

The next day we showed up on time for our first lesson at Stage 3. We were met by a rather condescending and unsympathetic middle-aged acting teacher named Harold. "So, you gentlemen are singers," he greeted us. "Have you done any summer stock, been in any school plays?" It was obvious to us that Harold considered Tommy and me to be a couple of rock 'n' rollers who had no business on this side of the studio lot. He proceeded to put us through a series of strange diction exercises where we blew imaginary bubbles and read from a script filled with alliteration.

By the time we got to role-playing some scenes with each other, Harold was anything but encouraging as he critiqued our performances. After a few weeks we realized that our private lessons and our rent-a-coach were beginning to take a toll on our self-confidence. We rationalized that, just as we approached our songwriting, it wouldn't be wise to appear too calculated and unnatural when it came to our actions and reactions. Far be it for us to ever be over-rehearsed.

Even though we had virtually dropped out of acting school, the studio was arranging to have guest star roles written for us so that we could appear in all of the sitcoms that Screen Gems had on the air in 1969. Since now the segments for the various shows were beginning to be scheduled, we realized that the time had come when we would be expected to hit our marks and say our lines. One Friday afternoon Kevin handed us each a call sheet stating that our services would be required on Stage 1 early the following Monday.

We arrived early for our seven a.m. call on the set of the long-running favorite, *I Dream of Jeannie*. We were escorted to the wardrobe department where it was decided that we should just wear what we already had on. Next, the makeup lady worked her magic, and then we were taken out onto the set where we met the producer, and he introduced us to the actors.

The show's beautiful co-star, Barbara Eden, was warm and friendly to us right from the beginning, which helped put us at ease in an unfamiliar situation. All of our scenes were with Eden and Larry Hagman, and as we began filming, the director, crew, and the two renowned actors went out of their way to make sure the whole experience was a lot of fun for us. Everyone on the set was extremely generous and patient with their two novice actors.

In the script, Jeannie and her "master's" vacation plans are put on hold because his boss's wife couldn't find a band for her charity event. Jeannie resourcefully puts a band together using guys she randomly finds on the street—us. First she zaps us with her famous wink and we find ourselves in a room together. Then they employed some sixties low-tech special effects. They nailed our shoes to the floor and laced them tight to our feet so that when Jeannie zapped us again to keep us from leaving, we could lean forward at a forty-five degree angle without falling over on our faces.

Jeannie takes her new group to audition for a high-powered record executive, and Tommy and I were surprised as we got ready to shoot this scene to see that the part would be played by someone we had both known since 1961, producer Phil Spector. Finally, she gets so caught up in managing the group that she has no time for the vacation. In the end

Major Nelson is surprised to find that the vacation that Jeannie finally agrees to is actually a tour for the band. In the fade-out scene, Tommy and I are spotted riding atop giant luggage trunks in the back of his convertible, singing our record, "Out & About."

When we reported for duty we noticed that we had been given a fictitious band name in the script. By mid-morning Kevin had heard about it, and within a few minutes, he was able to get the producer and director on the line at the same time. In his boomingly charming voice, he explained to them that the main reason his artists had been booked as guest stars on their show was to garner some early promotion for their own upcoming Screen Gems program. Before we knew it, the script supervisor was handing out revised pages and we were told that we would be playing *ourselves* in the episode.

♥

On December 19, 1969, Tommy and I reported for another seven a.m. makeup call. This time, it was on the set of the popular series, *Bewitched*. By now, we had already guest starred on other shows like *The Flying Nun* where we had a wonderful time playing alongside its brilliant star, Sally Field. So Tommy and I were a little more relaxed and beginning to feel like old hands at this acting game.

Half asleep, I climbed into the barber style make up chair and an artist began to smear pancake on my face. An actress in the next chair cheerfully said "Good morning" and tried to make some pleasant conversation. I nodded and semi-consciously mumbled something sociable, which to her must have sounded less than sincere. Without opening my eyes I could feel the energy from the two makeup artists get tense.

Then, with the calmness and finesse of a pro, the actress softly disengaged saying, "I didn't mean to break your concentration. We talked yesterday, but I guess you don't recognize me without my makeup."

She was right. I had just met Elizabeth Montgomery the previous day. The show's producer, William Asher, had introduced us at the read-through. My eyes shot open and I sat up like a scolded schoolboy as I offered an apology for my disrespectful behavior. I threw in something lame about not having my coffee yet. But as we chitchatted during the makeup session, nothing I said brought back the warmth that I had heard in her voice when she offered her opening "good morning."

In the script, "Serena Stops the Show," once again Tommy and I play ourselves. Elizabeth, as her mysterious cousin, witch Serena, writes a song and has her heart set on getting Boyce & Hart to perform it at her cotillion, which was to take place somewhere off in the cosmos. To illustrate our popularity, the opening scenes show us nearly having our clothes ripped off by a mob of overzealous teenage fans.

But when Serena tries to book us, our manager tells her we're way too expensive and, besides, we're booked up for years. So she casts a spell on us that causes our fans to start ripping up our 8 by 10 glossies instead of our clothes. When the cover of *Daily Variety* declares our careers to be in the toilet, we have no choice but to accept Serena's cotillion gig.

We had written a song called "I'll Blow You a Kiss in the Wind," which had just been released as our first single on our new B & H Aquarian Records. They decided to use this for Serena's song in the show. First, she auditions it for Samantha and Darren in their living room, and at the end, of course, we perform it among eerie lights and swirling clouds at her Cosmic Cotillion.

Throughout the shoot, Ms. Montgomery was very professional, but she always kept a cool distance. I felt deservingly embarrassed by my self-centered behavior in the makeup chair and decided to not even tell Tommy about what I had done. Tommy radiated his dependable trademark charm during and in between our scenes with the beautiful star of *Bewitched*, but even he was unable to elicit a warm response from her.

At the end of the week, all of our scenes with Elizabeth had been successfully completed. As we were saying our goodbyes, she said that it had been a true pleasure working with us. I was surprised to hear that her voice was full of the original energy and charm of the greeting back in the makeup room. As I watched her leave the set, still wondering at her change in demeanor, it finally came to me. Montgomery had played *two* roles on this show! While all during the week, I was expecting the reactions of the loving, warm-hearted Samantha, apparently Elizabeth Montgomery had not wanted to break *her* character. I realized that all of our scenes had been with Samantha's scheming cousin, Serena, the epitome of cool, calculating, and snooty.

Years later, when Quentin Tarantino hosted *Saturday Night Live*, in his opening monologue, he referred to "Serena singing 'I'll Blow You a Kiss In the Wind'" as the "greatest event in the history of television." Of course, to you and me this may appear to be a slight overstatement, but on August 4, 2004, on the *Tonight Show*, Tarantino explained to Jay Leno the reasons for making such a rash claim.

He said he had grown up watching *Saturday Night Live*. At 14 or 15-years-old, he told himself, "Someday I'm gonna be famous and I'm gonna host SNL." He said he remembered watching the one rock 'n' roll episode of *Bewitched* where Serena had written a rock song for Boyce & Hart to sing. As he sang along in his bedroom as a teenager, Tarantino visualized singing this song in his opening monologue when he hosted *Saturday Night Live*.

Nineteen years later, he actually was asked to host the show, and he actually did convince the writers that he should fulfill his nineteen-year dream by singing our song. I checked You Tube, and there for all the world to see was Quentin Tarantino singing his bigger-than-life version of "I'll Blow You a Kiss in the Wind" with his big band arrangement and his wild choreography on *Saturday Night Live*!

CHAPTER 35

I've Got Steve McQueen with Me

Three weeks starring in the main showroom of the Flamingo Hilton in Las Vegas and two months to prepare! When Kevin made the deal, the Flamingo gave us an unexpectedly large amount of money, but since we weren't well known enough to fill this type of venue, the agreement obligated us to hire a co-star who was. Tommy, Kevin, and I looked over their list of acceptable names. The first call we made was to Zsa Zsa Gabor.

On a sunny fall Friday afternoon we drove to her estate in Bel Air, through the gates and up the long driveway to her mansion. Zsa Zsa's secretary led us to the smartly appointed living room and we waited. In a few minutes she swept into the room, dressed to the nines and looking dazzling as always.

The Hungarian star was around fifty at the time, and she still possessed the regal beauty that had always been her trademark. Kevin made the introductions. "Kevin tells me they want us to work together," she started. "Well, you're both very good looking boys and would make fine leading men, but what on earth would we do together, Dahlings?" With a smile and a wink, Boyce blurted out "I could paint your toenails on stage!" Between Tommy's eccentric charm and my quiet smile we made friends that day with the undisputed queen of glamour.

Kevin, trying on a new hat as Las Vegas producer, outlined a few ideas for the show. There would be a role reversal "hat and cane number" with Tommy and Bobby in tie and tails and Zsa Zsa in a hippie dress with leather fringe. Then we would do a contemporary song in casual outfits while Zsa Zsa wore a glamorous sequined gown. The opening comic would field questions for her from the audience, leading to her pre-arranged punch lines. Tommy and Bobby would do their hits, a medley of songs they had written for other artists, and jokes and production numbers with beautiful Las Vegas dancers.

Zsa Zsa left the room and returned with a few pages of her own material—classic Zsa Zsa Gabor lines like, Q: "I broke up with my fiancée. Should I give back the ring? A: But, of course, Dahling. But you must always keep the stone." We left with an agreement in principle. We would commission top designers to come up with a glamorous new Gabor wardrobe for the show. We would hire top comedy writers to spice up her special material. We would hire her entourage of dressers, stylists, and assistants. As for her part, she would show up and look beautiful.

We held auditions at CBS Television City for dancers and settled on two who were very talented and also happened to be gorgeous. For our opening act we hired a brilliant comedian named Sandy Baron whom we had befriended after meeting him when we did the *Della Reese Show.* For Zsa Zsa's dialogue we hired a comedy writer who had been recommended by Columbia named John Amos, and he started sketching out special material for the show. It was the same John Amos who later became the respected actor/star of TV shows like *Good Times, Roots, West Wing* and *Men in Trees* and movies like *Coming to America.*

Kevin had been working mostly behind the scenes in his latest role of Las Vegas producer, but now we experienced it first hand as he presided over rigorous rehearsals of our solo songs and the numbers with the dancers. He arranged for us to play a two-week stint at a supper club in San Francisco called Bimbos in order for us to have an out-of-town tryout for the Boyce and Hart part of the show.

On opening night, I came off stage after a hokey hillbilly dance number with thirty seconds to change into my white brocade tux for a serious song. I had no idea the suit had come back from the cleaners about three sizes smaller than when I'd sent it in. The band vamped for what seemed like an eternity. Finally I had no choice but to go on in my high water pants with the zipper only half way engaged. The next morning's *San Francisco Chronicle* entertainment review bore the headline, "Brand New Farce Hits Bimbos."

We re-tooled the show with a new choreographer, new numbers, new special material. This meant we had even less time before opening night to rehearse the new dance routines. The pressure on two untrained dancers to appear professional doing something as foreign as a Fred Astaire "hat-and-cane" production number became oppressive. The mood in the Hollywood rehearsal hall was tense as Tommy and I crammed to learn the new steps.

Kevin had been on edge all afternoon as Tommy and I struggled to keep up with our girl dancers. Justifiably unhappy with our performance, he became more and more offensive as he shouted orders. When I voiced an objection to his tone, Kevin bellowed, "Why don't you just sit down and cool off." Fuming and frustrated are two traits not typical of my behavior, but I felt that I had been trying as hard as I could, and his remarks weren't helping. I heard myself booming, "No, YOU sit down! The last time I checked, I still sign your paycheck every week!"

A few weeks later, as I got to know Barbara, one of our dancers, she confided to me, "I never really noticed you until that moment." She had obviously seen Kevin as the boss and Boyce and me as a couple of hired hands. But, salary not withstanding, it was beginning to become clear that he was no longer working for us; we were working for him!

Long before this incident, I had begun to realize that Tommy and I had become way too comfortable with our new lifestyle and too dependent on the services that Mathews was providing us. In any city Kevin could get us into the most exclusive restaurants and private clubs with a phone call. He sent us on a weekend trip to Rome aboard a new 747 that Boeing was delivering to Alitalia Airlines. He would arrange to have special awards given to us and then write our acceptance speeches on the way to the events.

We both saw Mathews as our Col. Tom Parker, but now I watched with concern as the bond that had been developing between Kevin and Tommy was now turning into more of a father and son relationship. I had the feeling that the natural connection Tommy had shared with me back in our more relaxed days was being slowly transferred to a partner more suited to his energy level. A story that Tommy told me illustrates the fun that the two were having together and the closeness that it had engendered.

One weekend Boyce and Mathews decided to fly up to Vegas to clock the competition. I opted to stay behind for some silence and freedom. With both Sinatra and Elvis appearing that week, the town was packed, and after an evening of revelry, in the wee hours of the morning, they realized that they were ready to retire in a town where there were no hotel rooms to be had. As usual, Kevin concocted an outrageously clever plan.

He put in a call to the front desk at Caesar's Palace. "This is Mathews from Columbia. I've got McQueen with me and I need a room." "Yes, Sir, Mr. Mathews." "Only thing is, he's a little soused. I'm going to bring him in through the kitchen and I don't want any of your staff staring at him." Tommy (who had a similar body type to Steve McQueen) donned a golf hat and staggered along, head down, through the long corridors of the hotel's underbelly as Kevin led him to the suite.

Now reports of Mathews' dark side were reaching our ears too frequently to ignore. Mostly they still involved verbal abuse of employees, and we had even witnessed some of it ourselves. Ever since early fall, I had been urging Tommy to take a serious look at how our good reputations, and perhaps our fortunes, were at risk. But by this time our abilities to communicate with each other had reached an all-time low.

I remember staring straight ahead as I sat in the shadows with Barry and Tommy in his 1929 Cadillac that was parked out in his driveway. The three of us had retreated there late one evening to escape the din of the party that raved on inside Tommy's house. Tommy, alone in the back, was addressing Barry who sat firmly in the driver's seat, dutifully trying to mediate the discussion. "Tell Mr. Hart that without Kevin, the TV division wouldn't even talk to us." Barry dutifully complied, "Without Kevin, the TV division . . ."

Joining the ridiculous game, I replied, "Tell Mr. Boyce that Kevin's getting out of hand and I'm afraid of totally losing control of our own careers." "Well, you tell Mr. Hart that he doesn't know jack about the TV business or anything else he's talking about." Soon it wasn't a game anymore. The communiqués were getting louder, more personal, and closer together, leaving no space for Barry's instant replays.

Finally in December, after Kevin's Napoleonic side was becoming more visible daily, I called a late night summit, and Tommy finally agreed that we were going to have to cut the umbilical cord and let him go. "But we can't tell him right now," Tommy reasoned, "because we open in Vegas in two weeks, and that would disrupt everything." I knew that Tommy was stalling, but he had always kept his word to me. As a compromise, I agreed that we would give him his notice right after opening night at the Flamingo.

♥

A few weeks before our scheduled opening in December of 1969 we took the show, including Zsa Zsa, her mother, Jolie Gabor, and her entourage, to Honolulu for a full dress rehearsal. We all went out to see the Don Ho show on the evening of our arrival. Then, Boyce stayed up way past my bedtime getting to know Zsa Zsa and her mother, Jolie Gabor. On December 7th, U. S. Navy officers escorted Boyce, Gabor, and me to the middle of Pearl Harbor where we laid a wreath at the site of the USS Arizona as a memorial to those who gave their lives there on that day that will live in infamy.

As we checked out of Honolulu's beautiful Kahala Hilton, where our party had been lodged for the week, the hotel manager took Tommy, Kevin, and me aside and informed us that none of us would be welcomed back to this hotel in the future. It seems that sometime during the night Zsa Zsa had found the right moment in the hotel lobby to draw a black mustache on the life size portrait of the chain's founder and her ex-husband, Conrad Hilton.

At the close of 1969 the entire troupe flew to Vegas for our three-week engagement at the Las Vegas Flamingo Hilton. The evening before our opening, Zsa Zsa, Tommy, and I had dinner together at Benihana. That was the night that she and I really started to get to know each other.

After a couple glasses of wine she began to get comfortable with us, and we all shared a lot of laughs late into the evening as she told us hilarious stories of her early life.

Opening night was finally upon us. We had invited our lawyers, accountants, employees, and our families. Our parents and our friends, Shirley and Del Shannon, Samantha and Micky Dolenz, and Rosmari and Brian Hyland, had all flown in. But when we added the names from Zsa Zsa's invitations, the guest list began to look like a Who's Who of forties and fifties movie stardom. To our amazement, out front on opening night were Betty Grable, Kathryn Grayson, Terry Moore, Arlene Dahl, Anne Francis, Howard Keel, Margaret O'Brien, Edie Adams, Peter Marshall, Barry Sullivan, Joi Lansing, Phyllis Newman, Steve Lawrence, and Eydie Gormé, and the list continued.

At the after-the-show reception, we barely had time to greet all these legends of the silver screen, but I particularly enjoyed chatting with one who had always been a personal favorite of mine, Jeanne Crain. The star of *People Will Talk* with Cary Grant and Rodgers and Hammerstein's *State Fair* was still gorgeous and very gracious.

The flashbulbs were popping continuously in the reception room. One photo, taken as Barry Richards chatted briefly with Mary Wilson of the Supremes, ended up a few months later gracing the front page of the *National Star* under the caption: "The White Man Who Broke Up the Supremes."

Although she had invited him, Zsa Zsa had told us that her ex-husband, Conrad Hilton, probably would not show up at his own hotel since he was eighty-two at the time and rarely appeared in public. "Yeah!" we were thinking, "that, and the trail of defaced portraits you've left in Hilton lobbies the world over." But he must have had a sense of humor, because, sure enough, there he was in person.

Conrad Hilton, the man who had built the multi-national hotel empire from a fleet of run-down rooms in a Texas boomtown, was friendly and down to earth as Zsa Zsa introduced us. "You know, the show was really entertaining," he said as he stood and chatted with Tommy and me at the reception. "I enjoyed it very much. I was just thinking as I watched it that you should take this thing on the road. You know, where they would really love this is in Europe! You should just pack it all up and head to Europe." Zsa Zsa liked the idea, and when she told Kevin, he began making arrangements right away to do just that.

Our audience of friends and strangers gave us a warm reception, and both the dinner show and the midnight show went off without a hitch. Zsa Zsa was resplendent in her new outfits; Sandy Baron was funny; and Tommy and I sang our hearts out, hit our marks, and got into a groove with the dancers. Mathews had commissioned filmmaker, Chuck Braverman, to put together a film montage depicting moving reminders of what a great country we live in. The hundreds of quick-flashing images ran on a large rear projection screen behind us as we sang the "I Wanna Be Free" finale.

The next day *The Hollywood Reporter* printed this about our Las Vegas debut: "The duo makes a thoroughly solid impact. Their talents are formidable and they have a very natural affability and sparkle. Top of the heap status is theirs if they choose to pursue it."

We retired late, still basking in the afterglow of one of the biggest nights of our careers. But downstairs, in the high stakes world of high rollers and lowball losers, danger was lurking that would spell the end of the industry that had become Boyce & Hart.

CHAPTER 36

I've Got a Bad Feeling About This

While we had been preparing our show for Las Vegas, I noticed that my old friend Barry Richards seemed to have become a permanent houseguest, occupying what used to be Tommy's bedroom at the Boat House. As much as I loved Barry, after a while I had begun to miss my privacy. But in order not to hurt his feelings, I decided that instead of speaking to him directly, I would put my psycho-cybernetics to work. I began to visualize Barry moving on to a better situation for himself, one that didn't involve him living in my house.

Well, thoughts are powerful things. While we were busy rehearsing, Barry had auditioned for and landed a job as a singer/dancer in the Juliet Prowse show. They say there are no coincidences. The only thing I can tell you is that the very same week that we opened at the Flamingo, Barry opened directly across the Las Vegas Strip at Caesar's Palace in the Juliet Prowse show. He had moved out of my house, but somehow, three hundred miles away in the desert, he had ended up living only yards away.

One afternoon near the end of our first week at the Flamingo, Tommy called me from his room and blurted out, "Kevin's disappeared!" "What do you mean, disappeared?" I queried. "He hasn't answered his phone or the door to his suite all day. I checked with the band, the dancers, the choreographer, the hotel management. Nobody's seen him since last night's show." My reply expressed the queasiness in my stomach, "I've got a bad feeling about this. Let me call you back."

I hung up the phone and dialed the Flamingo's entertainment director. "No, I haven't heard anything from Kevin today," he offered. "Thanks," I said, my heart racing. "Listen, I'd like to come down and pick up our check for the first week." "Oh, no" he replied. "Mathews was in the office yesterday and he picked up a check for all three weeks." Now I was really concerned. By this time, Boyce had come down to my room and I told him what I had just learned. His face went ashen.

We decided to walk down to the hotel lobby and start asking around. A few minutes later, the entertainment director found us there and added another piece to the bad news puzzle. "I checked with the pit bosses and one of them told me that Mathews was down here at the crap tables last night and late into the morning. The word is, he was losing heavily."

We called our business manager in Los Angeles and gave him the sad news. When he flew in two days later with a new infusion of funds to pay Zsa Zsa, Sandy, our band, dancers, and crew, he told us he had done some further auditing of the books back at the Columbia lot. In Kevin's offices, he had found unpaid bills that made the Flamingo misappropriation look like chicken feed. We were on the hook for a mountain of additional expenditures that Kevin had failed to tell us about.

That evening, as Tommy and I were coming off stage after the dinner show, the stage manager handed Tommy the telephone. It was Kevin. "Don't say anything out loud, I'm in hiding, but I need to talk to you guys. Meet me behind the ball toss at *Circus Circus*. Don't tell anyone where you're going." Feeling like characters in a real life cloak and dagger movie, we jumped into a cab and soon found Kevin, obligatory trench coat collar pulled up around his head, at the exact coordinates he had described.

"Look, I'm really sorry, guys," he began. "I've had this long-standing problem with the IRS. I just thought maybe this time I could get even. Anyway, I'm leaving town for a while. How much can you guys let me have to tide me over?" I'm sure Kevin understood my answer from the incredulous look on my face as I slowly shook my head in disbelief and stared at the floor. But as I said, Tommy's friendship with Kevin went deep. He pulled out his checkbook and wrote our former Colonel Tom a check for five thousand dollars.

But the real damage could not be measured in dollars and cents. It was psychological, not financial. For the rest of the engagement, it felt like we were on automatic pilot. Now, Boyce & Hart was no longer that solid alliance that could face any challenge. In earlier days we would have viewed this betrayal as a momentary setback. "Hey, who needs him anyway," Tommy would have said. "We're the ones who write the hits and create all the magic." But that wasn't true anymore. Mathews had created his own wizardry. He had taken our self-image and doubled it. But then, just as easily, he had gambled it away on a loaded game of chance.

From the moment I had met Tommy in the little recording studio, he was all about confidence, spontaneity, charm, and trust. Trust in himself, trust in the future, and trust in others. Now, I felt totally helpless standing beside Tommy, silently trying to understand what he must have been feeling that would make him no longer want to be Tommy Boyce, the "star," my partner and my friend. I could see that Tommy was deeply shaken and profoundly disillusioned. You think you know someone and then something happens that makes you realize that no matter how close two people are, they are still separate individuals with unique, complicated, and unpredictable thoughts and feelings.

On the night of our last show, when I walked into our backstage dressing room, I felt that same detached, uncomfortable energy as I watched Tommy across the room slowly pulling on his favorite boots, ready to go onstage. My natural way is to keep my distance when I sense that people need to be alone.

I softly said "Hey" to Tommy in my usual greeting, and he casually gave me his trademark double thumbs up as he walked out the door. Onstage, Tommy hit every cue and energized the audience with his singing, playing, and his sincere love of entertaining. The audience believed that Tommy was having the time of his life, and he had me trusting that the worst was behind us.

But the next morning as we sat silently eating lunch together in the hotel dining room before our flight back to L.A., Tommy calmly and clearly announced to me that he was quitting the business. "Quitting the business?" I involuntarily parroted in a high-pitched tone of shock.

"What do you mean?" I felt my entire emotional foundation instantly evaporating. "I just don't want to do this anymore," Tommy murmured in a tone just the opposite of mine.

Anyone who knew us might have thought our conversation was staged and I was being Tommy and he was playing my part. Tommy was always the assertive, extroverted salesman. But in a complete change of roles, I was the one nearly standing on the table unleashing torrents of fast-paced speech and unrehearsed, but deeply sincere argument. I reasoned. I cajoled. I laid out all the logic in black and white detail, using my best skills of persuasion. It may have been the most open, honest, spontaneous, articulate, and desperate moment of my life.

I tried reminding him of all the work we had done to get to this golden threshold of opportunities. We had a successful nightclub act. Thousands of dollars-worth of special material and costumes were already paid for. We had offers to tour Europe with Zsa Zsa before our return engagements in Las Vegas. We had a successful recording career and owned a recording company. We had our own TV show in development at Screen Gems. At the end of it all, I realized that all Tommy was thinking was, "Yeah, but we don't have Kevin."

I knew Tommy well enough to know that if he walked out the door still feeling the way he did, that would be the end of Boyce and Hart. In that café booth, in that unforeseen, electric, critical moment, I had given him everything my psyche could muster to convince him not to give up on our partnership. Nonetheless, Tommy's entire being reflected the damage his confidence had sustained, and nothing I did or said could change the way he felt. He would have none of it. He was through. He stood up, left money on the table for the waitress, and walked out without flashing the cashier his trademark smile or saying another word.

♥

When one member of a duo quits the business, that's pretty much it for the act. Unable to fulfill my contract with Screen Gems/Columbia without Boyce, I had no option but to execute the termination agreement that they had quickly drawn up, and this meant paying them back the large sums of money they had advanced us. As we signed the last of the papers, a man slightly younger than us, in an expensive silk shirt and a gold pinky ring, asked if we could have our belongings moved out of our offices and off the studio lot by the end of the week. I put some things in a box, carried it alone to the parking lot, sat in the passenger seat for several minutes, and then drove my new, black Lincoln out past the security guard.

I sat at home alone at my kitchen table for the rest of the afternoon and into the night. No music, no TV, and the phone never rang. As the shadows from the trees created patterns on the floor and walls, I thought the same thoughts over and over. I kept feeling that for three years, I had been pinned to the nose of a runaway train, held upright by the sheer power of its inertia. Now, in a blink, the whirlwind that had been my life had come to a screeching halt, just as if someone had slammed on the brakes. Someone had. It was Tommy Boyce.

Emotionally, my entire being slid down over the cowcatcher and poured out onto the tracks. I remember how lonely those first few weeks were. Tommy had been an everyday part of my life for more than five years. He was with me when our youthful optimism had catapulted us forward, oblivious to the odds against finding our dreams. He had gone with me to the hospital to welcome Bobby, Jr. into the world. It was the smile in his eyes that had reflected my own as we spied the first sparks of our success. He was the one who had shared the pain of broken relationships. And he was there, the other pillar sustaining the structure of our dreams, when they finally found fulfillment. I was suddenly a stranger in a strange land without Tommy's partnership, creativity, charisma, and friendship.

Unexpectedly, after several empty days, he stopped by my house to say hello. I was very glad to see him and we drove down the hill to one of our favorite cafes for a sandwich. It felt great hanging out with him. During the course of our conversation, he floated the proposition that maybe we could continue working together as an act, after all. Surprised to hear those words coming from Tommy's lips, I displayed a cautious interest while hiding my excitement. But before I could say how much I would like that idea, he added that there would have to be one condition.

Tommy removed all the charm from his voice and his piercing eyes looked directly at me when he said, "but I will be the only one to make all the decisions from here on out."

This was the second time in as many months that I felt utter shock upon hearing a single sentence from an old friend. For a moment, I toyed with the idea of going along. I thought that if I could have gotten the words out, "Sure, I'm fine with that," then maybe things would be like they once were.

However, I knew myself too well; and I knew Tommy too well, to think that I could ever go back to the days when I was just tagging along. After a long pause, I slowly shook my head and managed a dispassionate, "I don't think so, Tommy."

A month or so after the day of Tommy's ultimatum, he called to say he was headed up to Eddie Fisher's house and asked if I wanted to go along. As we wound through the Hollywood Hills, he told me that he had moved out of Sunshine Park and was staying in a beachfront apartment building in Venice, one of the investments he and I had made the year before. Tommy looked rested and sounded like the "star" Tommy Boyce, but there was something in his eyes that made me feel uncertain that the man I was looking at was indeed the Tommy I knew. Then suddenly and totally unrelated to what we were talking about, he threw me one more unexpected curve. Thrusting something in my direction, he said, "Dig my new business card." On it were three words, "David Tucker, Poet."

CHAPTER 37

Aliens Stood at the Foot of His Bed

"You want to drive out to the desert for a few days?" I asked my friend Barry. "I want to get as far away as I can from show business and anybody and everybody that has anything to do with show business," I grumbled. Barry said we could probably use his Aunt and Uncle's vacation cabin in Yucca Valley, thirty miles north of Palm Springs in the high desert near the Joshua Tree National Monument.

With Barry in the front passenger seat and our jackets and small overnight bags in the back, I navigated my Lincoln Continental toward Riverside where we picked up the keys from Uncle Leonard. Then we drove for another 90 minutes, exited the highway and finally found the nearly deserted neighborhood of modest vacation homes miles from nowhere. We set our bags inside the cabin and decided to hike to the top of a nearby mountain before dinner.

When we reached the rocky crest we sat down to survey the spectacular panorama and breathe in the warm desert air. Almost immediately, we both became intrigued by a strange white igloo-shaped structure that sparkled unexpectedly in the sunlight below. Looming ominously in the distance, it was the only landmark that interrupted the endless array of sand, desert brush and cactus. Making a mental note of the dirt roads and the lay of the land, we jogged down the hill, hopped in the car and set out to quench our curiosity and find this mysterious building.

After ten minutes of careful driving down narrow, dusty two-lane desert roads, entertaining ourselves all the way with improbable scenarios like two kids on an adventure, we came within sight of our goal. I pulled my dirt-covered car up in front of the strange, white, wooden dome. The forty-foot-high structure, larger than it had appeared from a distance, was deserted. It was surrounded by a locked chain link fence, and on the fence was a sign that read: "The Integratron: World's First Anti-Aging/ Anti-Gravity Machine—Information: Giant Rock Airport." Now, we were hooked.

For another ten minutes we followed the occasional arrows farther and farther into the desert. Finally, we saw it. It was a giant rock alright! Arising out of the endless expanse of flat, off-white desert terrain, a massive four-story rock of gray granite stood on its end, towering over a small dirt airstrip. In front of the landing strip, there was a small cinder block building with a weatherworn sign reading, "Café." Feeling like bit players in a Clint Eastwood spaghetti western, Barry followed me as I cautiously pulled open the wooden screen door and stepped inside. We nodded to the twenty-five-year-old Hispanic waitress as we slid onto bar stools in front of the long 1940s counter and ordered pie and coffee.

We had driven for hours. We had long since left the highways and the main roads behind and ventured so far out into the desert that we were secure in the accomplishment of our goal: removing ourselves about as far as possible from the Hollywood scene. But before the coffee was poured, Barry and I heard the roar of a small airplane engine. We watched as it landed in clouds of dust, taxied in and came to rest in front of the café. Out stepped the pilot and his two passengers: Denny Cordell and my friend, Leon Russell.

"Bobby! What are you doing here?" a bewildered Leon Russell asked as he strode through the door of the Giant Rock Airport Café with his companions. Whirling around on my bar stool, I observed myself encountering the number one most surreal moment of an already dreamlike adventure and heard myself stammer, "Hey, we just kinda stumbled onto the place. What are *you* doing here?" Leon sat down with us and ordered iced tea. Then he explained that he and his partner had an appointment to see George Van Tassel, the inventor of the Integratron.

Denny said that Van Tassel was looking for investors to help him finish his controversial experiment. In less than five minutes, a strong-looking, balding man in a worn Air Force jacket and dark slacks walked through the door. He smiled and warmly welcomed Leon and Denny and then began telling the most fantastic tales of his life and his invention.

Van Tassel's voice was soft, slow, and deliberate, and his demeanor evoked sincerity. He said that he had been awakened one night many years ago, from a deep sleep by aliens who stood at the foot of his bed. He tried to rouse his wife, but the visitors had prevented her awakening. Van Tassel told us that in this, and subsequent visits with these extraterrestrials, they had instructed him in the design and construction of the Integratron. He said United States Air Force officers had once landed on his small airstrip and demanded information about its design.

When it came time for George Van Tassel to conduct an actual site tour inside the Integratron for his potential benefactors, he glanced apprehensively over at Barry and me, the two intruders. Leon came to our rescue. He said "Are you kidding? Bobby's got more money than any of us." And so we were allowed to tag along.

I felt an eerie shiver as I entered the dank, forty-foot-high dome, white cobwebs everywhere. As he led us through the belly of the beast, Van Tassel pointed out, " This has all been constructed completely out of wood, without using any nails or metal of any kind. When it's completed," he continued, "these giant wooden paddles will spin like a gyroscope at high rates of speed just clearing the inside of the dome." He told us the Integratron's purpose would be threefold: life extension, antigravity, and time travel. "In the first run-through a few years ago," he claimed, "we successfully extended the life of a small mouse long beyond its expected years."

After the tour Leon, Denny, Barry, and I went back to the tiny airport café to digest what we had just seen and heard, along with a couple of burgers. I had first met Leon Russsell, the singer and virtuoso pianist whose stellar career has spanned five decades, soon after moving back to Hollywood. Boyce and I had been invited to a session he was co-producing to watch Gary Lewis and the Playboys record one of our songs. Soon the three of us became good friends.

Leon remembered some fun stories about Tommy Boyce from the sessions he had produced with him as an artist before Boyce & Hart became singing partners. Barry chimed in with a few memories of the times when we had visited Leon's large house on Skyhill Drive, near my place in the Hollywood Hills, and how on any given day you might find twenty musicians, their girlfriends, hangers-on, or just plain squatters who had taken up residence there.

Leon flipped his long salt and pepper hair back with a flick of his hand and glanced at the ceiling as he spoke, "Well, I didn't know anybody when I got here from Tulsa. This is why I've never regretted helping out the Oklahoma kids when they land in L.A." But Leon wanted to reminisce about the days when he would come to see me at various nightclubs around L.A. Even then, his lifestyle of sharing had made Leon a mentor of almost cult-leader status, and he would arrive with an entourage that would sometimes double our crowds as they walked in the club to watch Gerry, Larry, Billy, and me play the blues. After promises to keep in touch with each other, Leon and Denny boarded their chartered Cessna and disappeared into the sky.

We returned the following evening, to find the place filled with twenty-five neighbors who considered this to be something like their church. Each attendee was given an opportunity to speak, and we heard some fascinating testimonies as our attention rotated around the circle.

A man in a cowboy hat on the other side of the bar remembered that when they used to hold their Friday evening meetings and meditations in the small cave-like room that was nestled into the base of the Rock itself, the windowless room would sometimes be filled with an unexplainable bright, glowing light.

Then, a grey-haired lady in her fifties talked about how the indigenous Chemehuevi people of Joshua Tree had considered the Giant Rock to be sacred. She said that before the white man came, only their chieftain was allowed to go near it to commune with the spirits of the rock people who had predicted that the rock would one day split open to herald a new age.*

When my turn came, I said that I had practiced TM meditation for years and had recently become interested in the teachings of Paramahansa

---

* On February 21, 2000, at 8:20 a.m., a thirty-foot slice of the rock spontaneously split off, revealing a gleaming, white granite interior.

Yogananda. When they heard his name, the group chimed in their approval and Van Tassel said that Yogananda was a very holy man.

The next morning we left the magical desert realms behind and drove back to the land of the mundane.

♥

Three months later, on March 13, 1970, I was awakened by a telephone call from Leon Russell. He said, "Bobby! I'm putting together a touring band for Joe Cocker and I want you to come with us. You'll sit behind the Hammond B-3 and sing "Turn On Your Lovelight" and a couple of other solos in the show. We're rehearsing down at the A & M sound stage today. You've gotta be there by two." And he hung up.

I thought about it for a couple of hours. But then I said to myself, "Hey, I'm a big star. Friend or no friend, I'm not going to just rush down and become a side man on a grueling road tour." I guess everything happens the way it's supposed to, but in retrospect, I think that if I could have checked my ego at the door, it would have been fun to look back and say that I had been a part of the legendary filmed musical event of that year, the *Mad Dogs and Englishmen Tour*.

CHAPTER 38

From a Hollywood Somebody to Just Some Body in Hollywood

When I got back from the desert, my answering machine was flashing its red light trying to get my attention. I wasn't sure if I wanted to hear any more messages about the chaos of my business breakup. I took a chance, and the first message was from my friend, Allison. She said there was someone special whom she wanted me to meet. It was her new roommate, Claudia.

Near the end of our last hurrah in Las Vegas, I had read a book called *In Search of Serenity*. It had helped me to realize that at thirty-one, maybe it was time for me to grow up and look inside myself for the ability to make a deeper connection and commitment. I had made a vow that I would stop my parade of surface relationships and hold out until I found that special someone, and amazingly, I had been able to keep that promise to myself for nearly a month now! Besides, I had never been a big fan of blind dates. I preferred to see what I was getting myself into ahead of time. And, in my present frame of mind, I wasn't sure I could work up the mojo to make any woman find me interesting.

When I finally got around to calling Allison back a couple of weeks later, she recognized my voice and immediately said, "Too late! Claudia is already out of town." Then she said something that made me shoot straight up in my chair: "She's back in Chicago shooting her Playmate of the Year layout."

During the couple of weeks before Claudia Jennings was due back in town, I concentrated on cleaning up the mess that had been our business empire. Instead of talking to agents and the media about bookings and interviews, I was spending my time talking to lawyers about settling up and winding down an abandoned corporation. The bookings had become court dates and the interviews had been replaced by depositions. Instead of a Hollywood somebody, now I was feeling like just some body in Hollywood.

Allison didn't have to wait for a delayed call back from me when she left a message that Claudia was back in town. I was definitely ready for some new feminine energy in my life. When the big day arrived, I looked through my closet and decided on an outfit that I had sometimes worn on stage. It was a very stylized white suit with a six-inch high collar. Around seven, I arrived to pick Claudia up for our first date, and Allison let me into the large three-story house in the Hollywood Hills that she shared with Claudia and two other roommates.

Then, she appeared. I was expecting beautiful; she was gorgeous. As she was seated for dinner at Diamond Jim's Steak House, Claudia's long strawberry-blond hair flowed off her shoulders and arranged itself perfectly without her fussing with it at all. She was warm, playful, and engaging, and she made me laugh easily. I was disappointed when she said she needed to get home early because she was tired from her trip and still needed to unpack.

I let several days go by after our first date before calling Claudia again. I didn't want to appear too anxious, and besides, I needed to find just the right occasion for the all-important second date. The perfect answer to my dilemma came in the form of a printed invitation to attend an evening of music performed by Jimmy Webb at the Dorothy Chandler Pavilion in the Music Center area of downtown Los Angeles. But, when I finally called her back, Claudia told me that she was leaving town two days later for a six-week tour of Europe with a girlfriend. My heart sank, thinking that I had waited too long again, but then she said she'd be happy to be my date for this special event.

As I was escorting Claudia out through her front door, I caught a brief glimpse of the two of us together in the full-length mirror in her foyer. Claudia had gotten dressed up for the occasion in a beautiful long gown and I wore one of my more formal but over the top outfits, debonair by seventies standards. It was the first variation on a scene that would be repeated many times over the next five years: Claudia on my arm as we attended parties, movie premiers, concerts, and music business galas. It felt so naturally comfortable as we settled into our front row seats and chatted while we waited for Jimmy's show to begin.

I had met Jimmy Webb five years earlier, when he was an engineer at a demo studio on Melrose Avenue. But it wasn't long before he had established himself as one of the great American composers with songs like, "Up, Up and Away," "Galveston," "Wichita Lineman," and "By the Time I Get to Phoenix." He invited Boyce and me to his New Year's Eve party in 1967, and before we left he took us upstairs and played us an unreleased tape of his masterpiece, "MacArthur Park."

But half way into this date night, as Claudia and I watched, Jimmy introduced a medley of two songs that he had not written himself. He told his audience of fans and music business luminaries that these pieces had been an inspiration to him early on, and that he considered them to be two of the greatest songs of all-time. The first was the Everly Brothers' classic, "Let It Be Me." The second was "I Wanna Be Free" by Tommy Boyce & Bobby Hart. It was an unexpected and appreciated honor, but more importantly, it topped off a perfect second date with a girl who, until now, hadn't known a lot about what I did for a living.

As I eased the Lincoln to a stop in front of her house on Gramercy Place, Claudia leaned over, put her arms around my neck and looked straight into my eyes. "I'm not into one night stands," she said, "If you want to see where this is headed, and I think you do, this has to be an exclusive arrangement."

We communicated often while Claudia was in Europe. And this long distance relationship turned out to be a blessing in disguise. It was my first experience in years with really taking my time and getting to know someone without any pressures or expectations. I knew more about her childhood, daydreams, fears, and aspirations from our long talks than I think I had known about any other woman in my life since Becky. I didn't have any reservations as I carried Claudia's suitcase and boxes into the Boat House when she returned from Europe.

♥

In April of 1970 Barry Richards won a trip to Russia on *The Dating Game*, and instead of coming back to L.A. when his prize trip had ended, he made London his home base. There he secured a booking agent and began a series of singing tours, performing in the capitols of Europe, the Near East, and Africa. When he signed a record deal with *Cream Records*, Barry suggested that the company engage me to produce the sessions, and I took Claudia along with me to London for the dates.

Warner Brothers Records had been talking to me about recording for them as a solo artist, and when I let them know that I'd be in London producing Barry with members of the London Philharmonic, they asked me to also cut a couple of big string sessions with myself. When they put me in touch with the head of Warner Records in England, it turned out to be none other than my old friend Derek Taylor.

Barry met us at Heathrow, and we took a cab into the city where we rented a mews house in the Cornwall Gardens section. The next day Derek met Claudia and me at a pub near his office to welcome us to town and then invited us to visit him and his family at his home in Sunbury. After our reunion he made sure that our names were on the lists of all the most exclusive London nightspots.

When we weren't recording, Claudia and I spent our days shopping on Carnaby Street and Kings Row and our nights exploring the vibrant club scene. When we saw that Chicago would be performing at the Royal Albert Hall, I called an old girlfriend of mine who was now married to one of the members of the group. Tickets were waiting for us when we arrived at the stately old theater, and we enjoyed the fantastic concert from front section seats.

At George Martin's Air London Studio where we were recording, I ran into my friend Richard Perry, who was producing Harry Nilsson's *Nilsson Schmilsson* album in the next studio. Harry had become close friends with John Lennon and Ringo Starr, but it was Paul McCartney who had stopped by the studio the day before. Richard told me that Paul had offered, "Hey, let me sing backup on this song. I'm the world's greatest background singer."

♥

A few years earlier at the Old World Restaurant on Sunset Boulevard in L.A., manager Alan Pariser had introduced me to George Harrison. Alan stopped me as I walked by the sidewalk table where they were having lunch, and we chatted for a while. I mentioned to George that he and I shared a love for our chosen spiritual teacher, Paramahansa Yogananda, and his face lit up. He told me that he had personally given away hundreds of Yogananda's *Autobiography of a Yogi* and always kept a stack of copies in his car.

If you look on the cover of The Beatles *Sergeant Pepper's Lonely Hearts Club Band* album, there in the paste-up crowd of luminaries you will find the faces of all four fully enlightened gurus of the path of Yogananda's, *Self Realization Fellowship*: Mahavatar Babaji, Lahiri Mahasaya, Sri Yukteswar, and Paramahansa Yogananda. He told me that day that he always handed out the books with this verbal endorsement: "There's a miracle on every page."

♥

I had met Harry Nilsson in the early sixties when he was a struggling singer/songwriter and working as a teller at the Bank of America on Hollywood Boulevard. One evening, after a day of recording at Air London Studios, Harry and Richard Perry invited Barry, Claudia, and me to join them for a visit to the home of the Bee Gee's Maurice Gibb and his wife, recording star Lulu.

We arrived at their stately Georgian mansion in St. John's Wood and were cordially welcomed by the Gibbs. I had met Mrs. Gibb, the lovely, Scottish powerhouse singer, Lulu, in 1967 when she, Tommy, and I were guests on the *Pat Boone* TV Show. The four of us had sung "I Wanna Be Free" together and she had done her 1960 international smash, "To Sir With Love." We got a chance to reminisce for a few minutes that evening before she and Claudia started talking about girl things.

It was an evening of fascinating conversation with some of the greats of musical history. Maurice, often called the quiet member of the Bee Gees, was relaxed on his home turf and was anything but reserved on this memorable evening. Richard told stories about his studio work with Carly Simon, and Nilsson talked about the play he was writing at the time, *The Point.*

Back in L.A., Claudia and I resumed our new routine as a Hollywood couple. Claudia's career was beginning to come together as her modeling success had become a springboard to a busy schedule of film work. While I stayed busy writing songs at home, Claudia was spending more time on the road working than she did with me. She would either be off on location for one of the more than twenty movies she made during those years or on Broadway, where she received rave reviews for her acting performances.

Within two or three months, the Boat House had started to seem a little too crowded for Claudia and me and the guests she would invite to stay with us. So, after six memorable years, I traded in my bachelor pad and we moved up to a much larger home on Pyramid Drive, only blocks away in the Hollywood Hills. Renting the modern architectural structure with seven levels that opened under one giant ceiling, would give us time to find that perfect house to buy where Claudia and I could create our new domestic lifestyle. Soon after moving in, we found out that our next-door neighbor was Harry Nilsson.

I often worked in the afternoons in my music room, which was situated up on the top floor of the seven levels. Perched above our property, was a street cul-de-sac where three or four young neighbor kids liked to hang out after school, and it was within earshot of my music room. My singing must have been within the kid's earshot as well because one day, as I was slaving over a hot piano, I heard one of the rude little ne'er-do-wells yell down in my direction, "Hey, Mister, why don't you play us another one of your stupid songs!"

Well, it was only a matter of a few days later when Micky Dolenz stopped by to visit his good friend, Harry Nilsson, next door. The Cul-de-sac Kids got very excited when they looked down and spotted Micky getting out of his car in Harry's driveway. They began chanting at the top of their lungs, "Hey, hey we're The Monkees . . ." I listened for several minutes with a smile on my face. They had no idea that my greatest revenge was hearing the kid's joyous rendition of "another one of my stupid songs."

CHAPTER 39

Well, There You Go, Hart, You Left $200 on the Table

One morning after we had been together for a few months, Claudia invited me to go with her up to the Playboy Mansion West to meet Hugh Hefner. Apparently it was a big deal to get a boyfriend on the guest list, but she said "We've been together long enough now to be seen as a couple, and Hef says he's looking forward to meeting you." We arrived early on a warm summer evening and joined the six or eight other guests. Hef, as he likes to be called, had recently purchased his new, twenty-nine room, West Coast home located in the exclusive L.A. suburb of Holmby Hills.

He was cordial and seemed to enjoy showing me around the grounds. We walked the quarter mile that was his newly landscaped back yard where tons of dirt had been imported to provide an infinity view of nature. We stood there looking down on the green palate of trees and endless lawn of the adjacent L.A. Country Club golf course. Hef and I talked as we took the long stroll back to the house, and then I had a brief tour of the stately mansion.

As evening shadows lengthened, Hef proposed a game of Monopoly and we settled around a table in one of the well-appointed sitting rooms of the gothic structure. I felt Claudia lean close and take my hand under the table as we prepared for the game to begin. I was soon to find out that Mr. Hefner took his Monopoly very seriously.

"I'll be the banker," Hef said in his most assertive voice of the day. "Which piece do you want Bobby?" he asked, adding, "Anything but the hat." I chose the thimble and Claudia picked up the cannon. Turning his focus away from me, Hef placed the tokens on the "Go" square of the Monopoly board. "I'll just give these a little shuffle," he said in a much softer voice as he very skillfully shuffled the Community Chest and Chance cards, placing them face down near the center of the board, "Gotta make sure we have an even playing field."

"Let's get you some cash, Mr. Hart. Don't spend it all on one property." Hefner dealt out $1,500 in Monopoly money like a seasoned pit boss in Vegas. His hands were almost a blur as he counted out my one to five hundred dollar bills. "Let me just organize the title cards so that when you buy up all these properties I can get them over to you quickly," Hef said as he looked up and smiled at Claudia.

With a flick of his wrist Hef placed the dice in the center of the board. "Go ahead Bobby, let's find out who goes first." I calmly rolled the dice and got the lowest number possible. "Not a promising sign there, Mr. Boyfriend of the beautiful Claudia Jennings," Hefner observed, as he moved into competition mode.

I had never prided myself as being an aggressive competitor when it came to board games. It seemed to me that the object of these contests was having fun, and I was always happy for whoever happened to win. But, just as though a bright interrogation bulb had been switched on over my head, it suddenly became obvious to me that Hef was using the game of Monopoly in a very different way. Within ten minutes of realizing that I was on trial in some bizarre court of social acceptance, I had already failed my evaluation. Apparently I had committed one of the most glaring faux pas known to Monopoly pros around the world. I had neglected to ask for my $200 for passing "Go." "Well, there you go, Hart. You left $200 on the table and you may live to regret that here in a few minutes," he warned.

Hef was right. Within twenty minutes, he had taken possession of most of my money and all of my properties. "Don't worry," he consoled, "There aren't too many who can keep up with me in this game. You have to know the odds, get out of jail early, and show no mercy. Monopoly is a lot like real life. Luck plays too big a role to risk letting another player stage a comeback. Then, he looked around the table and added, "Who's hungry?" Hef shook my hand and gave Claudia a quick kiss on the cheek as we moved to the dining room.

On the drive home that night, Claudia gave me a subtle lecture about staying more focused when I was around Hefner. "Hef has a genius IQ, and he uses games like Monopoly as a method of sizing up new acquaintances," she said, "and it's easy to lose his respect if you don't stay on your toes." Mentally, I was toying with my rebuttal, "Hugh Hefner might have to reawaken *my* respect if I ever see him again," but I let it go when Claudia added, "But don't worry about it. I was very proud of you tonight."

Although we never became close friends, he was always a gentleman and over the next few years, my name was on the guest list for all his social events.

♥

"Bobby, you don't know me, but I'm a fellow songwriter and record producer." Early in 1970 Claudia was off on location shooting *Willie and Scratch* when out of the blue one morning, I got a call from a man who said his name was Danny Janssen. "I got your number from Barry Richards," he volunteered. "I've written a bunch of hits for Bobby Sherman, like 'Little Woman' and 'La La La (If I Had You).'" "Oh, yeah, I know your work," I interjected. "Congratulations, Man! Those are some great records. What's going on?"

"Well," Danny said with an energy that told me he knew how to sell himself, "I'm doing a lot of work in the youth market these days, you know the pre-teens, and I've been making some really good money writing songs for the Saturday morning cartoon shows. I've just finished a series for Hanna Barbera called *Scooby Doo*." Anyway, I was calling to see if you'd like to help me with this new cartoon project they're doing called *Josie and the Pussycats*." I felt Danny's energy humming through the telephone wire and had to admit to myself that I liked his confidence and style.

After my partnership with Tommy Boyce had ended, I had written by myself and with my friend Brian Hyland. I also co-produced Brian for Uni Records, enjoying making music again, especially with an artist who possessed a voice like his. But I was anxious to continue my career with a full-time writing partner. I had just read Yogananda's booklet, "The Law of Success," and had been trying to apply some of its principals. Now this phone call had me thinking that maybe this stuff was working way faster than I had expected!

A short time later, Danny invited me down to watch as the last few finalists for Josie and the Pussycats were auditioned at the Capitol Tower in Hollywood. I felt like I was inside Van Tassel's time machine as I dressed for work that morning, and over breakfast, I told Claudia, "What a great life I live: from Monkees to Pussycats."

There was an array of very talented auditioners, but finally three young singers were chosen: a very pretty red-head named Cathy Dougher as Josie; Patrice Holloway, younger sister of Motown artist Brenda Holloway as Valerie; and for the role of Melody, an All-American, wholesome-looking blonde named Cheryl Jean Stopplemoor. Fresh from South Dakota and barely nineteen, Cheryl Jean was pure talent with a striking face, beautiful personality, and lovely voice. For this, her first major project in show biz, she had changed her name to Cherie Moor.

Promptly at ten a.m. a few days later, Danny Janssen showed up at my door, sporting an enthusiastic smile. He carried a cassette tape recorder and a yellow pad under his arm. I welcomed Danny into the new Jennings and Hart residence on Pyramid Drive and escorted him up to my seventh level writing room.

Danny was affable, talented, and down to earth, and we found a natural and easy rapport right from the beginning. His raspy voice and relaxed style reflected his Minnesota background. I sat back and took a slow breath, letting him take the first steps in our new relationship. "If it's all right with you, Bobby, I've got a couple of ideas," Danny said without looking up from his tape recorder and yellow pad, "Can I just sing you this little verse?" He presented his song ideas in almost a shy way while at the same time exhibiting a self-assured confidence that let me know he was absolutely positive that his contributions were definite hit material.

Within a couple of days, we had created and refined two songs for Josie and the Pussycats, "You've Come a Long Way, Baby" and "With

Every Beat of My Heart." Danny tried to list the writer's credits as Hart and Janssen, but I explained, "I've had good luck with Richards & Hart and Randazzo & Hart and ever since my Boyce & Hart days, I've insisted on second billing. Like Tommy always said, 'It just sounds better.'"

When the sessions were set, I met Janssen at the recording studio and he introduced me to Cherie Moor and the other two girls. The studio musicians found the right groove for the tunes and the tracks came out sounding like hits. The girls all sang great. They were very professional for their young years, cooperating fully with the constructive suggestions Danny and I offered. And I never once had to break up a wrestling match!

A few days later, Danny invited us to attend a pool party at his home in the Valley. When Claudia saw Cherie in a bikini, she wasted no time in asking her if she would be interested in posing for *Playboy*. Stunned and surprised, Cherie stammered her objection, "Oh no, I'd never do anything like that." Claudia smiled and backed away, reclining next to me in the sun with her umbrella drink. "'No' doesn't always mean 'no'," she whispered.*

---

* Cheryl Stopplemoor (Cheryl Ladd) was featured in *Playboy* spreads in 1978 and 1979 after starring as Farah Fawcett's replacement in the popular television series *Charlie's Angels*.

CHAPTER 40

Sunshine Acres is On Fire!

Claudia had big news to tell me when I got home from the studio near midnight. "I finally landed a big-league talent agent to represent me," she gushed. Within weeks, he negotiated her a substantial role in a revival of *Dark of the Moon* opposite Rue McClanahan and Marcia Wallace. When she finally returned, I couldn't wait to pick her up at the airport and see that smile again. But it would be only weeks before she would be off on location again for her next project.

By the end of 1971, Claudia had already made four movies, and she had made friends in every one of them. On December 20th, we celebrated her twenty-first birthday and then hosted a Christmas party for eighty guests at the Pyramid house the following week. Claudia's guests were actors and models; mine came from the world of music. Tommy Boyce and Del Shannon were there. Football legend turned actor, Jim Brown, brought my old friend, Keely Smith.

All of Claudia's coworkers that I met painted the same picture: "She never got upset, never complained, and always had a kind word for her coworkers." It wasn't long before she took my knowledge of what it meant to care about people to a whole new level. During one of my phone conversations with Bobby and Bret, she overheard me talking to Becky about how her car had broken down again. One of the prizes Claudia had received when she was chosen Playmate of the Year was a new Mercury Capri, and I had no sooner hung up the phone than Claudia said, "Why don't we give her the Capri. I've been looking around for a used Mercedes anyway."

When Marcia Wallace came west to seek movie work, she stayed with us for a few weeks. Wardrobe assistants, script supervisors and crew members like Peggy, Dennis, and Gwen all came for extended stays. When the house of our friend, the actress Sally Kirkland, burned down, and she had been left with only what she was wearing, Claudia took her into her walk-in closet and said "Take anything you want." "Anything?" she asked. Claudia repeated, "Anything!"

♥

As I drove to a business lunch one day while Claudia was on location, my attention locked onto a public service announcement that was coming over my car radio. "Anyone interested in helping inner-city kids with their homework in the evenings, call this number." While reading Yogananda's writings, I had been observing a common theme. He seemed to be constantly stressing the importance of selfless service, along with morality, meditation, and love for God. "I may not have gone very far at cultivating the last three," I told myself, "but now I'm really ready to work at having some service to others in my life."

That evening, I made the call and signed up for my night shift as a homework tutor. When actress Marcia Wallace, who was staying at the house, heard about my plan, she said, "I've been looking for something like this." So once a week, fueled by See's butterscotch suckers and a profound sense of altruism, Marcia and I would drive an hour to a public library in a depressed area of Watts where we would play substitute parents for an evening.

The sweetness of the fifth and sixth graders that we worked with made it easy for us to form a bond that left us melancholy when one of our regulars would fail to show up. I wondered if the fun and satisfaction I was receiving would cancel out the good karma I had hoped to chalk up for my serviceful efforts. As I arranged my head on my pillow the night of my first tutoring session, my mind drifted lovingly back to my very first role models in selflessly dedicating their lives to the service of others.

I was fourteen. Jimmy Dingman and I were driving down a deserted, unpaved desert road beneath a warm Arizona sun. I bounced along, riding shotgun and feeling shyly pleased at the rare opportunity to be alone with one of my heroes. Jimmy pulled to the shoulder and got out of the pickup truck. As the cloud of dust from our speedy journey overtook us, he made his way around the hood and opened the passenger door. "Go ahead, slide over" he said smiling, "take the wheel." Jimmie was my father's age, and for this day of my teenage rite of passage he would be a surrogate father, the very role that he had been born into this world to play.

While I was growing up, Jimmy Dingman was the pastor of the Apostolic Christian Tabernacle, our sister church in Mesa, and a family friend. But the all-encompassing dream that for seventeen years had been fervently nurtured in his heart and in the heart of his saintly wife, Vera, was to someday build an orphanage where they could care for the children that no one else wanted, a home where they could love the unloved.

Theirs was a small, poor church, so Jimmy set up a photo studio in one room of the parsonage and took portraits and school pictures. He bought a set of molds, which he filled with concrete to make flower urns and sold them in the church parking lot. The Dingmans built a malt shop in the front yard of their home and sold ice cream and my favorite carbonated beverage they called a "cherry-lime Rickey." Soon the place was so popular that it was expanded into a cafeteria, and Vera began cooking for the local jail. All the while, Vera and Jimmy would save every dollar they could, an arduous task while raising five children of their own.

Finally, with the help of the Mesa Optimist Club, the Dingmans were able to sell their house and put a small down payment on a 125-acre plot far out in the desert that held some dilapidated buildings and a deserted western movie set. They had been talking for years about little else than their children's home, and we all knew that it would be called *Sunshine Acres*. Jimmy and Vera were grandparents with no income, a mortgage on a property that contained a house with no windowpanes, no electricity, and a well with a broken pump. But Aunt Vera told us that the night they moved in, she and Jim felt very strongly that they should never solicit money and never turn a child away for lack of finances. "God impressed on us that night that this was His work. We will take care of the children and He will take care of the finances."

This November day, I had come with my family to visit Sunshine Acres. Jimmy had proudly given us a tour of the new girls dormitory that had just been completed. "The girls have been moved in for about a month now, and they love having a place of their own," he said. "We put all of our best beds in here and friends dropped off some used furniture." After the tour Jimmy told us that the kids were all off attending a picnic in Mesa, and he invited me to ride along as he drove into town to help bring them home.

"Don't hold the steering wheel so tight," he was cautioning. "Just feel the road and adjust slightly left or right when you need to. You have to let the clutch out slowly while you push down on the gas pedal." Neither Mom nor Dad had thought it prudent to allow me behind the wheel of our family car in the city. But here on this deserted, dusty road Jimmy was filling me with a big dose of confidence along with his helpful instructions.

We had no sooner reached the picnic site when a call for Jim Dingman came in to the park office. His face was ashen when he stepped out moments later. "Sunshine Acres is on fire!" he said. He and I rushed to the truck and Jimmy drove the old clunker near the top of its speed. By the time we made it back, the main buildings were engulfed in flames. My father was on the roof of the kitchen holding a limp garden hose, dousing coals that were falling on the dry shingles while the rural fire department did their best to control the blaze. But the new girls dorm could not be saved. The girls began to cry when they saw that their new home had been destroyed along with all their clothes and toys. The fourteen girls had to move back in with the sixteen boys and sleep on pallets on the floor.

In her 1969 book *The First 500,* Aunt Vera quotes the Bible verse "All things work together for good" and tells about how she found it true in her own life. Incredibly, the extensive radio and newspaper publicity that came from this horrendous event began to put Sunshine Acres on the map. One by one, families, retirees, corporations, government agencies, and humanitarian clubs and organizations came forward offering help in a myriad of ways. Though Uncle Jim and Aunt Vera have passed, the modern campus and facilities that is today's Sunshine Acres thrives as an eternal monument to two of the most selfless people I have been blessed to know and the others who work to keep their dream alive.

CHAPTER 41

Stopped in Its Tracks
by a Tragic Hand of Fate

"Bobby? It's Danny." Janssen called one morning after Claudia had left for an audition call-back. I've got an idea. You know, for my cartoon projects, I've been working with a whole bunch of great young studio singers. But there's this one kid from Virginia who really stands out. His name is Austin Roberts and he has a terrific voice. I'm thinking we sign Austin to a recording deal and try to place him with a label." At our next meeting, Danny played me some of Austin's work and I whole-heartedly agreed. We wrote four songs for our new artist, and then made an appointment to play them for an old friend.

Wes Farrell had recently moved to L.A. to produce the music and records for a new television show, the Partridge Family, a job that had been earmarked for Tommy Boyce and Bobby Hart, had we not parted ways with Screen Gems so abruptly. Wes signed Austin to his newly opened Chelsea Records. Danny made the business arrangements, and we booked a smokin' studio band and made some great tracks. Austin was personable and enthusiastic and sang the heck out of our four new songs. In late summer Wes released his first Austin Roberts single, "Something's Wrong with Me," and by the end of 1972 Jansen & Hart were back in the top ten.

Before I met him, Danny Janssen had already written *The Partridge Family* TV theme song with Wes Farrell. One day Janssen made the suggestion, "Wes likes my writing, and I know he likes yours. Why don't we try to write some songs together for *The Partridge Family?*" The result was that at least one Janssen & Hart song ended up on every one of *The Partridge Family* LPs and even the David Cassidy solo albums. The group also recorded songs I had written with Tommy Boyce and Jack Keller, giving me more Partridge Family writer credits that anyone except for Wes himself.

The production of our first Austin Roberts album marked the beginning of a five-year period when Danny and I worked almost daily, ten to six in the studio when we weren't writing at home or in the Chelsea offices. At our most prolific during this time, we managed to write and produce an average of over fifty songs a year as Wes kept us busy with one production project after another in return for the publishing rights to our songs.

Just as Austin Roberts' second release "Keep On Singing" was taking off, it was stopped in its tracks by a tragic hand of fate. Wes called us with the news that his gifted head of national promotion had died unexpectedly of a heart attack. As a result, the record only made it halfway up the charts, peaking at Billboard's #50.

Helen Reddy and her husband, William Morris agent, Jeff Wald, had moved to Los Angeles in 1968 and settled in my neighborhood on Outpost Drive. Although I had met her briefly at different music business functions, most of our real conversation centered around pitching songs to her and dropping off demos at her house in the seventies.

She later told me, "Jeff and I were driving across country on tour when "Keep On Singing" came on the radio. It was soon after the death of my dad and I was really touched when I first heard Austin's version of the song." Danny and I had written a lyric, loosely based on Janssen's own experience, of a singer who loses his biggest supporter, his dad. "It was like listening to the story of my life," she continued, "I told Jeff, 'Keep an eye on this song. If it doesn't go top ten, I want to cut it.'" It didn't and she did, and this time it did rise close to the top, peaking at #15.

♥

On an overcast L.A. morning, an international delivery truck pulled up to our Pyramid driveway and unloaded a giant wooden crate, almost big enough for me to stand in. I pried open the heavy lid and discovered a trove of hundreds of primitive African wood carvings in all shapes and sizes. There was no note of explanation, but Claudia and I surmised that it could only have been sent by our long absent, world-traveling troubadour friend, Barry Richards. Even in the big Pyramid house, it was impossible to display all these wonderful gifts, so after a few months, we began offering the carvings to friends who would express an attraction to one piece or another. Every time we looked at one of the carvings, we sent out a silent "thank you" through the ether to our benefactor, wherever in this wide world he might be.

We were able to pinpoint his exact coordinates when he painted this word picture upon his return.

Barry looked out from the stage of the *Don Quixote* at the colorful mix of tourists, off duty guerilla fighters, and blood diamond traders. It might have been "Rick's American Café" in *Casablanca*, except that there was an eight-piece band playing where Sam would have been sitting behind his piano.

As he sang "My Cherie Amour," Barry could feel the breeze created by the chorus line of Brazilian dancers that whirled around him in their colorful sequins and feathers. They, like he, had been imported into the seaside city of Luanda to provide a distraction for the locals from the harsh realities of the Angolan civil war. At the break, Barry joined a statuesque light-skinned beauty named Janeeza at her table. "What do you do when you're not having drinks at the *Don Quixote*?" he asked her. "I could tell you, but then we could never see each other again," she replied with a provocative smile.

Two days later in his seaside apartment, Janeeza threw Barry a curve. "You know, Barrita, since you are leaving in a few weeks, I know a way that you could make a lot of money for the both of us." Barry tried to change the subject. He had already intuited an aura of intrigue around Janeeza that went beyond the level he could be comfortable with or even interested in. But a few days later, she brought her subject up again as Barry straightened his tie before leaving for the club. "Look at these," she said unfolding a black velvet bandana to reveal several shining, uncut diamonds. "They look small, but they're worth a fortune," she smiled. "I could give you an address in London. We're talking about thousands of dollars here." Barry looked her in the eye for full impact. "I could sing 'Diamond Girl' for you in the club tonight, but I'm not a smuggler."

Trucks filled with armed soldiers roared through the streets as Barry walked to the *Don Quixote* the next evening. During the first set, he looked down and noticed two sinister looking men at Janeeza's table. Joao and Savimbi shook his hand as she introduced them between shows.

"I liked that song you sang to Janeeza," Joao opened. He seemed cordial enough when he smiled. "And I like the way you sing." The band was vamping the intro to the midnight show, and as Barry was excusing himself from the table, a sober Savimbi slipped something in his jacket pocket and gave his parting shot. "I hear you'll be going back to Europe soon. Janeeza says maybe we could do some business together."

There was a loud argument in Barry's room that night. As he undressed, Barry had reached inside his jacket to retrieve Savimbi's business card and instead pulled out a one thousand U.S. dollar note. "Look, Honey, you know how I feel about you, but I thought I made it very clear. I'm not interested in getting involved in this kind of business. If we're going to remain friends, then you're gonna have to respect that." Janeeza gathered her things, snatched the bill from Barry's dresser and stormed out into the humid darkness. He never saw her again.

A few evenings later, as Barry looked out and down the long expanse of white sandy beach from the open-air porch of his bed and breakfast lodging, his eyes caught a lovely, statuesque native girl walking alone. Utilizing his unique talent, he was by her side in a matter of seconds. "Where you off to?" She understood his question, although she spoke little English, and motioned for him to follow.

They had walked hand in hand for nearly half a mile when she pointed out their destination. Barry could see several local men in the distance setting up ten-foot bench seats for what appeared to be an open air movie theater on the beach. The two sat together as the film rolled and our friend heard the opening strains of Tommy Boyce & Bobby Hart singing the movie's title song, "Where Angels Go Trouble Follows."

I learned these stories when Barry finally returned to America two years later. His opening question to me then was, "Where did you put all my statues?"

♥

"Hart! How come you've never written a song about *me*?" Claudia, in a playful mood, surprised me one afternoon. It was a fair question to put to a songwriter. "They're *all* about you," I replied, smiling. "No, no" she continued. "The only way I'll believe you is if it has my name in it. It's gotta go 'Claudia Jennings, I love you, Claudia Jennings.'"

A few days later I wrote her a song. As a favor, Jimmie Haskell wrote a beautiful arrangement, and we slipped it in at the end of one of our string sessions. I made a cover sleeve with her picture on it and presented the record to her on her twenty-second birthday, along with a diamond necklace. There was no contest. I could see her green eyes become teary as she listened to her song. It was titled: "Claudia Jennings."

CHAPTER 42

No, Really, There *Is* No Budget

The air was thick with the intoxicating fragrance of pittosporum blossoms as Claudia and I negotiated the long driveway to inspect the two-story Georgian mini-mansion sitting back on a hill on Woodrow Wilson Drive. We had looked at a ton of houses that were on the market over the last year. Each time the offering would lack either the aesthetic charm that Claudia envisioned or the green-forested nature and privacy that I required. One afternoon in the spring of 1972, she called me at the Chelsea offices and announced, "I think I found our house." We moved in over the Memorial Day weekend.

The winding driveway culminated at a motor court, which revealed the classic Connecticut-style house. It was perched near the top of a hill and looked down on a valley, green with mature trees. The orchard held avocados, oranges, grapefruit, lemons, plums, figs, yellow sapotes and mulberries. We made a bedroom of the large space that had once been the dance studio of legendary dancers and movie choreographers, Marge and Gower Champion.

It wasn't long after we had settled in when Becky called one afternoon to share her continuing concern with how both Bobby and Bret had been struggling with their schoolwork. Over the next few days Claudia and I had long conversations about how to help. I finally agreed with her premise that the boys needed a change of environment and that Bobby should come to live with us. Now we had to convince Becky. We redecorated one of the bedrooms, and in the fall, eleven-year-old Bobby Jr. moved in.

♥

"Hey, Dad, watch this!" Bobby was crouching low on his skates and zooming around the rink, holding his own as he applied the skills he had acquired from years on his skateboard. A moment later, Claudia was showing him how to whip her by him to increase her speed as she approached from behind. She was wearing her pink hoodie and sweatpants, but her attitude and energy reflected a much darker purpose as she circled the rink with resolve. Tonight, she had come to the skating rink on business.

On an early fall evening in 1972, the three of us had driven to Burbank and pulled into the parking lot of the Moonlight Rollerway. Even before we walked in, I could hear the live organist groovin' his version of "Kansas City," one of my old favorites from the *Prelude*. The moment we entered the rink, it was like a flashback to the fifties.

Claudia was a favorite of Roger Corman who owned American International Pictures, and he wanted her for the lead role of Karen in his new roller derby movie, *The Unholy Rollers*. All she had to do now was prove that she had the skills for this physically challenging part. I sat on the sidelines and watched the wonderful world of color and energy spin around me in this small, but dynamic universe of sacred everyday humanity. I divided my attention between my two family skaters and the thoughts that were rolling around in my consciousness.

I was still at a loss as to how to create a traditional father and son connection with my boys. Claudia hadn't been willing to take on two boys this early in our relationship, so we had enrolled Bret into Treehaven, a private school in Tucson. My days, and some evenings, were taken up with my work, and with Claudia gone so much, I was afraid that we still weren't providing Bobby with the attention and guidance he needed.

My dedication to Claudia was unwavering, but now I was experiencing emotional ups and downs that I hadn't counted on. I well understood her determination to achieve her goals, but now it seemed like she was becoming even more driven, just as I was trying harder to balance my outer life with time for my inner spiritual goals.

I watched as Bobby pulled off the rink and skated over to me with a grin. I gave him a hug, and when Claudia joined us, we all left the rink arm in arm, in arm.

♥

Even if it's a low budget film, a movie set is always an exciting place to visit. There's an energy in the air as dozens of young directors and cast and crew members scurry around, performing their assorted talents. As the cameras rolled, I watched Claudia zoom around the track, taking down her opponent with a ruthless thud, and when the cameras stopped, I saw her laughing with her new friends—real roller derby skaters who had been hired as extras.

One of the main reasons she was so excited about doing this movie was that Corman had told her about the brilliant new kid he had lined up to edit the film. The newcomer was already establishing a buzz around town and had just finished directing his own film for AIP called *Boxcar Bertha*. I had never heard of Martin Scorsese, but Claudia always seemed to have the latest inside information when it came to anything related to her industry.

Vernon Zimmerman, the *Unholy Rollers* director, approached me one day as I watched the filming from the sidelines. "How would you like to do the musical score for me? There's no budget, really," he said with a friendly smile. "I'm not kidding; the producers are giving me a thousand dollars for music." I smiled back without saying a word. Vernon shrugged his shoulders in a weak silent apology, hoping that he hadn't offended me.

Of course, it was Claudia who had put him up to it. She knew the importance of music in movies and she wanted to do anything she could to make this one as good as it could be. "If there's anyone who could pull this off it would be you," she cajoled me later that night. "I know it's a big favor . . . but, for me?" she pleaded. I agreed to try. I mentioned my dilemma during a conversation with Don Graham the following day. "You've got to talk to Marvin Schlachter," he ventured. "He runs Arc Music. They own all the early Chuck Berry hits and a ton of other oldies. I'll give him a heads up that you're going to give him a call."

The next day, I phoned Schlachter and I made him an offer he could have easily refused. "The total music budget is one thousand dollars and I'd like to give it all to you," I dangled. "All I want is to be able to use as many of the songs as I need from your catalog." I heard what sounded like a laugh coming from the New York end of the phone. "It's a thou' you wouldn't otherwise have," I bargained. Marvin agreed to take the "thou."

My next call was to an old friend in Seattle named Jay Gigandet. Jay had been Tommy Boyce's manager for a time before I met him, and we had stayed in touch over the years. Jay was managing a local fifties retro group called Louie & the Rockets. I told him, "I can get your guys some big screen time in a major release movie if they're willing to come down to L.A. gratis and pre-record the music for the film." Jay paid for his group's trip down to L.A. I paid for the recording studio time. Danny Janssen and I wrote one original song, "Stay Away From Karen," to serve as a theme, and Louie & the Rockets tore up the studio with some great old fifties tunes.

The boys had a fabulous time filming their scene in a real Hollywood movie. Later that night, Barry, Danny, Don Graham, and I took them to a Chuck Berry concert in Anaheim and they got to meet the rock 'n' roll legend in his dressing room after the show. Soon after appearing in the movie, Louie and the Rockets changed their name to The Unholy Rollers.

CHAPTER 43

Floating Above the Shroud of My Own Expectations

Being part of the "show" with Claudia on my arm as we frequented the Hollywood scene had been fun for me in the beginning. There were media-covered celebrity parties and exclusive music business affairs. We received backstage passes from the hottest acts and had front row seats at their concerts. We were photographed, dressed to the nines, as we walked movie premier red carpets. It made me feel like somebody special and I could see in Claudia's eyes that all the attention was having a similar effect on her. I easily slipped into my role as the "I've-got-it-made" pop star counterpart to Claudia's glamorous, charismatic, woman rebel persona.

But, soon, even my inflated ego was able to easily recognize that the novelty had begun to wear off like spray-on glitter from a papier-mâché façade, flashing its last sparkle as it floats to the stained concrete floor below after the red carpet had been rolled away. It hadn't taken long for the inferno of this public life pressure cooker to begin to overheat our personal nervous systems.

Claudia and I had our honest love for each other in common, but we had conflicting professional and personal ambitions, and the tensions were beginning to wear on both of us. It wasn't just my loneliness when Claudia was away so often on location; there was also a growing discord during the times when she was at home.

On a Saturday evening in August, Claudia and I arrived at the mansion for one of Hef's annual "Midsummer Night's Dream" gatherings. At these events, and at all of his Sunday movie nights that we had attended, there was never a shortage of movie stars and always an abundance of beautiful, young girls. Now that I was in a committed relationship, being surrounded by beautiful girls wasn't nearly as interesting as it might have been three or four years before.

Claudia was always right at home in this unique setting and this night, as always, she was reveling in the attention she so naturally attracted. After a while, as usual, I wandered off on my own. I strolled around the mansion until I found a small, empty parlor filled with books. I sat down on a comfortable, forest green, velvet loveseat, sipped on my club soda, and let the insistent thoughts play over my mind. Although I loved her very much, I couldn't ignore the cracks that were beginning to appear on the pages of our fairy tale.

An hour later I found Claudia enjoying the hot water in the grotto. She was not happy that I had left her alone for so long and told me so as I struggled to hear her voice over the sounds of laughter and water jets. I joined her in the pool, but tonight the spectacular grotto area with its multicolored, underwater lights, soft candlelight, and even the stained glass lit from behind in the ceiling of this manmade rock cave didn't seem so glamorous.

At home, Claudia had been continuing to press for a wedding so that we could raise children in our beautiful little house on the hill. But, at the same time, she would give tough feminist magazine interviews purporting that she didn't believe in marriage and would never succumb to the institution. I told her if we could get through six months without a major fight, I would propose. These days, we were lucky to make it through three.

In the early seventies my substantial income from The Monkees and Boyce & Hart records had taken a sharp decline. It was a momentary setback until the royalties from my new hits would start to arrive. But Claudia had told me back then, "When I was still in school, I made a vow to myself that I would do whatever it takes, but I will never be poor." Over the ensuing years she would remind me from time to time that she had a standing offer from real estate tycoon, Stan Herman, to set her up in a nice house in Beverly Hills. I knew he had been in the ballroom that evening, probably sweetening his offer. An uneasy stillness hung over the car as we drove home that night, both still wearing the terrycloth robes we had donned from a stack that was always available in the pool house.

Then there was the disparity in how we expressed our spiritual natures. Day after day, I would witness examples of Claudia's natural kindness, empathy, generosity, and service to others. Over the last three years, her compassion had inspired me to work at being more open, service-oriented, and caring. She was completely supportive of the alone time I required every day for my meditation practice and was fine with my penchant toward reading inspirational books. But in spite of all her innate spiritual qualities, she had a non-negotiable aversion to organized religion.

Once I shared with Claudia a story I was reading, about the Benares saint, Lahiri Mahasaya. As we sat in our twin wingback chairs in front of the fireplace, I interrupted her to ask if she wanted to hear it. She nodded and put down her book.

Although he held a day job, Lahiri Mahasaya spent his free time in the evenings teaching and meditating with his students who flocked to his living room from all over India. After some time, Lahiri's wife Kashi Moni began to feel ignored and on this particular night, she had come to his room to upbraid him for spending so much time with his disciples and not earning more for the family's care.

Suddenly, in the middle of her scolding, Lahiri vanished into thin air. Kashi Moni was confused and frightened, but then she heard her husband's voice resounding from every corner of the room, "*Divine* wealth is what you should be seeking." When she looked up, she found her husband levitating near the ceiling of the room, surrounded by angels. Begging for forgiveness, she bowed in awe and immediately asked to become his disciple. I closed the book and smiled at Claudia.

"Well, don't expect me to do that to you," she announced sternly, breaking the stillness with a mildly frustrated shake of her head. I hadn't thought it necessary to explain, but now I heard myself saying, "Are you kidding? I'm pretty sure it's going to be a few lifetimes before you find me floating near the ceiling. I just thought you'd enjoy hearing a cool story." Unimpressed, she picked up her book and went back to reading her novel.

♥

"Bobby, it's Lester," the familiar voice on the phone began, "The movie composer Dominic Frontiere was just in my office. He often needs to come up with theme songs for the pictures he scores, and he's looking around for a new lyricist. I told him that you're the guy to fill that bill, hands down." "Thanks, Lester," I said with a hint of skepticism. "Would I know any of his work?" "Oh, yeah. He's composed the music for a ton of TV series like *Outer Limits, Rawhide, The Fugitive.* He does all the John Wayne movies, that Clint Eastwood hit, I think it was *Hang 'Em High* and dozens more." "Cool!" I reflected with renewed interest.

The next morning Frontiere called me, and we arranged to meet at a small Hollywood coffee shop. Dominic was friendly and charismatic and wasted no time selling himself to me as we slipped into a booth. "BMI just told me that I'm their top earner," he opened, referring to the society that collects royalties for composers when their music is played on radio and television. It took no more than his opening line to impress me, knowing that BMI provided a major part of my income.

Apparently, he had already done his homework on me, and all I ventured when Dominic told me about his new movie project, *A Name for Evil,* was, "Sure, I'd love to try to do a lyric for you." Just before sunset that evening I stopped by Frontiere's Beverly Hills home and he handed me a tape containing his completed melody. It wasn't until I got home and began to play the cassette over and over, that I realized this partnership would demand a whole new set of writing skills and a work discipline beyond anything I had previously faced.

When I worked with Tommy or Danny, we would often be writing the melody and lyrics almost at the same time. There was always a combined energy and the fun of bouncing ideas off each other. But with a movie composer, I was expected to sit alone at my house and attach one syllable to each musical note of an orchestral melody that didn't sound much to me like a pop song. And some way, I would have to make the words sound natural, poetic, and sing-able. To sound conversational, the words would need to go high or low with the melody, in the same way the natural inflections of the words would flow up or down if you were to speak them aloud. I wanted this opportunity, so I jumped right in with painstaking effort and worked late into the night.

The next afternoon I arrived at Dominic's home, ready to demonstrate my work. His wife, Sicily, sat in as I gave my best performance, singing my lyrics to his melody. As I finished, I could see that she was wiping her eyes, and she asked me to repeat some lines that had particularly touched her: "There's a trace, of peace on your face, and the sun's always shining behind it. You go there, without leaving your chair, while I run around trying to find it." "Dom, what a beautiful lyric!" she said, as she gave my hand a congratulatory shake and then took her hot tea elsewhere in the house. Dominic nodded his head in agreement and then asked me to listen to the new melody he was working on for his next movie.

Over the ensuing years, I've been asked to write lyrics for other movie and television composers, most notably the talented Alan Reeves. Alan and I have become good friends, and he continues to call on me to collaborate in writing theme songs to accompany his various motion picture scores. Although this kind of lyric writing remains a challenge for me, I now find great satisfaction whenever I've been able to stretch beyond myself and come up with a lyric that rises beyond the shroud of my own expectation.

After a couple of years of supplying lyrics for all of Frontiere's movie themes, I suggested that he, Danny Janssen, and I collaborate on the melodies as well as the lyrics and try to come up with more commercial theme songs for the hit James Caan-Alan Arkin cop-buddy film, *Freebie and the Bean*. After hearing the demos, Warner Brothers asked me to sing the lead vocals for the two songs and then released them as a single on their record label. When *Freebie* was made into a television series a few years later, the new producers re-used our same theme song and asked me to re-sing the vocals.

No More Back Door, Overcrowded Dreams

Wes Farrell's record company and publishing operations occupied the entire tenth floor of the high rise, 8086 Sunset Building. At ten o'clock on a Monday morning I arrived at the Chelsea Records offices, as I often did, for a writing session with Wes and Danny. Wes entered the writing cubicle where I sat at the piano and greeted me with a question, "Guess who I just signed to an album deal for Chelsea?"

Tommy Boyce and I had remained friends. We spoke on the phone regularly, and we would see each other from time to time. But it was Wes and not Tommy who told me he had been signed to record an album with his new band. Soon after, Boyce invited me down to the studio to hear some of his recording in progress, and I was surprised to hear that he was cutting heavy rock tracks. Just before the LP was released, I picked up a copy from a stack on Wes's desk. The artist on the record was listed as *Christopher Cloud* and the cover featured a grey cloud, which floated ominously in front of the band, totally obscuring Tommy's face. Once again, Boyce had chosen to disguise his identity, avoiding any suggestion that he was trading on his past successes.

At my next breakfast with Wes at the Polo Lounge in the Beverly Hills Hotel, over our usual plates of shirred eggs and chicken livers, he hyped, "I'm lining up the next record production project for you and Danny. I can't tell you who it is yet, but it's an established artist and a big star. You're going to be blown away when you find out." A week later in his office, he told Danny and me, "I've set up a meeting Wednesday at

251

three for you two to sit down and get to know Vikki Carr and her manager. She wants to go in a more commercial direction and I think you guys will be the perfect fit in the studio."

In the studio the process turned out to be completely different from any of the other acts I had produced. Still a youthful, beautiful woman, Vikki was also a seasoned professional in a way that surpassed any other artist I ever worked with. There was no need to look for that perfect take, redo certain lines, or make vocal composites. On almost every song she would walk into the vocal booth and nail the performance with perfect pitch, great phrasing, and soulful expression on the very first take. Vikki had the wonderful ability to focus like a laser while working, and then when her work was done, to relax and be playful.

After the success of Ms. Carr's *Ms. America* album she asked us to produce her next album, *Live at the Greek*, which would be a double record set of her entire live show. Danny and I rented a mobile recording studio and recorded a weekend of her performances. I took turns with Danny as we went between the truck and sitting in the audience enjoying one of the most polished, sincere, and talented entertainers in the business.

On the first day, as I watched the full orchestra rehearsal from the twentieth row of the empty, beautiful outdoor amphitheatre, I was stunned to see that even with no audience, Vikki Carr would cry sincere tears when she sang her emotional songs like "It Must Be Him" and "With Pen In Hand." Between numbers she would sometimes talk for several minutes, conveying moving thoughts harvested from her life and experience and strengthening her rapport with her loyal audiences. The orchestra would underscore these intimate moments with heartfelt music, and I noticed that they were playing the theme from *Days of Our Lives*.

At the first band break I introduced myself to Bob Florence, Vikki's talented orchestra leader and arranger and thanked him for using my song, knowing that when the record came out there would be a song royalty for Boyce and me. A moment of sparring ensued as Florence surprised me with, "If you're recording this thing, I'm not playing *your* song. I'll write something of my own for the talking bits." "I'll tell you what,"

I replied, smiling, "You write a couple of background pieces, and Danny and I will publish them. How does that sound?" Bob Florence stuck out his hand and coalesced, "It's a deal," as he walked back to his podium.

Bob titled his compositions "Soap Opera Music" and "Morning of a Faun," and I dutifully listed them with the other songs when I turned in the label information to Columbia Records. When *Live at the Greek* was released, I noticed that the publishing information for the two new music compositions were not listed in the credits with the other songs.

The next morning on the phone, I pointed out the omissions to a royalty manager at Columbia. "What do you mean?" he retorted, feigning ignorance, "That's just background music while the artist is talking." "That's right" I replied, "But you know as well as I do that a record company has to pay songwriter royalties for any music they use on a recording." Our first royalty statement confirmed that the manager had been quite aware of his copyright obligations all along.

♥

"Bobby, how'd you and Danny like to produce the Raiders?" Keith Allison had been working as a full-fledged member of Paul Revere and the Raiders for a couple of years when he called me at our Woodrow Wilson home. "You guys have been writing great stuff and having hits, and because of our longtime friendship, Paul asked me to see if you'd be interested." "I'd love to produce the Raiders," I said without hesitation. When I told Danny, he was delighted, being a longtime fan of Mark Lindsay and the boys just like I was.

I arranged with Keith to have Columbia Records draw up the agreements, and Danny and I started thinking about song concepts for the perennial group right away. To me, they had always been America's own junior Rolling Stones, but with an entertainment bonus of comedy when you saw them in person. For over a decade, they had consistently turned out some great records, and now they were just coming off their highest-ranking single ever, "Indian Reservation."

Just as we were gearing up for the Raiders sessions, I took a call from Keith. "I don't know what's going on over at Columbia," he started. "But the word has come down that they will not authorize Janssen & Hart to produce any sessions with any of their recording artists." "What?" I was stunned. "Yeah, I know," he said. "I don't know what the deal is, but Paul asked me to give you a call and tell you how sorry he is that we won't be able to work together." I paused for a moment. Then I said, "I think I might just know what the problem is. Let me call you back."

I had been producing records for Columbia for nearly a decade, ever since Tommy Boyce and I cut our first Barry Richards sessions for them in 1968. Music icon Clive Davis had been president of the company for many years, and during that time he, Tommy, and I had become good friends. He had given us valuable career advice and even invited us to attend the yearly Columbia convention in Puerto Rico one year. By 1975 Clive had moved on to start his own label, Arista, but I felt that I had a cordial relationship with his successor.

When I called the new Columbia Records president's office in New York he picked up on my first try. "I had a little discussion with your Royalty Department on the last Vikki Carr record," I confided. "That can't be the reason," he said after I told him the story of our being apparent victims of blacklisting. "Let me check it out and I'll get back to you." He never did, and he never again returned my calls.

Of course, I had heard stories about others being blackballed and refused employment, but you never think it could happen to you in this day and age. Janssen and I discussed the matter and decided that since we weren't hurting for work, our time and energy could be better spent on creating new projects rather than fighting a mega corporation in court.

♥

After my "Hello?" the caller started right in without a greeting. "Listen, Bobby, I've got this great concept for a song that I know will have a special interest for you." I recognized the voice of my old friend Sandy Baron one morning back when Claudia and I lived at the Pyramid house. "When can I come over and lay it on you?" Sandy and I had remained friends since our first meeting when Tommy and I had guested on the

Della Reese Show. Although he made his living primarily as a comedian and an actor, I knew that Sandy had also had a bunch of songs to his credit.

A couple of days later, I made him a cup of coffee in the kitchen and then we retired to my writing room near the piano. "Look, man, I know how you feel about human rights . . . the sacredness of every living being and all that, 'cause we've talked about it. You know, Bobby, this country's not out of the woods yet when it comes to racial prejudice." I silently nodded my agreement and took a sip of my coffee. He intentionally dropped a couple of quotes from Dick Gregory, a campaigner for civil rights who Sandy knew I admired. I could tell by his tone of voice and pacing that he had been thoughtfully preparing his presentation to me, so I sat back and let him continue. "I've been tossing around this song idea for months but I need some help to get it right. Then last week it came to me, BAM! Bobby Hart!"

"Why me?" I shot back with a smile. "Look, you probably don't even realize how many message songs you've already written," he informed me as he got out of his chair, stood near the window, and sang out in full voice, " *'Hey, hey, we're The Monkees, and people say we monkey around, but we're too busy singing to put anybody down.'* You can't tell me this song isn't the perfect coming of age anthem for every young generation."

"And how about your lyric for the Let Us Vote campaign?" Sandy leaped forward and played my piano standing up like Jerry Lee Lewis. "The time is now and the feelin's right, to look at things in a better light. We're old enough to lend a helping hand; together we can build a better land." I was surprised that he knew the words to that one. Sandy turned around and sat down, looked me straight in the eye, and continued in a more subdued key.

"And every time I heard you and Tommy sing "I Wanna Be Free" when we worked in Vegas with Zsa Zsa, I felt your message went deeper than just a love song. "I'd be watching from the wings and when I'd hear the words 'I wanna be free, like the bluebirds flying by me, like the waves out on the blue sea,' I'd hear a soul crying out for the God-given right to make their own choices." I felt a slight blush creep over my face, feeling that Sandy may have given me more credit than I deserved. "All right, already," I pleaded, "What's your idea?"

"You know, I co-wrote a big hit for Lou Rawls last year called "A Natural Man." It was kind of a black emancipation anthem. Now, I know it's time to write something honoring the struggles of the Latino community. I want to call it 'Chicano.'" There was a sudden and powerful silence in the room as he finished, and the perfect timeliness of the idea washed over me. Smiling, I calmly put down my coffee, reached for my yellow pad, and within 45 minutes Sandy and I finished writing a song that expressed our mutual beliefs, hopes, and vision for a future in which the racial walls between all human beings would be toppled as flat as the one in Berlin.

When Sandy heard that I was working with Vikki Carr, he suggested that she would be the perfect voice to introduce the song we had written in 1971. In the sixties, Vikki Carr had changed her name to better assimilate into the American music scene, but she was fiercely proud of her Latino heritage. Although the subject was quite out of character from her usual material, she agreed to record our song, "Chicano." I stood near the piano in the studio listening as she repeated the lyrics after me,

Descendants of an Aztec culture, ancient and supreme, Children of the mystic sun god, you are kings and queens, No more back door over crowded dreams, Chicano! No more need to hide, Sing it out with pride, Chicano.

CHAPTER 45

You Took a Gig
on Christmas Day?!

I had become good friends with an Italian ball of energy named Christian De Walden after his mother had introduced us over Thanksgiving dinner in 1972. I helped him get started in the music publishing business and now he was constantly traveling the world, building a music catalog and a reputation as an international business mogul.

One morning early in 1975, I picked up his unexpected call. He said, "I just got back from Thailand and a promoter there wants to book The Monkees for some concert dates. Could you give Micky a call and see if the guys are up for it?" Over the phone, Micky told me that Michael Nesmith had made it clear he was not interested in touring with The Monkees and that Peter Tork had sort of dropped off their radar screen. When I reported back to Christian, he thought for a silent moment and then suggested, "Well then, why don't you and Tommy team up with the other two?"

On a Monday afternoon David Jones, Micky Dolenz, Tommy Boyce, and I met to discuss the proposition at Carlos and Charlie's, a restaurant on Sunset that Micky owned. Our lunch reunion turned out to be so much fun that we decided that if the promoters made it worth our while, we'd all be amenable to giving it a try. As we got up from the table, I shook hands with my three old friends. "This could be a lot of fun," I offered, looking Tommy straight in the eyes. "Let's go make some money," Boyce said with a smile that reminded me of the old days. He gave me a pat on my shoulder and headed out the door.

Once we had signed on, Christian began promoting the tour to begin in July of the following year, expanding it to concerts in Japan and several other Asian countries. When word got around about our tour of the Far East, an American booking agent named Tony Rico approached us with offers to play concerts throughout the States. Because of contractual limitations, we couldn't call ourselves The Monkees, so we decided on the uncreatively obvious billing of Dolenz, Jones, Boyce & Hart.

We put together a program called *The Great Golden Hits of The Monkees Show,* starring "The Guys Who Sang 'Em and the Guys Who Wrote 'Em." We sang Monkee hits and Boyce & Hart hits, a repertoire that didn't require much rehearsal. Davy choreographed some moves, Micky put together segue bits for comedy relief, and we just clowned around and had fun. We asked Keith Allison to put together a band, come along as our musical director, and open the shows with a twenty minute warm-up set.

On June 21st, 1975, we arrived, not knowing what to expect, in St. Louis to play our first show at the Six Flags Over Mid-America theme park. A few fans began to trickle in as we made our way to the stage for a brief sound check. When I returned after an hour on the roller coasters, I noticed that the venue was nearly full. But none of us expected the twenty-two thousand kids that showed up that day. In one afternoon we realized that ten years after *The Monkees* show had first hit the airwaves, there was still an audience who was interested in the guys who sang 'em and maybe even the guys who wrote 'em.

We asked Abe Somer to test the waters for a Dolenz, Jones, Boyce & Hart record deal, and the first company he approached, Capitol Records, signed us and released two albums. It was great working with my old friends again, especially Tommy. We wrote together for the LP and had a great time on the road, playing auditoriums, stadiums, and nearly every amusement park in the continental U.S.

My new part-time performing career coincided symbiotically with a shift in Danny Janssen's focus. He had been spending more and more of his time and energy on his real estate investments. Now, his business dealings had moved to the forefront of his interest, just as I was spending much of my time on the road.

♥

"Hey, Hart!" Claudia greeted me with that thousand-watt smile as I picked her up at LAX on her return from her latest location shoot. After *Unholy Rollers*, she had made *Truck Stop Women*, *'Gaitor Bait*, and *Death Sport* with David Carradine in quick succession, and played guest-starring roles on a number of TV shows like *The Brady Bunch*, *Cannon*, *Streets of San Francisco*, and *Ironside*. For a few days it would be like old times, but then the old conflicts would surely arise before one of us would be off again for our next engagement.

At this point, when I talked to Claudia from the road, the subjects of our conversations were more domestic than romantic. Like when I returned the message that was waiting for me when Dolenz, Jones, Boyce & Hart checked into the Sheraton in Philadelphia: "Hart! You've gotta wire me some money tonight. The dentist says Bobby needs a couple of fillings and the water heater died." It was getting harder and harder to reach Bobby when I called in from the tours. He was usually out with his friends.

♥

I pulled my latest black Lincoln up in front of Treehaven and parked. My fourteen-year-old son Bret was standing there waiting for me with a few of his friends, and when I got out, he introduced me around. One shy little girl, I recognized immediately. It was Wes Farrell's daughter Dawn, who had enrolled here for school after Wes had divorced his first wife, Joan, and married his second, Tina Sinatra. I gave Bret a big hug, and he took me inside to show me his room and the pig he had been raising for his agriculture project.

I had called ahead and gotten permission for a few days spring getaway for just the two of us. I'd flown into Tucson for special weekend events at Bret's boarding school before, but they were always structured programs, and Becky and her family would also be there. On the phone to Bret I had proposed, "How about we just get in the car and drive down into Mexico, do some sightseeing?" He said "Sure, that'd be great," and I had driven most of the 450 miles and stayed overnight in a motel in order to arrive at the school early on a Monday.

We crossed the border at Nogales and I pointed the car south through the Sonora desert. A line of spiny saguaro cacti stood sentry along the I-15 guarding the stately, purple mountains in the distant background. And above, white cotton-ball clouds floated in a perfectly clear blue sky. As for the sightseeing, after hours of driving, the terrain didn't look all that much different from the deserts we had left behind us in southern Arizona.

But it was a chance for father and son to be alone together and try to get to know each other a little bit better. At first, it was hard to find common ground, when our lives and interests were so obviously different. I could easily envision the loneliness that must have been a part of Bret's everyday life, from being away from family for the first time at a young age. "It'll be great when you come over when school's out in June," I started awkwardly, trying to penetrate the surface of his feelings about not living with either his mother or his father for most of the year. But Bret stayed true to the persona of independence and self-sufficiency that he had presented ever since childhood. "Naw, it's okay," he said. "I've got a lot of friends."

We drove for hours through the villages of Magdalena de Kino and Santa Ana, sometimes in silence and sometimes commenting on the panorama that unfolded before us. Here and there, Bret would point out plants and igneous formations that he was learning about in school. Just before sundown, we reached Hermosillo, the capital of Sonora State where we stopped at a small hotel. It was plain but clean, and after a tasty supper of chicken, rice, beans, and corn tortillas, we settled in for the night.

I can't say that the conversation was that much more spirited on the return drive the following morning, but with every mile, I could feel a loosening of the restraint between us and a strengthening of a warm, unspoken bond. As we pulled into Tucson in the early evening, I clung to the feeling that Bret and I had forged the beginning of a promising friendship. And I was sure that neither one of us wanted the feeling to be over just yet. We found a coffee shop for dinner and drove around until we spotted a theater where we watched *One Flew Over the Cuckoo's Nest* together.

It was late when I returned Bret to his boarding school and hugged him goodbye. And there was an emptiness in the pit of my stomach as I watched my son growing smaller in my rear view mirror. We waved to each other until I could no longer see him in the darkness and I drove off into the black Arizona sky.

♥

"You took a gig on Christmas Day?!" she yelled. A relationship coming apart can be blamed on a hundred little things or on nothing at all. This excuse was as good as any to break the camel's back. When I told her that our three weeks of concert bookings in December would have us away through the holidays, Claudia was inconsolable. She saw it as a conscious choice on my part to be away from her at a time of the year that held so many happy memories for us. When I returned from the road in early January, she had moved out.

In April I lent out my house for one of Sally Kirkland's Hollywood networking parties, and Claudia showed up unexpectedly. She told me she had missed me and wanted to know if we could give it another try. It was a blissful couple of months, but by the time I visited her in Nevada City on the set of *Moonshine County Express*, I think we both had already realized that in spite of how much we had wanted to make it work, it just wouldn't work.

CHAPTER 46

Too Loose to Be Circumscribed by the Mouse and His Handlers

On the 4th of July weekend, 1976, Dolenz, Jones, and Boyce & Hart arrived at Disneyland to play some of our final American shows. Soon after finding our dressing rooms, I discovered that the happiest place on earth was probably the most controlled environment that I'd ever performed in since the Copacabana goons had laid down the law back in the Teddy Randazzo days.

We were treated by the park militia like just another one of the rides, and our performances were expected to begin and end at the exact preordained minute that they had specified. This tight schedule, they told us, was to avoid any conflict with the other Mickey, who would be leading his light-show parade right by our outdoor theater just one minute after our final bow. Since our shows were much too loose and spontaneous to ever be circumscribed by the Mouse and his handlers, we found ourselves constantly in the doghouse alongside Pluto.

David Jones had brought along a gregarious young friend named Derek, just a year or so older than my boys, and he soon became the pack leader as they roamed the park. Derek showed Bobby and Bret how easy it was to go directly to the front of the long lines of patrons waiting for the rides. "All we had to do was tell the ticket taker that we were the sons of one of The Monkees," Bret proudly announced to me that evening. It was a raucous weekend for the three and for my boys, their first, and maybe their only, encounter with trading on their father's celebrity.

Peter Tork, who had heard about our concerts on the radio, reappeared from obscurity, called Micky and was invited to join us on stage for the final Sunday evening show. Peter strapped on the bass and traded lines with Dolenz on "I'm Not Your Stepping Stone" to the delight of the sold-out crowd. I looked out at the sea of young fans and their families, many of whom hadn't even been around ten years back when The Monkees had been unleashed on an unsuspecting nation. As we prepared to leave the land we loved after a year of touring across America, this seemed to me to be a zenith moment, a farewell concert that continued on well after the mouse and his parade had passed us by.

The next week Jones, Boyce, Hart, and Dolenz, in an arm cast from a hang gliding accident the week before, handed our passports to Christian de Walden as we boarded the Singapore Airlines flight for our long-anticipated tour of the Far East. When we de-boarded and entered the Tokyo airport, we found ourselves surrounded by hundreds of screaming Japanese fans. Halfway between the original Monkeemania and 1976, all of their original albums had re-charted in Japan after one of their songs had been used in a popular television commercial. Now, we were finding out that their popularity had remained even stronger here in Japan than it had back home.

We signed autographs for the excited fans who waited eagerly behind stanchions, well controlled by the airport police, staying as long as we could before being hurried off to a major media press conference inside a meeting room at our hotel. We did television talk shows in the afternoon and then played our first concert at a US military facility in the evening.

A day later, a ninety-minute bullet train ride took us to Shizuoka for a sold-out show. It afforded an opportunity to see the beautiful Japanese countryside and the ingenuity of a densely populated culture and their use of space. Then it was back to Tokyo for an afternoon concert in the giant Hibiya Park stadium as guests of a popular Japanese group.

The Zutrubies had visited us in Los Angeles back in the spring, bringing gifts in the venerable Asian tradition. They told us then, "Sometimes in our country we have been compared to The Monkees." That day in their country provided one of the most singular experiences of the tour as the fans in the audience actually put on a show for us. Apparently, the stadium was occupied by members of different fan clubs. The fans in each section had dressed in their own signature color, and all of them were bearing large placards. In planned synchronicity, the fans in each section would stand and move to the music while arranging their cards into colorful patterns and messages to the performers.

Two days later Dolenz, Jones, Boyce & Hart returned the favor and invited the Zutrubies to share the bill with us for another concert at Tokyo's Yubin Chokin Hall. Capitol Records brought in their equipment and recorded what would later become our *Live in Japan* album. As always, we sang The Monkees hits and the Boyce & Hart hits, but by now we were including a few cuts from our studio LP. I looked out into the audience of radiant faces as I took the stage to sing my lead on "I Love You and I'm Glad That I Said It." Girls were screaming my name, and it felt wonderfully exciting, just like eight years earlier back home in America.

We had no sooner unpacked in our Singapore hotel than we were spirited away to the local police precinct. Christian de Walden had pulled a coup by arranging for us to be the first American rock group to be allowed to perform in the authoritarian, Southeast Asian city-state of Singapore. To obtain our work visas, he had painted us as non-threatening, clean-cut purveyors of good-time music. But he had warned us that we would not be allowed off the plane if our hair had not been sheared short enough that it would not touch our collars.

The members of the Singapore police department were not cordial when we entered the building. Christian approached the watch commander's desk and announced our arrival. The captain loudly spoke something in Malay and several uniformed officers surrounded us. Feeling like criminal suspects, we resisted our usual inclinations to be friendly and playful and immediately adopted the serious demeanor of our interrogators. Then, Tommy, Davy, Micky, and I were taken away separately and shown into drab, gray holding rooms.

I stood at attention while an armed officer walked around me slowly, scrutinizing from a range of only inches, each thread, hair, and bead of sweat. I held my breath, knowing that our concert was hanging in the balance. Finally, we were all brought back to the watch commander's desk where Christian presented him with copies of all the lyrics we would be performing that night.

Laboriously, he and his cohorts pondered each line, presumably checking for secret subversive messages. After we were dismissed, we waited until our driver had pulled out of the compound and we were well out of range before any of us dared breathe a sigh of relief or crack a smile. Then, we all laughed out loud when Davy suddenly began singing a subdued version of "I Wanna Be Free."

♥

It's hard to imagine the creeping, standing, crawling journey from the Bangkok Airport to the modern high-rise Dusit Thani hotel in the world's worst traffic jam as being a source of inspiration. But the two-hour trip to the hotel where we would sing and stay afforded me a close up view of the spiritual ardor that permeated the people of Thailand. Busses and trucks, large and small, and even little three-wheeler motor cars, had been lovingly decorated with colorful, ornate images of Buddha, Shiva, Krishna, or Christ.

And intersection after intersection would reveal elaborate corner street altars, which they called "spirit houses," where statues or paintings of multifarious deities had been lovingly garlanded with beautiful fresh-cut flowers. This surprising visual panorama must have triggered something in me because I found myself no longer hearing the frenzied sounds of the snarled traffic, but instead heard the warm and compelling voice of Dr. Faulkner preaching to my childhood Apostolic Temple congregation about the importance of learning to love God. After all, I thought, wasn't this the basic tenet of all the world's religions?

Granted, these were not silent prayers of the heart. They were gaudy outer displays, showy and ornate. But I was struck to witness firsthand a society whose love for their objects of devotion was so ingrained that it was considered perfectly normal to display it for all to see. My meditations fit perfectly with my personality and background; they were a form of devotion that was private and silent. In contrast, the beautiful people of this exotic culture had needed and found some more external ways to help them remember the first commandment.

A thousand times my preteen ears had heard a myriad of preachers commanding me to "love the Lord thy God with all thy heart, with all thy soul and with all thy mind." I had done my best to feel that love for the invisible ruler of the kingdom of heaven, not so much because I blindly accepted this recurring instruction, but because of the intuitive belief in its importance that had been a part of me since early childhood.

Behind closed eyes and on bended knees, my young heart had tried, with varying results, to tap into that river of love that should be flowing effortlessly between a child and his Creator. Since it seemed nearly impossible to love a God that I didn't even know, my upbringing had tied me mainly to the Lord Jesus as my *Ishta*—my chosen deity, a form I could visualize.

The emotion I felt from witnessing the religious devotion of the Thai people stayed with me late into the evening as I peered out the window of my seventeenth floor room at the Dusit Thani. Far below, I had watched the controlled chaos of masses of humanity going about the business of their lives. Suddenly, I felt very alone, so far from my home and my family. I was a stranger in a stranger Siam than I had envisioned. And yet, sitting on my unfamiliar bed and immersed in a culture so foreign and exotic; still I felt a natural sense of security, as though I were safe in the arms of the divine Mother of my religious background.

Sweetly, I began to feel the familiar peace of meditation budding inside of me and a slow melting away of levels of stress and emotion that I hadn't even known were there. I felt the whirlwind of restlessness that surrounded our rock 'n' roll tour begin to settle down around me like leaves falling after the wind stops blowing. The longer I stayed in this stillness, the more my consciousness expanded beyond just me.

Intuitively, I had long known that the peace of the planet is directly proportionate to the peace created in the lives of the individual souls who live here. Whenever I was given the opportunity, I had written songs that would broadcast my beliefs in the importance of peace and kindness. I had wanted that kind of a world, but I knew I needed to work harder on myself to create it within and around me.

♥

Keith Allison and I entered the brightly lit, glass-front bookstore, up the street from our hotel in Taipei, Taiwan. As we wandered through its spacious aisles I said, "This looks like a Barnes & Noble and a Tower Records combined." "Yeah, but, something's different," Keith pointed out. Every book cover and every record jacket had been faithfully reproduced and looked exactly like the ones you might purchase in the States.

But when Keith picked up a record and handed it to me, I saw what he meant. "Look! There are no copyright notices on any of these." No publisher, no paperback writer, no recording artist, no composer or lyricist would see a penny of these profits. Someone had purchased one original of each creation and reproduced it in huge quantities with no thought, let alone remorse, for the years of work and millions of dollars it had taken to bring these products to market. Some of the charm of this exotic country evaporated at that moment.

The next morning we drove to the airport and prepared to leave the Far East. It had been a wonderful opportunity to see some beautiful parts of the world and immerse myself in cultures I might never have had a chance to experience. We had performed in Hong Kong; Kauala Lumpur, Malisia; Singapore; Taipei, Taiwan; Bankok, Thailand and for a week in Japanese cities, and all the international audiences were just as gracious as the ones back home. I left with a deep feeling of gratitude for the blessing of seeing firsthand the impact that our music has had on people all over the world.

In the days after our tour of the Far East, the group took time to recuperate and reassess. Then, within weeks, two of our four cast members unexpectedly pulled up stakes and moved to higher ground. Independently and suddenly, Tommy Boyce and Micky Dolenz relocated to England.

CHAPTER 47

You Say the Queen Was Toasting You?

"**B**obby!" It was Christian de Walden on the phone. "I think we should go to MIDEM this year," he suggested. The international music trade show, held every January in Cannes, France, is a place for buyers and sellers of music to get together. "I can make more deals in one week over there than I can traveling around for months. But it'll go a lot better if you show your face, too."

To keep my off-weeks productive during my year and a half of DJB&H touring, I had formed a production company with Barry. We talent searched, auditioned, signed several artists to recording deals, and began placing them with record labels. MIDEM would be an opportunity to shop our new artists and songs to the world market and to temporarily get my mind away from Claudia and my intense sadness.

I called Tommy in England. "Yeah," he said, "I was thinking of going over too. I'll meet you in the South of France, and we can hang out. Hey, you know what?" he added as a second thought. "Why don't you come back and spend a couple of weeks with me here in London on your way home?"

After a productive week in Cannes, we said goodbye to Christian and flew to Heathrow together where we booked a cab to Tommy's flat near Hyde Park. He had only been in London for a few months, but it was more than ample time for Boyce to acquire a cadre of new friends, and he proudly introduced me around. For the two of us, there were late nights of reminiscing and spinning tales from our checkered past. But none were more captivating than the stories he told me of his new life since relocating so suddenly to jolly old England.

Feeling directionless after the demise of Boyce & Hart, David Tucker, Christopher Cloud, and finally, DJB&H, he had decided to wipe the slate clean. "Alice and I just wanted to start all over, and just try to make it on our own," he said.* "I've changed my name to Tommy Fortune!" I quickly calculated in my mind as I listened, computing that this was at least the fifth time Tommy had decided to change his name and his persona.

The scene came alive for me as Tommy painted his word pictures. As though I were standing in the back, I could see him perched on his stool in the small basement club with only a dozen tables and fewer patrons. He was singing his heart out, delivering Hank Williams' "You Win Again" and other songs from his youth with the same passion he had emoted to an audience of twenty thousand fans only months before. On his picking hand, he wore a white leather glove. "Just to set me apart," he explained. And in between songs, he did his Dylan impressions and effortlessly streamed his charming patter to the patrons, just as he had done at KiKi's piano bar so many incarnations earlier.

Funds were low and times were tough for Tommy Fortune as he carried "Alice" to his job, night after night. Starting over from scratch was an exercise that would tax his endurance.

He was finding out that anonymity could be a cruel taskmaster, demanding both self-deprivation and humility, two traits that did not come easily for Tommy. Then, just at the lowest point of his hope, a customer in the coffee house who had recognized him brought some life-changing news.

"You're Tommy Boyce, aren't you? Congratulations on your new hit." Tommy smiled back, protecting his disguise but too curious to let it go. Seeing the confusion in Tommy's eyes, the Englishman continued. "Don't you know that you have a record in the top ten?" The popular British retro group, Showaddywaddy, had re-recorded his Curtis Lee hit, "Under the Moon of Love," and he was back on the charts again.

His cover blown, Boyce allowed Abe Somer to negotiate an exclusive writer's agreement for him with Rondor Music. With this he was able

---

* "Alice" was a reference to his guitar, which Tommy affectionately called "Alice Long."

to forgo the meager coffee house paychecks in favor of weekly advances from his new publisher while he waited for his Showaddywaddy royalties. "They got me writing with a new partner over here," he shared, one cold, foggy evening. "His name is Richard Hartley, but now he's going by Ricky Fame so we can be known as Fame & Fortune."

"Dig this, Hart. The other night, I was in a club and when I looked over, there was Queen, raising glasses and toasting me for my success." "The queen was in a nightclub, and she was toasting *you*?" I enquired suspiciously. "Not the Queen, you clown. Freddie Mercury, you know, Queen!"

One evening, we stopped by and visited Micky and his new wife, Trina, in their Cornwall Gardens flat. Micky had gotten a job with a British television network, directing children's programming and the pair seemed quite happy. Dolenz, Boyce & Hart laughed as we recapped highlights of our recent tour for Trina and reprised a song from our show in honor of Jones, "Oh yes, I wonder . . . what he's doin' tonight."

A few days later, Tommy accompanied me to the airport and shook my hand goodbye. I grabbed my bags and started for the gate. As I waited for my security check, I looked back across the lobby and witnessed one more time, a smiling Tommy Fortune. He was offering me his long-established salutation that, to me, always meant, "Hey, everything's cool." His two fists were held close to the chest and his thumbs were pointing straight up. It would be many years before I'd see him again.

Claudia's car pulled up behind mine on a small side street near the Sunset Strip. She parked, jumped into the front seat next to me and closed the door. It was so nice hearing Claudia's voice when she called unexpectedly the night before. "Hart, we need to talk," she said. For a moment, my heart leapt, thinking that, like me, maybe she was having second thoughts about our separation.

But as we sat in the Lincoln, she soon made it clear that she had arranged this meeting to talk about a financial settlement between the two of us. Claudia had found a West Hollywood condo that she wanted to buy and she needed the down payment. It was hard to listen to her talking about how excited she was about this new property in the same way she had once talked about our house on Woodrow Wilson.

The meeting didn't take long. I didn't need time to consider her offer; I wanted her to have whatever she needed. She acknowledged that I had probably contributed ninety percent of our income during our time together; still she hoped for half of the appreciation in the value of the house. Her face softened when I said, "Look, I never would have found the place without you. It was our house together and you deserve whatever makes you feel comfortable." A few minutes later, I watched her drive away, leaving me feeling lower than I had before she called.

CHAPTER 48

I Could Feel Her Mother
Go Limp Before I Finished

"Good morning, Self-Realization Fellowship" I heard a lady's voice announce cordially. I felt suddenly paralyzed and unable to say why I had called! After an uncomfortably long pause she volunteered, "How may I help you?" I realized I hadn't taken a breath since I dialed the number, so I inhaled and calmly responded, "I'm calling to sign up for the lessons to learn *Kriya Yoga.*" With a sympathetic smile in her voice, the lady with a British accent offered, "Just a moment and I'll connect you to Membership Services."

A year's study of Yogananda's SRF lessons would be required, I learned, before I'd be able to apply for the highest technique of Kriya Yoga. I provided my name and address, promised to send in the twelve dollars to cover the cost of printing and postage, and hung up the phone. I leaned back in my high-back chair and watched the orioles playing in the eucalyptus trees through the window of my second-story office/library.

This morning, as I had slipped through the lacy curtains that separate sub-consciousness from the waking world, something had made me think about the present year, 1978, and the fact that it had been an entire decade since the first time I read Paramahansa Yogananda's *Autobiography of a Yogi.* I had felt then an immediate soul intuition that here was a man who had an intimate relationship with God, and one who could actually lead me down the same path he had followed to find Him.

A thousand thoughts raced through my mind as the leaves gently swayed in the midmorning breeze. I wondered how I could have let ten years go by without signing up for the lessons that I was sure would improve my life-long striving to live a more spiritual life. Was it because of my fantasy: that I would one day leave this materialistic West and find the meaning of life directly from the lips of some holy man in a snow-capped Himalayan cave?

Was it because I was afraid that I would totally fail for the first time in my adult life? "No," came the inner reply, "It's been years since I was afraid of failing at anything." Then, not wanting to face it head on, the truth sat down anyway and looked me straight in the eyes. "I wasn't ready to do the work!" Well, I'd asked for the truth and it hit home hard. My delay could only be blamed on the fact that I wasn't committed, disciplined, or sincere enough to fulfill my end of the bargain. I was nearing forty and still looking for fulfillment in all the wrong places. Was I really willing to change? Well, at least now I had taken my first step.

♥

One of the closest moments I ever had with my father happened a few weeks later. "Yogananda says that Kriya will actually rearrange the cells of the brain by working with subtle electric energies in the spine," I quoted. Dad had arrived on the weekend, and that night he was visibly stimulated by this kitchen conversation. After a few minutes he said, "It's been years since I've been able to talk to anyone like this." I smiled and continued, "He says that our habits have created "grooves" in the brain that make us behave in certain ways, even when we know we shouldn't."

"I really am excited about the ancient yoga techniques that I'm learning in the lessons," I told my father. "But, the intimidating part for me right now is what Yogananda calls *yama-niyama*. The foundation of this path, he said, would be the moral and spiritual precepts expounded by all religions." I knew that even Dad could see that my current lifestyle wasn't living up to the guru's how-to-live guidance. Although it seemed far away from my present capacity for accomplishment, I felt a knowing intuition gnawing away in my conscience that, sooner or later, I would have to do the work that would start to take me closer to that ultimate realization.

♥

Barry was sprawled on the floor as I riffed on the Hammond B-3 I had installed next to my bed. "I've probably released twenty-five singles over the years," I mused as I played. "But except for Boyce & Hart, I've never recorded an album." "Hey, you sounded pretty good on that song we were working on last night," Barry encouraged. "Why not go for it?" We immediately began amassing songs for what would become *The First Bobby Hart Solo Album*.

Serendipitously, Teddy Randazzo pulled into my driveway the following week in his Winnebago. He was needing time and space from an East Coast divorce and I invited him to move in for an extended stay at the popular Woodrow Wilson heartbreak hotel. Bobby Weinstein flew out for a couple of weeks and we wrote songs together that ended up on records that Teddy produced with the Stylistics, on my solo LP or on both.

Now, with a wealth of material, I bought a block of time at a small studio in West Hollywood called Star Track and put together a great band that included two old friends. Vince Megna flew in from Milwaukee with his wife, Connie, to supply all the guitar parts while Larry Taylor, former Candy Store Prophet, was there to contribute his trademark bass. To top off the cake, I asked my friends Sydney and Marin to join us for the background parts.

Barry and I decided that we'd like to break in the material in front of a live audience before heading into the recording studio, so he got on the phone and booked us all for a two week engagement in a small club in Van Nuys. It would be a chance to get the band tight and help us narrow down our song list by gauging our patron's reactions to particular pieces. It was like the old days at the Prelude, but instead of twist music, it was seventies urban R&B–pop, and we had a great fortnight groovin' the nights away in the Valley.

There was a low-hanging fog the night I pulled into Claudia's driveway. She had sold the condo and traded up to a fixer-upper house in Laurel Canyon. I slid a cassette of my finished album into her new Bang & Olufsen stereo, and she sat down with me on the carpet to concentrate.

She had tears in her eyes when the music of the last cut finally faded to an end. In the silence, she looked up and said, "Hart, I'm so proud of you."

♥

On a beautiful Monday morning in late September, Claudia stopped by the house unexpectedly. Right away, I noticed a change in her demeanor. Over the last four years, her party life had taken its toll. But she had put a little weight back on, she was clear eyed, and she looked good. Claudia told me that she had been studying and taking her acting more seriously. "And, I've made up my mind to break it off with Stan for good," she volunteered.

I knew that she had been living with Stan Herman at his seaside house in Malibu off and on for a couple of months now. She had resisted his advances all these years, and now the wealthy real estate broker had finally won his prize. It was not a good match. I kept hearing there were too many parties. Claudia had complained to mutual friends that Stan was controlling and possessive. But now for the first time in years, I could see that Claudia was fully committed to turning her life around.

"I bet you thought you'd never hear me say this, Hart, but I've come to you for some help." It was not the old Claudia that I knew. "I've cleaned up my act; I'm trying to do all the right things, but I just don't know what to do," she said. "All those years I watched you meditating and trying to become better person. I just couldn't admit to myself that you knew something I didn't. But I'm ready to listen, and I know you can help me." There was a sincerity and a pleading in her eyes. I knew that it had taken a lot of courage for her to break through the stone wall of her lifelong resistance to religion in any form and to ask for help from any man.

I held her close for a few moments and waited for her breathing to calm. "Why don't you go into the meditation room for a few minutes and just watch your breath," I suggested. "What do you mean *watch* it?" "I mean, don't try to control it in any way. Just observe, as if you were watching someone else breathing. It'll slow your mind down so you can concentrate on one thought at a time."

Claudia looked at me for a long pause. Then she walked over to the familiar little room under the stairway and sat down on the meditation mat. I closed the door and said a prayer of peace and harmony, visualizing her in God's light as I waited. In ten minutes time, she opened the door and seemed to float over to where I waited on the bed. There was a miraculous serenity on her face that I had never seen. She had obviously had a deep experience and she didn't want to talk.

"Paper and pencil," she whispered. I found Claudia something to write with and she spent the next ten minutes transcribing her thoughts. When she finished, she handed me the several pages, looked in my eyes, and murmured a soft thank you. A few minutes later, Claudia hugged me a heartfelt goodbye and walked out the door. I listened to her car head down the driveway and out into the street. Then, I looked down at the journal that she had placed in my hands. It began "Hart, you knew. You always knew."

♥

On October 3rd, the phone rang in my downstairs apartment. Barry and I had been listening as a talented singer/songwriter named John Battan played us a tape of some of his compositions. "Is this Bobby Hart?" a female voice inquired. "Yes it is. Who's calling?" "I'm one of the secretaries here at *Playboy*," she answered. "Mr. Hefner asked me to call to make sure you knew that Claudia Jennings was killed this morning in an automobile accident."

A shudder of cold anguish shot through my body. The shock of the news instantly drained the strength from my legs and I quickly sat down. I heard the voice on the phone say, "Mr. Hefner said I should call you first, and he asked if you would please contact the family." "Ye . . . yes, I will, I stammered with a dry mouth." I knew the voice was continuing but it seemed to be coming from some distant and indistinguishable source, and I was no longer listening.

John asked if he could do anything and then respectfully packed up and left the house. Barry stood at the window gazing at nothing for several minutes—probably in as much shock as I was in. "What can I do?" Barry asked. I just shook my head. Barry gathered up some papers. I heard the door close and his car drive away.

It had been nearly four years since Claudia and I had ended our romantic relationship and life had moved on. But she was a treasured friend, and I had never envisioned a day when she wouldn't be in this world. As for myself, I had taken longer to heal, and the grieving that I had done during those years was as real as the loss I was feeling on this day. Somewhere in the depths of my mind, I had deeply believed that with a little more time, she would turn her life around and fulfill the dreams of success and happiness that were her rightful destiny.

As I felt the warmth returning to my face, I carefully stood up and turned toward my meditation room. As I sat cross-legged in lotus position, I tried in vain to still my whirling mind. So I began a practice of slow and controlled deep breathing, broadcasting thoughts of love and goodwill to this girl I had loved for ten years, as I visualized her making a peaceful transition into that land beyond our dreams.

She had seen the sun, rising low over the calm ocean on her left, as she drove her car north on Pacific Coast Highway. She hadn't slept, since she had been up all night with two girlfriends, bolstering herself with their moral support for the task ahead. She would drive to Stan's, gather up her belongings and drive away without an altercation. Near Topanga Canyon Boulevard, she must have dozed off. The car crossed over into the oncoming lanes and was struck by a large truck. The next morning the *L.A. Times* ran an obituary. The autopsy had shown no trace of drugs or alcohol in her blood.

"I'm so sorry to have to tell you this." I could feel her mother, Joan, go limp before I finished my sentence. But, like the pillar of strength she had always been, she asked the details and then said she would call me back after she had notified Claudia's dad and sisters. Later, Joan called to say that the family was asking if I would make all the arrangements. "Could we have a little memorial at your place? We'll fly out as soon as we can."

On a sunny October day, as gentle breezes blew the fragrance of pittosporum blossoms like incense through the mountain air, three hundred
mourners made a pilgrimage up my driveway. Movie stars, bit actors, girlfriends, boyfriends, doctors, lawyers, gaffers, and grips stood on a green
grassy terrace to say goodbye to a girl whose soul had touched each of
their lives in extraordinary ways. Jerry and Joan Chesterton, and their
other daughters, Julie and Connie, stood in ashen disbelief to be standing
at the end of the coming-of-age dramatic tragedy of a life that had seemed
so promising for the young Mimi that they remembered.

The service was informal. Claudia's close friends were there: Sally,
Marcia, Allison, Keith, Frank, Barry, waiting for their turn to speak their
tributes, along with others who remembered her from a singular kindness she might have expressed in passing. Marilyn Grabowski, Playboy
executive and close friend, repeated what she had said to me many times,
"I never knew anyone who didn't like her. And, once you were Claudia's
friend, you were her friend for life." Bobby, Bret, and a half dozen of their
school friends stood silently on the sidelines, staring at the ground.

Stan Herman made a brief appearance and then slipped away. The
previous evening, Julie completed the task that Claudia had begun on
her last day. When Stan opened the door of his Malibu beach house, she
bravely walked in and packed up all of Claudia's things. There were three
party dresses, some jeans and sweaters, headshots and snapshots of family,
both Chesterton and Hart. And, hiding in the bottom of a pasteboard
box, was a scratchy acetate record in a tattered sleeve bearing her picture
and the song title, "Claudia Jennings."

CHAPTER 49

A One-Two Punch of Life-Changing Events in Three Days

As I eased my car to a stop, I could feel the winds of change breathing inside me just as surely as the sweet scented breezes that blew through the stately old wisteria trees on Mount Washington. From 600 feet above Los Angeles, the lights of the city sparkled in the cool air like starlight on water. With respect for the incredible spiritual legacy surrounding me, I walked toward the administration building where Paramahansa Yogananda had lived for so many years, admiring the well-cared-for flower beds artistically placed throughout the manicured, park-like grounds of the International Headquarters of Self-Realization Fellowship.

As I climbed one step at a time up to the elegant walnut and oak entrance of this 1910 former grand hotel, I thought of a fact I had once read: "The steepest streets in all of Los Angeles are on Mount Washington." "What an appropriate metaphor!" I mused, "My path to peace has certainly been a hard and steep ascent." Although Mount Washington lives in tropical perpetual greenery, I reflected on the sacred bond it shares with the meditation caves of the frozen, snow-capped Himalayas.

I had finally applied, and tonight, February 1st, 1980, after a year of study and practice, I had come to be initiated into the higher technique of Kriya Yoga meditation, along with about two dozen other eager applicants. I entered the elegant and historic lobby and was greeted by a smiling receptionist who told me that the sacred ceremony would take place in the adjoining chapel. Before going in, I was drawn to the larger-than-life painting of Paramahansa Yogananda on the lobby wall, opposite the chapel entrance. I felt a wondrous emotion of love and connection as I gazed at the portrait, a comforting feeling like the one I had when my parents would come to assist me when I needed help as a child.

My attention was broken by the gentle sound of a gong being struck by a monastic. I was invited to come into the chapel for the Kriya Yoga initiation. As recommended, I had brought the traditional offerings from the disciple to the guru. I held a fresh flower, a ripe mango, and my financial donation in a sealed envelope. I knew that in this initiation, I would be taking a vow of discipleship to the guru. I looked forward to showing my gratitude, respect, dedication, and support by placing these offerings on the altar during the three-hour ceremony.

Back in my driveway I put the car into park and turned off the key. I felt such relief that I had overcome my mindset that I wasn't worthy to be a disciple of this holy man, and had finally begun to take charge of my unwillingness to change. I sat behind the steering wheel for a long time, squeezing my sandalwood beads tightly, in reaction to the intensity of my prayer. I held them close as I prayed that I would never lose my faith in God, in love, or in myself. Finally, I relaxed and enjoyed the deep, soothing sensations in my body and spine. In this calm moment, my mind remembered the lyrics to a song I wrote with Tommy years before:

> *It's all happening on the inside. Get to know yourself you'll be surprised what you might find. You know, somebody told me what life was all about. It all happens from the inside out. Come on and get to know yourself. Get to know yourself. It's all happening on the inside.*

The second, in a one-two punch of life-changing moments, happened only three days later.

♥

We shook hands, and as I looked in her eyes, she was looking back with what appeared to be a mystified expression on her face. It was as though she were thinking about something else rather than our introduction.

The echoing sound of Terry Costa's words saying, "Oh, MaryAnn, this is Bobby Hart," faded quickly away, along with my peripheral vision. All I could see now was this stunningly beautiful face.

Slowly, her expression turned into an enchanting smile that instantly grabbed all of my senses. It was sincere, sweet and slightly shy, but not timid. Her long blonde hair cascaded well beyond her gently suntanned shoulders, and her creamy smooth skin was radiantly youthful. I found myself frozen in time as I looked deeply into her shining dark eyes. Truly caught off guard by her innate, feminine poise, I was helplessly falling into the endless layers of their playfulness, charm, and mystery.

My dazed mind spun wildly, like a tornado in a junkyard. I knew there was little time for small talk. In a moment, we would be moving on up the steps and into a crowded house where commanding MaryAnn's full attention would require a boldness that did not fit my style. As I tried to stay in the moment, I felt myself ease back into bachelor autopilot, abandoning any thoughts of witty conversation and relaxing into my natural persona of quiet confidence. I packed every emotion and feeling that was cascading through me at the moment into a sincere smile and broadcast it through my eyes as I offered the simple words, "It was nice to meet you."

A couple of days earlier, Don Costa had called. "Hey Bobby, I just built a great studio behind my house. Why don't you come over and check it out?" On a nippy February evening, I ventured into the exclusive Trousdale area in the hills above Beverly Hills, with what might have been described as an entourage. In fact, it was just three friends: my sound engineer, Joe Cannizario; my writing partner, Barry Richards; and Don Graham, who was doing independent promotion of my records.

As Costa showed off his state-of-the-art control room, his wife, Terry, and the striking blonde, who had been writing songs with her in the main studio, walked through on their way to the house. It was the perfect cue for Don to invite us into his home for a drink. As I followed this vision in the white angora sweater and form-fitting brown leather pants up the steps to the Costa living room, Terry suddenly stopped, turned around and made this life-changing introduction.

Up early the next morning, I held off as long as I could and then I called my friend, Terry Costa. "What's the story on MaryAnn?" The reply was encouraging, "She's just getting out of a long relationship, but yes, she's single." Each succeeding morning, I would extend my standing invitation, "Why don't you stop by later. Maybe we could write something. Oh, and see if MaryAnn wants to come along." One afternoon later that week, they accepted. Soon the visits were occurring daily, and the time spent in song writing was giving way to fun and socializing.

It was a shadowy California evening, the kind when winter steals the light away too soon before the moon has time to rise. I had finally asked MaryAnn out on a formal date. A light drizzle was falling as we drove to the small, Italian restaurant. I broke out my umbrella when we arrived and escorted her in, enjoying the feeling of being closer to her than I had ever dared to be in drier weather. I looked across the table as we shared ourselves in conversation and the thought occurred to me, "This might be the most beautiful woman I've ever met."

I took a risk and told MaryAnn that when we were first introduced, I had seen a look in her eyes that I didn't understand. "It was as though you felt like you already knew me," I ventured. A knowing smile crept over her face. "Something extraordinary happened to me that night," she said. "When we shook hands, I saw and felt a flash of light that enveloped both of us and I felt a strong electric current. It instantaneously rushed down from my brain and into our hands, and I thought to myself, 'Wow! What was *that*?'"

As MaryAnn took a sip of wine at the end of her story, I thought of a phrase that Yogananda had used, "friends once more to be," and wished that I had been attuned enough to have shared her deep experience. Unfortunately, my earth-bound consciousness was still rendering me numb to those kinds of subtle energies. The wonder I was feeling at that moment was much more physical, my attention having been immovably locked onto the perfect outer form of this stunning twenty-nine-year-old beauty.

"Well, I was raised on the East Coast," she offered in answer to my question. "We were Roman Catholics, and I still go to church every

Sunday. God has always been a part of my life, but I guess you might say I'm more spiritual than religious." "I was a Protestant," I replied, not wanting to risk turning her off by talking about my guru on our first date. Still, I probably went further with opening up about my tightly-held spiritual life than I ever had with anyone else. There were so many very special things about this lady, and one of them was how totally comfortable I felt being with her.

In the candlelight her compassionate eyes became like pools of still, dark water. I could see a trace of sadness there, behind her sweet smile and friendly voice. Like me, she had experienced her share of life's disappointments. She talked about her need to finally find lasting happiness and to be free to discover her own, true path that would take her there. She wanted to be open and available to new possibilities. She believed that it was possible to have a relationship where she could give and receive unconditional love and unconditional loyalty, and she had total faith that what she was looking for existed. As she spoke, I listened better than I had ever listened in my life.

After dinner, we came back to my house and I played her my new single that was scheduled for release the following week. I knew that MaryAnn was a songwriter and that she must have a keen ear for music because Terry had told me that she had worked as a song screener, spotting potential hit songs for a major record producer and as a talent scout for a record label. So I was happy when she asked to hear my record over and over again, telling me how much she loved it. Later, as we stood softly talking on my front porch, I took her by the hand and led her down the steps to the red brick pool deck. There, under a sprawling jacaranda tree, in the misty aurora, MaryAnn and I shared our first kiss. It was St. Valentine's Day.

CHAPTER 50

I'm Surprised You Guys
Don't Suffer from Whiplash!

I had asked MaryAnn, "Would you mind if I meditate for a few minutes before we leave? We may be out late tonight." "One of the things I find attractive about you is your spiritual side," she said. "I really like the fact that you're so regular with your meditation practices. As we talked, a subtle and unique foundation of trust began growing between us. MaryAnn disclosed some of the dynamics of her childhood, teenage years, and her former marriage, and for the first time I felt comfortable enough to venture into areas that I had always withheld from others. I talked about my personal life from the beginning and was startled at what I heard myself saying. But MaryAnn's gentle encouragement, compassion, and openness had made it feel safe and natural.

♥

"Dad! She's taking all our furniture out of the house." Bobby Jr. was worried. "She put all our stuff out in the driveway," he reported excitedly. "It's okay, Bobby," I said with an understanding smile. "I think it's time we turned over a new leaf. Don't you think we could use a woman's touch in the house? I moved the furniture out into the driveway so we could have a garage sale this weekend."

The boys had an uneasy relationship with their new housemother. They were leery that everything was going to change, and of course, they were right. MaryAnn had a gift for style and interior design. She pulled up the old carpet to expose the beautiful hardwood floors. She had all the rooms painted, using bold but classic colors. On an early trip together to New York, she found a seventeenth century French armoire and had it shipped out West. She filled the house with other beautiful antiques and bought new furniture pieces that fit tastefully into each room.

There were other changes. MaryAnn had also filled our house with her aura of dignity and her innate sense of right and wrong behavior. After being awakened several times by late night visits from Bobby and Bret's crew, who would let themselves in and out at all hours, MaryAnn suggested that, for the first time since I moved into the house, I might want to have some keys made to fit the door locks. MaryAnn's process for making a house a home seemed to calm my teenagers' behavior when they were in the house, and influence their friends to invite them to hangout more in other places that may have been purposefully less peaceful.

♥

One reason I looked forward to summer every year was that my mom and dad would always come over for a visit. Dad was a "Jack of all trades," and there was no leak he could not fix nor home improvement desire he could not envision and craft. But now, we were also relating on a whole other level as we freely shared our feelings about God and what it means to live a spiritual life.

At Mom's urging, Dad had come to stay with me for a few weeks back in October when Claudia died. I knew that they were concerned about me, and it had been comforting to have him around during a hard time in my life. He had accompanied me to the morgue for the sad and uncomfortable task of identifying her remains. He had strongly suggested to some of my longtime houseguests that they give me some time and space so that I could do my grieving in private. I was sad to see him have to get back to Phoenix, but it was the holidays, and so I hugged him good-bye at the small Burbank airport and handed him a copy of Yogananda's autobiography. Now he was back, and he couldn't wait to talk about it.

"I think the book is great," he told me as he held a river rock in place for me to cement into our new garden wall. "The only thing I'm not so sure about is this reincarnation business," Dad admitted. "It's quite a departure from a lifetime of hearing about heaven and hell," he said with a deeply sincere look. "Well," I ventured, looking into his childlike eyes, "if we have to reap what we sow, isn't it comforting that through God's grace we have as many lives as we need to free our souls forever from the law of cause and effect." I could see Dad was ready for another trowel of mud, and I responded without a word.

He wrinkled his brow and I could tell he was thinking about it. Finally, he concluded, "It makes me feel like the universe is a whole lot bigger and more complicated than I can imagine. And the whole thing still sounds a little far-fetched to me." "It's not really important," I conceded, "Not nearly as important as learning to love God.

♥

I got a nice surprise in March when Linda Ronstadt released a great new version of "Hurt So Bad," which went top ten. The song was featured in her current album as well as the greatest hits collection that followed, and both LPs went platinum. I released two more singles as an artist as Barry and I continued to write together. We supplied the lyrics for a best-of English language album with Philippine legend, Freddie Aguilar, and had top-ten records. My continuing success kept my name in the trade magazines and the spike in royalties came along at the perfect time.

♥

"I'm surprised you guys don't suffer from whiplash, the way your heads are spinning around." MaryAnn's joking comment was aimed at Barry and me as the three of us motored down Sunset Boulevard one afternoon on the way to lunch. There was never a shortage of attractive girls along the Boulevard, and from my bachelorhood days with Tommy, up until this present moment, I had never even considered curbing my habit of savoring the beauty of each and every one as I passed them by. "You're bobbing your heads from side to side like windshield wipers," she said with a half-smile.

I was a little taken aback, not so much at MaryAnn's frank observations, but by the momentary realization that this compulsion had become such an automatic part of my behavior that I no longer even noticed that I was doing it, let alone how distasteful it must have seemed to my new love. I smiled and said nothing, but my mind was already plunging deep into a river of clever defensive rationalization.

I told myself, "it's a perfectly innocent little habit and it's been with me for so long that it's just part of who I am by now. But moments of introspection were unavoidable every time I would sit to meditate, and over time, my love for MaryAnn prompted a sincere desire to bring my behavior into harmony with my core beliefs.

I had known for years that changing one's self for the better was a major tenet of Yogananda's teachings. Now I realized I could no longer get by on my commitment to meditation techniques while ignoring the outer work. It was back to the foundation of yoga— learning to behave. Of course, deciding to do it was only the beginning. But I finally had the answer to the question that had puzzled me ever since my first experiment in philosophical reading back in Las Vegas: I hadn't been trying *nearly* hard enough.

♥

MaryAnn looked beautiful as the candlelight from the sparkling red and green table centerpiece caught her face. Her peaceful expression seemed to reflect the same emotions that I was feeling as we held hands, basking in the warm glow of the Christmas season.

We were at the home of MaryAnn's friend, Nancy Sinatra. And for us, the highlight of her gala party came after dinner as some of the guests gathered around the grand piano in her living room to share some traditional Christmas music and eggnog. MaryAnn and I watched spellbound as two iconic vocalists began to sing a duet, crooning the words of one of our favorite holiday songs. The first was, the American pop singer who Judy Garland called "the best jazz singer in the world," Jack Jones.

Jones was joined by the man who had co-written (with Bob Wells) the song they were beginning to sing, "The Christmas Song." Of course, it was none other than "The Velvet Fog" himself, Mel Torme. Hand in hand, MaryAnn and I savored the moment, lost in the spirit of our first Christmas together as two of the world's most celebrated voices blended to form the words, "Chestnuts roasting on an open fire . . . Jack Frost nipping at your nose . . ."

WILLPOWER

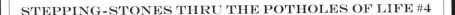

(1) MORE THAN ONE "YOU"?

I USED TO WONDER why I would so often rebel <u>against</u> doing the things I knew would be beneficial for me. I've sometimes felt that there were really more than one "me" living inside this body of mine. There was one who said, "I really do have to lose some weight this week." But then only an hour or two later, this other "me" told me "I've had a stressful morning. I owe it to myself to sit down and enjoy this doughnut with my coffee." So, if when I say "I," I mean the one who really wants to lose some pounds, then who is this other self who thinks it owes itself a doughnut?

(2) SECOND NATURE

RESEARCHERS IN THE FIELDS OF EVOLUTIONARY BIOLOGY AND BRAIN FUNCTION are now explaining mind as not single but many, and suggesting that "will" is just how we select which "me" (differing mind) we allow to call the shots at any given moment. Without will power, we just do the easy, immediately gratifying thing, whatever comes to us <u>second nature.</u> So if we call indulging our whims our <u>second</u> nature, what is our <u>first nature</u>?

(3) YOUR OWN HIGHER SELF

THE INDIAN YOGIS tell us that if you go deep enough, at your core there really <u>is</u> only one "you," your own "Higher Self, or the soul." They say that this is who we were meant to be and in fact who we really are, and that all those other selves are grafts on our souls, welded on by habit and tolerated because of inertia. Your higher self is that Self who always remembers what you really want, the one who will support you in all the actions you should take to make your life the best it can be in the highest sense. And, training ourselves to stay in constant touch with our Higher Selves has been called the essence of yoga. Just remembering <u>what it is you really want</u> in the middle of each of those troublesome skirmishes, when one of your other "yous" is trying to rationalize some quick gratification, can start you on your journey toward the best you can be.

CHAPTER 51

I Don't Think God Hears
Me Anymore

MaryAnn was looking out the window, watching the rows of towering palm trees glide by as we cruised down Santa Monica Boulevard on our way to have lunch in Beverly Hills. She was softly singing a Diana Ross song. I was surprised by the soulful quality of her voice. To me, it reflected the same kind of honesty I had always responded to in artists like Alison Krauss, Loretta Lynn, or even Leota Kidd. "That was beautiful!" I said, as I turned left on Canon Drive. Awakened from her reverie, she turned to smile at me.

"I think I should take you into the studio sometime," I ventured one day in 1981. I could see that MaryAnn was intrigued by the idea, but she said thoughtfully, "I don't think so, Bobby. I've never sung anything professionally, and I know it's not as easy as it looks. I was married to a singer for seven years and even when you're successful, it's a real grind." A few days later, I brought it up again. "Do you really think you could make me sound good?" she asked. "No, Sweetie, *you* will make you sound good."

During my next meeting with Christian, I shared, "You know, Mary-Ann has a real commercial voice and I think I'm going make her my next production project." I knew that he probably thought the love light in my eyes was interfering with the sound waves in my ears and maybe even my professional judgment, but, as always, his support was unwavering. "I just brought back this really hooky song from Germany," he told me. "Let me play it for you. Maybe you'd want to write some English lyrics and see how MaryAnn sounds on it."

Within a few weeks, Christian had secured the American rights to the song and we were heading into the studio. When she heard the instrumental tracks for her record, MaryAnn was excited and inspired. Although it was her first time before a microphone, her sound was magic, and she worked like a trouper to achieve the professional performance that I knew she was capable of. We made a music video of "Tell Me Why," and when he returned from his next trip abroad, Christian brought with him an offer from Polygram Records in Europe. When she signed her first recording contract, she decided to use the professional name, MaryAnn Hart.

"Tell Me Why" quickly hit the charts in Germany, and Polygram set up a European promotion tour for her. When the producers of Germany's premier television extravaganza, Music Laden, discovered the stunning beauty on the cover shot of her hit single, MaryAnn was promptly invited to appear on the popular program which was beamed weekly to millions of music fans all over Europe.

We were picked up by a Mercedes limousine and driven to a beautiful old hotel in the center of a lushly landscaped park in Baden. A small crowd of fans was waiting for MaryAnn when we came out to leave for the television studio, and she considerately autographed all their records and photos. She did a great job performing her record, and after the taping, was congratulated by some of her fellow performers who included Diana Ross, Trini Lopez, The Gatlin Brothers, and the English rockers, Bananarama. When her follow-up single also charted in Europe, the show flew her in for a return appearance, and Canyon Records signed MaryAnn to an album deal for Japan. It was like a blast from the past for me to watch her excitement as she experienced success on her own in the music business.

♥

"I'm going in to meditate. Why don't you say your prayers while I'm gone?" I ventured one summer evening. "Oh, I don't think God hears me anymore," was MaryAnn's forlorn reply. During our months together, she had been curious, and then intrigued watching me enter my little meditation room "cave" morning and night, and she had always been supportive.

But as she sat in prayer on this particular night, something akin to a miracle occurred, and after that everything changed.

"You won't believe what happened to me while you were meditating," she said softly as I came back into the room. I could see MaryAnn still sitting on the edge of the bed, but the despondency that I had witnessed just thirty minutes earlier had evaporated like morning mist in the sunlight. A peaceful smile was radiating from her face, which seemed to be bathed in the glow of an inner light. "Tonight, God showed me that He really *was* listening," she said.

Although she considers the details of her experience too sacred to share, I'm convinced that she had a profound spiritual encounter that night. From that moment on, MaryAnn was on a resolute quest to find God. The next morning, she began reading Yogananda's *Autobiography of a Yogi*, and only a few days later she filled out an application to begin receiving the SRF lessons. Within a year MaryAnn had taken Kriya initiation and was thriving on the spiritual instructions in the Master's writings.

Not since I first teamed up with Tommy Boyce twenty years earlier, had I been blessed to have a partner with whom to share the important goals of my life. Now, just like then, my partner's enthusiasm was making it so much easier for me to become re-inspired and raise my own efforts to a new level. This time, instead of redoubling my energy in the pop music field, I had the perfect environment to become more serious about my spiritual commitment. Being steady at my meditations had been a noble start, but now I needed to bring every aspect of my life into harmony with what I saw as a much higher goal.

Number one on my list of changes had to be my unwanted habit of placing my attention on every pretty face I saw. I picked up the lessons and began re-reading them with new interest, this time searching for help *with* (not a way around) my commitment to change. I began to understand how this lack of self-control, because of my strong habits, was robbing me of any chance of ever exercising free choice. I was acting more like a puppet dangling from the strings of habit than the child of God that I knew I was. I saw that without free choice, I had become a victim of inertia, unable to make the life decisions that would eventually bring me the peace, joy and happiness that I knew I wanted.

And for the first time, I recognized and actually became grateful for another benefit I was receiving from my new partnership. Every day, MaryAnn was silently but instantly reflecting my image back to me and allowing me to see myself magnified to full size through the perspective of her love and respect for me.

I picked up the lessons and read where Yogananda had written that in the battle of life, one has to learn to be a warrior and a hero. Self-discipline, he had said, was "a momentary bitter difficulty" that leads to greater happiness. But, if willpower wasn't enough, what I needed now was some effective armament worthy of the fight. One by one, the pieces began to fall in place for me like a jigsaw puzzle. The guru said that in addition to volition, habit can be outwitted by consistent replacement of bad actions with good ones and by the use of reason.

I began to practice catching each outmoded habitual action early enough to substitute one of more noble design. Feeling new confidence, I set out on a lifelong quest to develop a new paradigm of moment-to-moment awareness of my thoughts and actions.

Now I was ready to bring in the big guns of reason. My own wasn't developed enough, so I tried adopting the Master's reasoning: A stubborn, unwanted action can often be avoided by thinking about its likely consequences before you do it, mentally following it through to its logical, misery-making conclusion.

It was just one small habit, one that most men in today's world might consider to be just perfectly natural behavior. But for me, it was the beginning of making myself into the man I wanted to be. And, it wasn't just girl watching. Over time, it became easy to identify lots of habits that I had previously been unaware of, that now I could see were blocking my spiritual efforts. As I began to prevail at changing this one strong metal habit, I realized that, one by one, I could succeed at taking on all the unwanted others. It became possible to envision a future of infinite possibility. I embarked on an arduous campaign of trying to "shift my tastes" from inferior to more superior, distinguished pleasures.

♥

"Doesn't Self-Realization Fellowship have churches?" MaryAnn had often voiced her appreciation that I attended Catholic mass with her every Sunday, but had never asked about a church for Yogananda's services. "Sure, I think there are several of them in town," I quickly replied. "You wanna go check one out next week?"

A few minutes before eleven the next Sunday morning, MaryAnn and I were welcomed by an usher into the SRF Temple on Sunset Boulevard. The small chapel with its sparkling white walls, golden lotus sconces, and royal blue carpets gave off an aura of simple elegance. There were traditional American church features, such as stained glass windows and chandeliers, but the focal point was a gold leafed Indian-style altar. We were both pleased to see that one of the six pictures featured on the altar was a familiar Heinrich Hoffman likeness of the Lord Jesus Christ. We both felt deeply moved and connected to this unpretentious and straightforward Church of All Religions.

Within only days, we were making individual and collective decisions very differently than before. We noticed that our wine bill had decreased to zero, not by conscious effort, but because we had discovered that we wouldn't be able to meditate well after indulging in our usual glasses with dinner. The enthusiasm we had for our new lifestyle came from the joy we were feeling from applying the advanced yogic techniques and the principles of life that we had learned from Paramahansa Yogananda.

♥

"We've got a big decision to make." MaryAnn was looking at me pensively over breakfast one morning a Schwab's. I knew what she meant. She had signed with a personal manager to direct her budding career, and the centerpiece of his blueprint to break his new artist in the States was an extensive tour of the country that would include both promotional and in-person performances. In normal circumstances, it would have been happy news, but at this juncture of our lives, the prospect of taking the next giant step to international stardom was presenting a dilemma.

We were being asked to leave our vital support system behind to re-enter a familiar life that we both knew would be a major distraction, leaving us with little time for our new spiritual practices. Yogananda had written, "Environment is stronger than willpower." The dark cloud of indecision that had been following us around for weeks, finally bust open on a Monday morning when MaryAnn suggested talking with a monastic counselor.

"This is Brother Anandamoy. May I help you?" His voice was immediately recognizable from the many lecture tapes that we had been listening to for weeks at home and in our car. Patiently, he listened to our long story of MaryAnn's recording success and of the conflict we were feeling since we had been faced with her upcoming tours. Finally, he asked simply, "Do you have to do it?" "Financially, you mean?" I queried. "Yes, do you have to go on tour to make a living?" "No," we responded in unison. "Then I think you have your answer." We smiled at each other as we hung up the phone, letting out a harmony of deep sighs of relief. Although I had come to share the same conclusion independently, it had been Mary-Ann's decision to make.

MaryAnn handed me a cup of tea and began, "You know, one of my biggest blessings was proving to myself that I could actually have hit records as a singer. I guess in the back of my mind, it had been one of my desires since childhood, and I'm so thankful to you and Master that I had the opportunity to fulfill it. I got to look glamorous, I got to sign autographs, I got to be treated like a star. But I'm fully aware of everything else that goes with it, and I don't feel like I'm giving anything up. What we need right now is spiritual grounding." I looked up and MaryAnn's eyes were blazing with excitement. "This is exactly where I want to be," she said.

YOUR UNIQUE ROLE IN LIFE

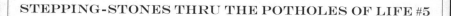

(1) LIFE AS A SYMPHONY

I like to look at life as one big symphony with God as the composer and director. To me it's obvious that the Power that ordains the exact orbits of atoms and planets would also plan a unique part to be played by each human soul in this Divine orchestra. Our first assignment is to IDENTIFY OUR OWN DIVINELY DESIGNED ROLE AND LEARN TO PLAY IT TO RAVE REVIEWS, not from our fellow musicians, but from the divine Conductor.

(2) FINDING YOUR UNIQUE ROLE

Ancient Sanskrit texts tell us IT'S BETTER TO PLAY YOUR OWN PART POORLY THAN TO PLAY SOMEONE ELSE'S WELL, whether performing an inspiring solo or a soft note in the background. As souls, we are already perfect, but often our upstart egos take over and start playing heavy metal in the middle of the Master Composer's magnificent arrangement. Playing the Conductor's vision, rather than our own, aligns us with His great power and adds His perfection to each of our performances.

(3) START FROM RIGHT WHERE YOU ARE

Pay close attention to YOUR OWN NATURAL SELF-EVOLVING PROPENSITIES. Try getting together with other like-minded positive energy people. Initiative is the power to create. Ask yourself, "Have I tried to create something that no one else has done?" Remember that the yardstick for measuring whether you've found your rightful place in the symphony of life is not wealth or power, but happiness.

(4) SERVICE TO OTHERS

Kindness is a natural reaction when we realize that we are all struggling with our parts. And performing your part well is in itself a service to all the other musicians. It can save the entire Divine symphony from sounding out of tune.

CHAPTER 52

How Can You Love God If You Never Think About Him?

"**B**obby, the academy wants to nominate "Over You" but there's some kind of procedural hang up." I was making song demos at the MCA recording studio on the Universal movie lot when I got the call from Lester Sill at Screen Gems Music. "I'm gonna have Betty Buckley call you and fill you in on the details tonight. Let's see if we can't get this straightened out."

In 1982 I had written a theme song called "Over You" with Austin Roberts, who was now a contract writer with Screen Gems, for their critically acclaimed new motion picture *Tender Mercies*. Robert Duvall plays an alcoholic, has-been country singer who finds his way back to recovery with the help of a young widow and her son. He has an ex-wife, played by Betty Buckley, who is also a country singer, and every time they cut to her in a nightclub scene, you hear her singing our song.

That evening, as promised, I got a call at my home from Betty Buckley. I knew she was a Broadway star, but I didn't realize until later that at that moment, she was starring as Grizabella in the Broadway production of *Cats*, a role which would win her the Tony award that year for Best Featured Actress in a Musical. It's even possible that she was calling me from backstage at the Winter Garden Theater.

Ms. Buckley's voice was cordial but concerned, and she was all business. "I've heard from some friends that several members of the nominating committee for the Best Song category have seen the movie and they love your song. I can't believe that nobody has submitted it!" My silence must have betrayed the fact that I had no idea what she was talking about.

Ms. Buckley went on but this time more slowly, like a second grade teacher might explain to a first grade student. "If you want your song to be eligible to be nominated for an Academy Award, the rules specify that the composers or the publisher must formally submit it to the academy for consideration. And the deadline has already passed," she said in a tone of exasperation. "Maybe if you write a letter explaining your ignorance, well, there's a slight chance they might make an exception."

The next morning, Lester had the contrite letter of explanation hand delivered to the MCA studio where I was recording. I signed it and sent it off by messenger to the Academy of Motion Picture Arts and Sciences. A couple of months later, when the Oscar nominations were announced, *Tender Mercies* got five: Best Picture, Best Actor, Best Director, Best Original Screenplay and sure enough, there it was: Best Original Song in a Motion Picture—"Over You"—from *Tender Mercies*—Composers: Austin Roberts & Bobby Hart."

On the afternoon of April 9th, 1983 the movie studio sent a limo to our Hollywood Hills home, and at about one o'clock MaryAnn and I rolled out of our driveway and headed down the winding narrow streets. We picked up Austin and his wife, Janet, at their hotel and cruised toward downtown Los Angeles on the Hollywood Freeway. As we approached the Dorothy Chandler Pavilion, we got in line with the dozens of other limousines and inched our way toward the red carpet.

"You can't love God if you never think about Him." The thought inexplicably resounded in my mind as we relaxed into our plush velvet theater seats. I had been trying to think of Him more ever since my first reading of the great spiritual classic *The Practice of the Presence of God* by the seventeenth century French Carmelite Monk, Brother Lawrence. He had taken the Apostle Paul's admonition "Pray without ceasing" literally and attained an exalted life of peace and tranquility by learning to never lose the thought of God.

Learning to commune with the Infinite, not just while you're on your knees, but while performing every profound or menial task of life, was a noble ideal and one that I aspired to. I was, however, finding this to be a momentous challenge. I bought a sports watch and set its alarm to go off every fifteen minutes as a reminder. But after only a few weeks, I was surprised to notice how irritated I would become by the rude interruptions to my "important" thoughts and actions. I realized that the ideal wasn't enough; you had to really *want* it deep inside. I relaxed and smiled to myself, mentally chanting the philosophy of Holland/Dozier/Holland—sometimes "You can't hurry love, you just have to wait," all the while resolving to keep on trying.

It was one thing to occasionally share a moment with my Heavenly Father during the relatively calm moments of my life, but quite another to remember Him in the topsy-turvy excitement of an Academy Award night. I sent a momentary thought of gratitude heavenward and turned to smile at MaryAnn. For both of us, it was great fun to be sitting in the middle of a theater filled with the biggest stars of the silver screen. I casually scanned the rows around us, careful to avoid looking like a tourist.

This was the cream that had risen to the top, the artists who had not avoided the hard work required to reach the pinnacle of their game, and for all, this was an evening of sweet recognition. While never failing to point out the highest goal of life, Yogananda had written volumes on the importance of also striving for excellence and success in this material world. And, I had gotten from him the feeling that it was perfectly wholesome to pause for a moment of pride after accomplishing a noble desire.

I had not yet met my friend, Michael Sembello, although I recognized him sitting two rows behind with the other nominated composers. Sembello was also a nominee. He was up for his hit single, "Maniac" from *Flashdance.* But it was another song from that movie, "What a Feeling," that took home the Oscar that night for Best Song of the Year.

I shared the happiness of the winners while basking in the satisfaction of my own nomination. It had lifted me up into the rarefied air of those who had been thrice honored. Now, I was a Grammy, Golden Globe, and Academy Award nominee.

Waiting for the show to get started, the long hours of taping and then driving across town to the parties had made for a long, exhausting day. It was after eleven by the time we pulled up in front of Spago for the renowned dinner party that the late legendary agent, Swifty Lazar, threw every year for those who had been nominated. Austin, Janet, MaryAnn, and I were all exhausted. We looked at our invitations; then we looked at each other and asked the limo driver to take us home, where we crawled in bed and watched ourselves on the TV news coverage. The reporters may not have known who we were, but they couldn't resist getting plenty of shots of my beautiful date, MaryAnn, on the Red Carpet.

The Golden Globe Awards, on the other hand, is an entirely different kind of evening. Much more relaxed and intimate, it's nothing less than a giant Beverly Hills dinner party. The elegantly decorated ballroom of the Beverly Hilton Hotel is filled with large, round, linen covered tables, and shining at every one of them, you'll find the brightest stars in the entertainment galaxy.

Two months earlier Austin, Janet, MaryAnn and I had walked down another red carpet and into the ballroom where we were shown to the *Tender Mercies* table. We found our place cards and looked around to greet the others at our table. We said hello to Tess Harper and Betty Buckley, the female leads of the film who sat to our left with their guests. To my right sat Robert Duvall, who had brought along three guests: they were his wife and another couple, Johnny Cash and June Carter Cash.

Tender Mercies was nominated for the Golden Globe Award for Best Motion Picture–Drama. Tess Harper was nominated for Golden Globe Award for Best Supporting Actress in the film. We all cheered when Robert Duvall beat Al Pacino for Best Actor in a Motion Picture–Drama. It was a great pleasure to meet and spend some time with one of Hollywood's most distinguished actors that night. When it came time for our song to be introduced, Betty Buckley took the stage and we complimented her on a great performance when she returned to the table. "Over You" was subsequently recorded by newcomer, Lane Brody, and became a real-life hit country single.

Later, I felt it was the right moment to move around the table and say hello to Johnny Cash. He introduced me to his wife, the great June Carter Cash. It was a thrill to meet a member of the legendary Carter Family. Modern country music can trace its origin back to her uncle, A. P. Carter, and the first generation Carter Family. I reminded Johnny that we had met years before when he had a small office in the same complex as my first manager/producer, Jesse Hodges. As we talked with fond remembrance about the early days in Hollywood when our futures still lay before us, once again for one brief moment, Johnny Cash and I were back in 1958, standing at the *Crossroads of the World*.

♥

One of the first people we met at the Self-Realization Fellowship church was an usher named Steve Kottish. It was Steve who invited us to start attending Tuesday night group meditations that were held in the home of long time devotees, John and Brenda Rosser. Brenda Lewis Rosser was the daughter of Yogananda's first American disciple and had known the Master since she was five. Soon, Brenda introduced us to her mother. John, Brenda and Mama Lewis became friends and we added them to our list of mentors on our new spiritual path.

During one of our first talks, John strongly admonished us with a word that he may have coined. "Routinize!" he told us. "Just make a routine of never missing your study, church attendance, service, and meditations. Soon the practices will become deeply ingrained habits, unaffected by your hectic schedules or whether or not you're feeling in the mood. And one day," he promised, "the inevitable results of your efforts, in the form of peace, joy and security, will have you looking forward to them."

At one point during one of our first Tuesday evening meditations, I opened my eyes and noticed that MaryAnn and I were flanked by two stars of the classic television series, *Gunsmoke*: on the left, Dennis Weaver and his wife, Gerry, and on the right, the towering, James Arness. After the meditation Steve, MaryAnn, and I went out for a bite, and Steve brought along his friend Gary Wright. As we talked, Gary and I found that we had a lot in common. We shared the same spiritual path. We were successful songwriters. We had both been artists on A & M Records.

We got to know Gary and his wife, Rose, sometime later when Mary-Ann and I were seated next to them at a banquet at an SRF Convocation, the yearly event where thousands gather from around the world for a week of classes in downtown Los Angeles. Gary began telling us about his many trips to India. Some years earlier he had been given a copy of Yogananda's autobiography by his friend, George Harrison, and George had introduced him to his beloved India when the two of them traveled there together in the nineteen-seventies.

Gary Wright told us that his pop/rock classic "Dream Weaver" had been inspired by a line in one of Yogananda's poems, *God! God! God!*, which includes the line "When my mind weaves dreams." It had made it to the top of the international charts in 1976, followed by a string of other self-penned and self-produced chart records. Before the dinner ended, Gary and Rose asked us if we might like to accompany them on their next trek to the sub-continent that they had planned for the fall, and we've been close friends ever since we shared that trip.

♥

Dad was always full of energy and lust for life, but when I picked him up at the Burbank Airport for his next visit, his mood could only be described as excited. All he wanted to talk about was reincarnation and he had brought along several books to bolster his newly reversed position on the subject. "I've been reading about all these cases where people have clinically died and then been revived," he shared as we drove toward the house, "and so many of them describe the same kind of experiences. Some of the people say their lives were completely changed by their encounters."

Dad was still animated as he, MaryAnn, and I headed to Toluca Lake for lunch that afternoon. "It's just that I've seen such a turn-around in Bobby this last year," he said, turning to address her in the back seat as I drove. "You know that Fern and I have thought the world of you ever since you first started dating our son. But we've noticed that you're both going through some kind of spiritual change, and I know it must be because of your new path. I picked up a couple more of Yogananda's books over at the Phoenix Temple, but now I think I'm ready to sign up for those lessons."

These few sincere words from my father now touched me more deeply than all the accolades, all the hit records, all the nominations. This was the recognition that meant the most—the understanding that Dad had been able to see some small results of my spiritual efforts. So much water had flown under the bridge of my life. How differently I now defined what it meant to me to be a distinguished person.

While MaryAnn and I were of course pleased that Dad wanted to take the SRF lessons, we were also more than a little stunned by his announcement. "What's Mom going to say about this?" I asked. "Don't worry, I'll still go to the Nazarene Church with her on Sundays. But I don't see any conflict with learning to practice meditation at home on my own. And your mother doesn't mind if I slip over to the SRF temple for the Thursday night lectures once in a while." Then, Dad's face lit up in a big mischievous grin as he added, "I told the ladies in the bookroom over there they could call me Nicodemus, since I'm like the disciple who went to visit Jesus by night so he wouldn't be recognized."

♥

As we drove toward Sunset Plaza for brunch on a Sunday morning after church, MaryAnn commented on something we had both observed in the SRF services. "I love how Master starts off every prayer with 'Father, Mother, Friend, Beloved God,'" she said. "Isn't it sweet! You can address Him in whatever aspect you feel closest to." I pondered her comments that night during my quiet time, and as the deeper implications dawned on me, I became overwhelmed by the realization that I could actually think of God as my friend. Simultaneously, tears filled my eyes as a feeling of intense gratitude filled my heart.

As a child, I had presumed to think of Jesus as a friend, but God had seemed so far off. I had been taught at Phoenix Christian High that He was omnipotent, omniscient, and omnipresent, but these were just theological concepts and it had taken twenty-five years for their profundity to hit home. If He were present everywhere and knew everything, He knew me, He knew my thoughts, He knew my feelings. The Master of the Universe, who was busy keeping the planets and solar systems revolving perfectly in their orbits, was still interested in *me* and my welfare. I could relate to Her as my Divine Mother, and cry until I was allowed to "sit on her lap," or I could talk to Him intimately as my closest friend.

One evening a few days later, a smiling MaryAnn proffered a wide-eyed proposal, speaking in the excited, childlike voice that I love so much: "I know! Let's have a race to God!" For Christmas in 1982, I gave her a small book of poems that I had hand written for her. One of them began with the lines, "'Let's have a race to God', she said. And before I could say 'Om' she was jogging ahead."

CHAPTER 53

Even the Trees Were Bowing in Our Direction

The faint scent of sandalwood was wafting over the heads of the thirty friends who had gathered in the small church on Sunset Boulevard, and on to the back of the chapel where MaryAnn and I waited, arm in arm. The soft sound of organ music and the defused sunlight streaming in through the stained glass windows was creating a beautiful atmosphere, exotic, yet peaceful. "Ready?" I whispered, as I pulled her close and looked deep into her sparkling eyes. It felt to me as if we were floating on air along with the incense as we began a journey that would last a lifetime, but would begin as we walked down this aisle, past the twelve rows of chairs toward the waiting minister.

Three years to the day had passed since that first Valentine's Day kiss in 1983 in the misty moonlight, and it seemed like we had been talking about getting married ever since. Finally, I had said, "I don't think we should wait anymore. MaryAnn, will you marry me?" A few days later, we met with the church's senior monk for the first time. Brother Bhaktananda had been a disciple of Paramahansa Yogananda and served as a monk in his ashrams since 1939. And long before this day, MaryAnn and I had become convinced of his saintliness.

"We'd like to get married," I started in. "Would you consider conducting our ceremony at the Lake Shrine?" Yogananda's beautiful ashram center in Pacific Palisades, a ten acre site with lush gardens surrounding a spring-fed lake where white swans glide, seemed to be the perfect, peacefully romantic back-drop for our nuptials. "No, it isn't possible for me to conduct your service anywhere else but here," he answered with a smile, "but I'd be happy to administer your vows here in our own little chapel." Without hesitation, we chose Brother Bhaktananda over the swans. From that day until his death at age ninety, he would become our greatest mentor, example and inspiration.

A month earlier, MaryAnn had taken me along with her to a small boutique designer that she knew where she picked out a fitted, white antique silk, floor-length gown. We sent out invitations for the ceremony and the reception at our home that would follow. We ordered a three-tier, pink and white wedding cake and planted pink tulips in full bloom in the rose garden, lining the brick pathway where the guests would arrive. Now, here she was, happily walking by my side, looking angelic in her gown and smiling brightly at all those who had come to witness our public commitment to each other.

As the wedding march ended, MaryAnn and I found ourselves standing before the Reverend Brother, where we were joined by her bridesmaid, Terri Costa, and my best man, Barry Richards. After an opening prayer and a few words about marriage, I turned to face MaryAnn for the rose ceremony. Nothing had ever felt as natural and right as this moment.

Her beautiful face was expressing security, support and love, human and divine. As we presented each other with single white and red roses, we repeated the first of our vows that had been composed by our Guru: "I am thine; thou art mine, that we may merge in God."

We stared into the incense fire that Brother had lit in a golden urn and repeated: "Body, mind and soul, we cast into the flame of love, to be purified into cosmic love for all mankind."

MaryAnn's brown eyes were gleaming as she sweetly and very consciously repeated all the rest of her vows to me, and I returned them in kind: "We will be loyal to each other, to demonstrate our capacity for divine loyalty." "We are united to fulfill the law of creation, and, through mutual love, to find the infinite divine love." "Even death shall not sever the bond of friendship which, through marriage, we establish in God."

Listening to the sacred words that were filling the air, I felt a sense of transformation in my consciousness. A lifetime of striving and uncertainty now seemed only particles of dust of a distant past. Now, there was a new sense of trust underlying all my dreams. It was a trust that was perfectly formed to fit seamlessly around the shapes of our two souls, a trust that when united with collaboration, would make miracles more than possible. Brother Bhaktananda pronounced us husband and wife, and began to shower us with rose petals, symbols of the blessings of God and the great gurus.

Falling in love with MaryAnn had been like falling in love with life all over again. Her willingness and ability to love all of me had already healed so many of life's injuries to my psyche. As a child, I had experienced my share of doubts, insecurities, fears. On several occasions in the nature of Oak Creek Canyon, I had come face to face with coiled rattlesnakes. But now as a Kriya yogi, I could see how infinitely more dangerous were the rattlesnakes of selfish desire and ego hiding in uncharted wilderness regions of thought and emotion. Gratefully open to the uniting of our souls for one greater, common purpose, we had inwardly renewed our commitments to help each other live in love and joy without fear or doubt.

At the reception our house was overflowing with everyone's love for MaryAnn and me. Individually or as a couple, all of our guests had a long history with us, and they appreciated what she and I had gone through to get to this moment of unreserved commitment. As I looked through the picture window, the breeze in the trees seemed to make the branches gently bow down in our direction, and in my heightened state, it seemed a symbol of God's approval and benediction on our gathering of love and friendship. It was a sacred day that I wouldn't have been capable of co-creating before I met MaryAnn and my guru, Paramahansa Yogananda.

♥

MaryAnn was sleeping soundly as I heard the pendulum clock upstairs strike midnight. But I was neither tired nor restless, just happy to be there, close to her. I melted into the serenity of the moonlight as it reflected off the water in the pool below the bedroom windows. Gradually I became aware that feelings of profound gratitude had settled into my heart, and I began to sense that this was an extraordinarily blessed moment. Gently, I moved to my nearby meditation mat and straightened my spine as I slipped into the yoga posture named after the lotus flower.

I could feel my heart overflowing with thankfulness for the new chapter of my life that this special day was heralding. Then, in timeless reverie, I watched as images of my life began to unfold in review across the screen of my stillness. It had been fraught with the same twists and turns that each of us face, and yet how incredibly blessed it had been!

How grateful I felt at this moment to have been born to loving parents who were both already striving to reach the divine goal of learning to love God. And, surrounding me with the support of the little spiritual family of our Apostolic Christian Church had only served to multiply my access to love. Loving God, I reflected, had been the goal of each and every one of these humble souls. Many were the Wednesday evening prayer meetings where I witnessed them pouring their hearts out in intense longing to draw closer to their Creator. I expanded my gratitude to the sincere seekers of all religions in all lands who were humbly contributing their sorely needed vibrations of peace and harmony to a chaotically disharmonious world.

With this thought came a new gratefulness for being drawn to a spiritual path that had provided me with a "user's manual," the divine wisdom that was answering so many of my "how to" questions. The spiritual path to God that Yogananda had introduced to the Western world seemed to have been created just for me, and had provided me with so many short-cuts to pursuing my divine goal. His royal path includes many sub-categories of Yoga and four of them had become especially meaningful: *Bhakti* (devotion), *Karma* (selfless service), *Japa* (using a mental mantra as a reminder that we are always in God's presence), and *Dharana* (meditation).

I watched again as a lonely eighteen-year-old Robert Luke Harshman stood on the corner of Hollywood and Vine, owning only a duffel bag and fifty dollars. Such deep feelings of appreciation I now directed toward that unseen hand that had guided me to creative success against terrible odds in an intensely competitive field within such a short amount of time, and toward the power that had allowed me to be able to support myself for all these years by doing the work that I loved. Intuitively, I knew that it had been God's amazingly personal and intimate Grace that had allowed me to simply relax and receive the love, beauty, and security of accepting my unique place in the universe.

I reflected that in my youth, like most others around me, I had been satisfied to try to wrench out a little satisfaction from the outer world of sensations. I had been searching for the same thing that everyone in the world searches for: happiness. The miracle of "being somebody" had seemed to manifest easily and quickly. But I soon discovered that real and lasting happiness in my life would require a miracle that was much deeper and harder to achieve.

My gratitude for the gifts of Grace that I had received in the music business was real, yet tonight I could see that in the second chapter of my life, Yogananda's compassion had provided something infinitely more valuable. He had urged us to set our sights on nothing less than the ultimate goal, the one that had been achieved down through the ages by those advanced souls that the world has known as prophets and saints: direct perception of, and communion with God! That night, my vows of renewed commitment would be just as fervent as the ones I had affirmed with MaryAnn in the afternoon.

This new chapter that she and I had just begun would be filled with our share of snares and challenges but it would also be fortified by the great good fortune of helping each other nurture our divine longings. Although we had not strayed as far into the destructive delusion as many around us, Yogananda had caught us just in time and reset our focus to a higher star. In the months leading up to our wedding, I had ended my daily meditations with a prayer for God to help us choose the best lifestyle for our coming years. I wanted to help create, with MaryAnn, our most loving and purposeful life together. And on a flight that might have been incredibly lonely, how deeply intensified was my appreciation tonight, that he had sent me someone with whom to share this adventurous journey.

Even if I still was not fully capable of *Bhakti*, that feeling of all-encompassing, devotional love for God that I knew would one day be mine, still tonight, these deep feelings of gratefulness were leading me closer to my goal. Until I could love God with all my heart, all my mind, all my soul and all my strength, I would be grateful for gratitude.

♥

"And, it isn't just me," I thought. A unique place in the universe has been assigned to each of us as one of God's treasured, immortal, distinctive, beautiful, and necessary sacred threads in the hallowed fabric of His universe. It was up to His children to dial back our rebellious egos enough to begin to weave ourselves gracefully into His master plan. Each one of us is an indispensible pixel in that bright, universal light of wisdom, kindness, peace and love!

If our little bulb is partially covered over with the darkness of ignorance and selfishness, then the whole, beautiful panorama of creation will be missing some of its loveliness. And, each of us is charged with the investment of figuring out how to let our own lights shine to their full potential and glory.

Taking personal responsibility for this kind of action is called *Karma Yoga*, the science of attuning yourself with the Divine by performing all actions with the thought of God and through selfless service to others. I remembered that Master had declared in his writings that "Life is chiefly service."

I had an awareness of that small, humble voice that tries to help and to guide and support us. In my mind, an image of the sun appeared, high above the earth, illuminating a world of swirling energy. There, I envisioned countless people busy with their lives; commuting to work, caring for their children, doing manual labor, frantically running after their rainbows. It was easy to identify myself in that huge collection of people hustling about, each with our own individual needs and desires unrelentingly pushing us forward again and again to act and to react.

Bygone scenes continued to drift past my mind like unique, pure snowflakes on a peaceful winter's night. I saw a twelve-year-old Luke delivering to the minister at the church a stack of fliers or donation envelopes that I had printed on the family presses. And like it was yesterday, I could hear his predictable response. Instead of slipping me a five spot for my efforts, Rev. Faulkner had always smiled and told me, "Thank you, Luke. You'll get your reward in heaven."

I hadn't fully appreciated it then, but tonight I instantly recognized that the times when I had done service for others, with no expectation for gratification of my own wants, seemed to purify my mind and open my heart more to the appreciation of the generosity of Spirit unselfishly working to help me. I felt such clarity and a resolve to intensify my *Karma Yoga,* my desire to serve, and to try to remember to dedicate all work to God.

"I love you, Lord. I love you, Lord. I love you, Lord." In the hallowed stillness, almost automatically, the whispered chanting of this personal, repetitive prayer (*japa yoga*) began to revolve through my consciousness. Whenever I had thought to silently chant these sacred words of affirmation, in the silence or in the din of life's battles, the practice had always expanded my heart to receive more of God's unlimited love. From time to time, I would change my mantra, "Thou and I never apart"; "Wilt Thou Come?, Wilt Thou come?" But always, encouraging my mind to constantly flow in this calming river of prayer had been a liberating blessing whenever I had been able to calm myself enough to remember to start it and keep it going.

As I reviewed my life, I became struck by the inescapable observation that every moment had presented a choice. Every thought, every action had either propelled me forward, or led me away from upliftment, inspiration, and my divine goal. Making the right choices, I concluded, had been a lot easier when the thought of God was already circulating in the background of my mind. And tonight, my mantra blended seamlessly with my appreciation, and my resolve to dedicate my actions to God.

Gently, I summoned my yoga tools of focus and concentration (*Dharana*) to go deeper within. Many years ago, I had become comfortable with the art of vividly holding a visual image in order to achieve a chosen goal. In fact, my success in the music business may have had more to do with *Dharana* than anything else. But this was different. There was no goal, no desire. I was more an observer of this special moment than an active participant. Within a few minutes I noticed that I couldn't tell whether my breath was flowing in or out.

After an unknown period of time in blessed meditation, visions of the faces of my family, life-long friends, creative partners, business associates, and fellow seekers came to me, all dissolving to a final image of MaryAnn's face. I felt my body suddenly take a deep breath and presently my senses were fully awake and aware of my surroundings.

I determined to do my best from this day forward, to take full responsibility for my actions while continuing to expand my faith in God's unlimited creativity, love, and connection to every living being. I would perform my roles for my family, friends, associates, and guru with as pure a selfless service as possible. I would try to remember this feeling and embrace the learning of life's lessons in an uncertain and turbulent world of ceaseless action and obligations, all the while focusing on the underlying power of all creation, the power of seeing miracles with your heart when your mind tries to convince you that miracles aren't possible.

I smiled and reverently bowed to the candlelit photograph of my Guru on the mantelpiece. The sweetness flowing back into my consciousness from his eyes could not be contained in my heart, and I could feel warm tears spilling out and trickling down my cheeks. It was a silent exchange of love between guru and disciple that, although overwhelming, I knew was only a taste of that divine ardor that would one day consume my soul.

He Was My Brother, My Eternal Friend

I've chosen to conclude my autobiography, not toward the end of the stories of my life, but with the new beginnings that started for me back in the early eighties. My marriage to MaryAnn, coinciding as it did with a deeper focus on my spiritual efforts, made that moment in time a most definitive and beautiful turning point.

Closing my story at that juncture should in no way suggest that I have reached the goals of my continuing spiritual journey. And, on the music side, I've never stopped being a professional songwriter, producer, and publisher. But as I continued working at my craft, I began an upward spiral of making more time for service to others, my spiritual study, and the life-changing practice of Kriya Yoga meditation.

This telling of my life has provided me with ample opportunity for bittersweet, nostalgic introspection. Throughout, I came face to face with traits cultivated and choices made, each affecting all the succeeding phases of my life. Although I hope you've enjoyed some of the stories I tell from my perspective, I've been more interested in reflecting on the spiritual lessons, some learned, many others still works in progress.

"Gratitude" continues to be the watchword as I relive the transformation of a shy kid from a small town in the Southwest to a confident conduit for creativity. Although there were many missteps along the way, I feel blessed when looking back at the times I faced life's challenges with perseverance and optimism. Had I failed to get up and start again each time I stumbled, it's a good bet I never would have realized even a small portion of my dreams.

Had I focused on worry or resentment every time I had a setback, or on anger toward those I perceived were responsible for my woes, it seems clear to me now that I would have only gotten better at worry, resentment, and anger. Had my life's many mentors never shared with me the power of visualization, the importance of stillness or the basic formula for creativity (desire + will = energy), my chances for success would have shrunk proportionately.

My friend Michael Sembello told me that when he first read Yogananda's autobiography as a teenager in Pennsylvania, he jumped in his car and drove straight to one of the guru's ashrams in California. He cornered the first monk he saw and said, "I'm here! I want to start meditating and do all those miracles like Babaji and the other saints." The renunciant inquired, "What do you do now?" "I sing and write songs," Michael answered. "Then, why don't you go off and sing and write some songs" was the wise monk's reply. Likewise, *I've* strived to continue to do my best at working right where life has placed me, while refining my priorities when it comes to how I arrange my time and energy.

The following is a brief timeline of my life and work since the events I've relayed in the last chapters of my autobiography:

In the early eighties Barry Richards and I wrote a power ballad called "I Need You," and when Greek superstar Demis Rousos added his memorable vocal, the record became a hit, going gold in nine major European countries. Over the years, this song has been recorded by many other international artists, reaching hit status in France, Brazil and Canada. Then, Lee Greenwood, a hot new country artist, included our song, "Think about the Good Times," in his platinum-selling album.

Although I continued to work with old friends like Barry, Austin Roberts, and film composer Alan Reeves, my main writing partner throughout most of the 1980s was a young MCA Music contract writer named Dick Eastman. When super-manager, Bill Dern brought his group of five inner-city kids from Boston out to Hollywood to record for their first major label release, he asked Dick and me to write and produce some of the album. The group was New Edition, and their first MCA album went multi-platinum, and included our single, "My Secret," which became an instant R & B hit in 1985.

In 1986 MTV ran *The Monkees* television shows non-stop for an entire weekend, exposing the group to a whole new generation of potential fans. As a result, The Monkees became the highest-grossing touring act of that year. When Arista Records president, Clive Davis, decided to re-release the original Monkees hits, he chose a song that Dick Eastman and I had written, "Anytime, Anyplace, Anywhere," to be one of two new songs included in the LP. Once again, another Monkees album ended up going platinum, and they included another Eastman-Hart song ("Long Way Home") in their follow-up Rhino Records LP.

Soon after this, a European record executive came across a song that Eastman and I had written called "If I Could Get to You" and thought it would be perfect for their artist, LaToya Jackson. He contracted us to produce the single for LaToya. In 1987 Dick and I went top-ten again with the follow-up to Robbie Nevil's smash hit, "C'est La Vie." Our song, which we wrote with Robbie, was called "Dominoes."

As I mentioned, in 1988 MaryAnn and I toured India with friends Gary Wright and his wife, Rose. It was a wonderful month of visiting our guru's pilgrimage places and other holy sites across the world's mother sub-continent. Since then, Gary and I have written many songs together, and he has recorded a number of them including "Your Eyes," "I Would Fly," and "Satisfied." Sharing the same spiritual path has made it very natural to incorporate lyrics of deeper metaphysical understanding into the songs we write together.

An early morning call from Nashville during Thanksgiving week in 1994 broke the sad news of Tommy Boyce's untimely passing. At his California memorial, I stood on a white sandy Malibu beach, holding hands in a circle with thirty of Tommy's friends, sharing sweet remembrances.

As the beautiful last rays of a bright red sun waited patiently before slipping beneath the waves, I spoke from my heart, and remembered:

We had been born only seven months apart and had grown up on country music in lower-middle class neighborhoods. We had the same amount of premature gray in our hair in our twenties;

each of us weighed exactly 127 pounds and stood five feet, eight and a half inches from the floor. In Canada they even titled one of our albums "Which One's Boyce and Which One's Hart?" Throughout it all, he was my partner, he was my brother, he is my eternal friend.

After his passing, Tommy's widow, Caroline, became proficient in copyright law and administration. Her work has been tireless as she interacts with Boyce & Hart fans around the world through social media. I'm inspired by her efforts to keep the Boyce & Hart music catalog vibrant for future generations.

I appreciate hearing my songs in commercials and I'm aware that my lyrics are sometimes used as teaching examples on college campuses. I get a kick out of coming across stuffed animals programmed to play one of my compositions. I enjoy hearing unlikely song interpretations, including popular bluegrass group the Grascals' as well as jazz artist Casandra Wilson's versions of "Last Train to Clarksville," the Sex Pistols "I'm Not Your Stepping Stone," and J-Love's and Alisha Keys' takes on "Hurt So Bad."

Three months before Tommy Boyce's passing in 1994, I lost my mother. I remember thinking then how different my life might have been without her early encouragement and loving support throughout my life. In the hospital, when they told her that she only had a short time left, she asked for writing material and began immediately planning her own memorial service. Both she and Dad were perfectly ready for their next adventures.

My Dad lived independently at home for another ten years before passing away peacefully at age 91 in 2005. We had spent precious time together—trips to visit his brothers and sisters in Ohio and Louisiana and those wonderful summertime visits when we would talk of God and carpentry. A couple of days before he left us, he excitedly told MaryAnn and me that a chorus of angels had come to sing for him as they stood around his bed. I remain so grateful for the blessing of having two wonderful parents to mold the values of my young life and to inspire my later years.

I remain close to my two sisters, two sons, five grandchildren, and five great-children, who all live in Arizona. They visit MaryAnn and me whenever their busy lives allow, and we spend time whenever we can with family at the forest chateau that my youngest sister Deborah and her husband, Mark, built near Sedona, site of the carefree summers of my youth.

In the last few years, I have focused much of my professional creativity on a musical play that I've been developing with four longtime business partners, Barry Richards, Klay Shroedel, Ron Friedman, and Don Loze. Klay, Barry, and I have written twenty-two original songs, around which Ron has skillfully woven the book for the show. *Uprising, the Musical* is a multimedia extravaganza set in a forest and centered around a peaceful, native tribe whose land is being decimated by a multinational logging operation. Veteran theater producer, Don Loze, will steer the ship once the project is launched.

I'm particularly gratified by the tremendous early response to *The Guys Who Wrote 'Em*, a new theater-length film that tells the story of Tommy Boyce & Bobby Hart. The documentary is directed and produced by film maker, Rachael Lichtman, who has put her fresh and stylized stamp on the film, and co-produced by Andrew Sandoval, foremost sixties music historian. Both producers are consummate Boyce & Hart fans. At their invitation, I have narrated the piece, which is being readied for release in theaters, television, streaming and on DVD.

I have agreed to accept speaking engagements and conduct teaching seminars on subjects that have always been a part of my life: manifesting creativity under any circumstance; the art of collaborative effort and partnership; and, my favorite, charting the journey to spiritual fulfillment by following one's true inner compass. I have also been asked by private, corporate, and government organizations to talk about that pivotal time of the 1960s and my experiences working to support the causes of Robert Kennedy and Martin Luther King, and about my part in changing the constitution of the United States to lower the voting age.

I continue my romance with the Hammond B-3 by playing organ for services at my local Self-Realization Fellowship Temple where I serve as chairman of the Lay Disciple Group, coordinating pilgrimages and other special events. I feel blessed to serve alongside two hundred+ dedicated members of the group, assisting the minister with the operations of the Temple.

Looking back now, it's easy to recognize that every soul who crossed my path in this long journey has had something valuable to teach me. I may have learned more from adversaries and setbacks than I did from the supporters and successes. I'm still putting one foot in front of the other by using my will and perseverance and by trusting in the power of Omnipresent Good to take me where I need to go. I embrace each day, aspiring to appreciate the past, live in the present, and remain open to the future's infinite possibilities.

I came to Hollywood with childlike dreams and no expectation of coming of age in the Age of Aquarius. Yet even during the turbulent sixties, Tommy and I found the primal power of focused creativity and the sheer sense of fun that comes from never taking this world too seriously.

We go wherever we want to,

Do what we like to do.

We don't have time to get restless,

There's always something new.

We're just trying to be friendly,

Come watch us sing and play.

We're the young generation,

And we got something to say.

That my music is appreciated and seen as valuable so many years after it was introduced, I am grateful. That my family is healthy and doing well, and that MaryAnn and I continue supporting each other in our individual efforts to grow and change ourselves for the better, I am grateful. That I am daily buoyed by the blessing and guidance of my deathless guru, I am humbled and eternally grateful.

Thank you for sharing my journey. I wish you a life of happiness and one as wonderfully blessed as my own has been.

Please visit BobbyHart.com for the latest updates.

Acknowledgments

I would like to express my sincere appreciation to

my friend and co-writer Glenn Ballantyne for helping bring this book to life with your colorful words and unrestrained ideas. Thank you for patiently luring me out of my songwriting habits of 8 lines and a chorus to a thousand memories and 110,000 words;

to MaryAnn Hart, Marcee Gutman-Ballantyne, Barry Richards, Andrew Sandoval, Caroline Boyce, Rachel Lichtman, Julie and Bill Belote, Don Graham, Rose and Gary Wright, Keith Jennings, Francis O'Neill, Vince Megna and Self Realization Fellowship, for your early encouragement, suggestions, and support for this project;

to Gareth Esersky and the Carol Mann Agency, Nancy, Kenichi, and Kenzi Sugihara of SelectBooks, Meryl L. Moss and everyone at MLM Media Relations, Emilie Pomerleau, Olga Vezeris, Steven Roche, Gina Herrera-Parker, Greta Hanson-Maurer, Judy McGinnis, and Janice Benight for your professional guidance and creative contributions;

to my friends: Hagen Smith for starting me off on a writer's journey; Gary Strobl for his Photoshop magic; to Micky Dolenz, Clive Davis, Peter Tork, Leon Russell, Paul Williams, Barbara Eden, Keith Allison, the Honorable Victor Reyes, Michael Kuhne, Carol Whitworth, Desiree Rumbaugh, Katie Silcox, Tom Capek, Mark Winkler, Drew Dix, and Jim Strain for your kind words;

to my family, Bob, Fern, Bobby, Jr., Bret, Andrew, Annie, Luke, Lucy, Brandy and Jeremy Harshman; Deborah and Mark Alyea; Rebecca Anderson; Melanie, Eric, Keanu and Selena Alvarado; Christie and Emily Barrett; Grace, Ricky, Katy, Debby, Joanie, Pat, John, William, John Sr., Melissa, Patrick, Elizabeth, and Stephen for your love and encouragement;

and to Tommy Boyce for thirty-five years of fun and friendship. I miss you.

Index

A

Abbott, Jimmy, 41
Abernathy, Ralph, 168–169
"Action," 90
Adler, Lou, 143
Agnew, Spiro, 165–166
Aguilar, Freddie, 286
Air London Studio, 225
Alamo, Steve, 95
Aldon Music, 82, 83
Aldo's Coffee Shop, 35
"A Little Bit Me and A Little Bit You," 135
Al Jolson Story, The, 30
Allison, Keith (Guitar Keith), 94–95, 109, 110
   coiffure, 143
   musical director, 253
   Where the Action Is appearance, 95
Alpert, Herb, 141
Alpert, Richard (Baba Ram Das), 96
Americana Hotel, 74
   performance, 75–76
American Bandstand (Clark show), 90, 177
Ames, Ed, 124
Amos, John, 205
AM/PM (nightclub), 71
A&M Records, 141, 301
Angels, The, 46
Animals, The, 112
Ann, Mary (the Twisting Doll), 42
   booking, 44
"Anytime, Anyplace, Anywhere," 315
April Fools (movie), *171*
Arc Music, 244
Arista, 254
Arkin, Alan, 250
Armed Forces Radio Service, 5
Army Reserve Unit, 4
Arthur Lee & Love, 93
Ascots, The (formation), 44
Asher, William, 201
Association, The, 144
Astaire, Fred, 206
Auditorium Arena, 129
Auntie Mame, 161

Autobiography of a Yogi (Yogananda), 174, 226, 272, 285, 292
Autry, Gene, 128

B

Babaji, miracles, 314
Baba Ram Das (Richard Albert), 96
Baez, Joan, 181
Baker, LaVern, 24
"Ball and Chain," 144
Bananarama, 291
Baron, Sandy, 205, 254–255
Barry, Jeff, 135
Beach Boys, The, 39
Beachcomber, The, 88
Beatles, The, 52, 100, 122, 128, 134, 142
   hysteria, 130
   songs, analysis, 103, 115
"Becky Baby" (writing), 12–13
Bee Gees, 191, 226
Be-ins, 95–96
Belafonte, Harry, 168–169
Bell Sound Studios, 84
   Hart recording session, 45–46
   "Hurt So Bad" recording, 86
Ben Casey (show), 110
Ben Frank types (hippies), 104
Bernstein, Carl, 188
Berry, Chuck, 244
Bewitched (show), 201, 203
   "Serena Stops the Show," 202
Bhaktananda, Brother, 306–307
Bhakti, 308
   capability, 309–310
B&H Aquarian Records, 184, 202
Big Brother & Holding Company, 144
Bimbos (club), 205
Bingenheimer, Rodney, 175
Bishop, Joey, 167
   meeting, 178
   phone call, importance, 185–186
Black, Jay, 61
Blackwell, Dewayne, 27
Bland, Bobby "Blue," 42
   influence, 141

"Blue Angel," 26
"Blue Bayou," 26
"Bluebirds Over the Mountain," 45
BMI
    contract, Mathews renegotiation, 184
    Special Citation of Achievement, 87
Boat House, 89. 98, 101, 115, 152, 167
    Harshman sons, visit, 172
Bobby Harshman Fan Club, 21
Bobby Hart and the Hearts of Joy, 163
Bo Diddly, 129
Bono, Sonny, 143
Booker T. & the MGs, 144
Boone, Pat (Palmer involvement), 17
Born Free (album), 127
Boston Tea Party, The, 94
Bowl-A-Rama, 44
Boxcar Bertha (movie), 244
Boyce, Caroline, 316
Boyce, Evelyn, 30
Boyce & Hart Day, documentation, 196
"Boyce & Hart Music Machine," 185
Boyce, Tommy, 29
    Bishop warning, 185–186
    career mode, 153
    Checker single, 57–58
    commercialism, 140–141
    confidence, damage, 213–214
    Corday meeting, 90–91
    dancing ability, 73
    death, 315–316
    exuberance, 159
    good news, 31–32
    Grand Ole Opry arrival, 197
    Hart, cowriting, 49–51
    Hart/Farrell, songwriting, 59–61
    Hart problems, 173–174
    Hudson, relationship (description), 53, 81
    Hudson, reunion, 152
    interaction, 33–34
    Kirshner employment offer, 83
    lyrics, change, 174–175
    Miami arrival, 147
    Monkees, music, 118
    NARAS performance, 175
    New York arrival, 37
    New York residence, 48
    other names used, *See* Christopher Cloud
        and Tommy Fortune
    parties, 153–154

    personality, 29–30
    radio market tour, 146–151
    Randazzo hiring, 71–72
    Screen Gems/Columbia Music offer, 83
    Screen Gems Television agreement, 199
    tour. *See* Dolenz, Jones, Boyce & Hart
        tour.
        father accompaniment, 190–196
    WIXY, on-air interview, 158
Brady Bunch, The (show), 259
Brill, Becky, 4, 12, 156, 242
    dreams, encouragement, 23
    Hart, reuniting, 80
    letters, 18–19
    marriage, permission, 5–6
    Phoenix move, 65
    Robert Harshman, arguments, 44–47
    sons, visit, 172–173
    support, 27
    wedding, 20
Bristol Hotel, 73
Brody, Lane, 300
Brooks, Donnie, 17, 65, 68, 163
Brother Anandamoy, 295
Brown, James, 129
    influence, 141
    Palmer involvement, 17
Bubble Gum Music, 94
Buckley, Betty, 297–298, 300
Buffalo Springfield, 144
Burdon, Eric, 90, 130
Burnette Brothers, 17, 24
Burnette, Dorsey, 17
Burnette, Johnny, 17, 113
Butler, Artie, 160
Byrds, The, 144
    coiffure, 143
"By the Time I Get to Phoenix," 224

C

Caan, James, 250
Caesar's Palace, 207, 211
Cajuns. *See* Gerry McGee and the Cajuns
Candy Store Prophets, The, 111, 113, 274
    album, 141
    Denver concert, 128–130
    Hendrix replacement, 150
    Monkees, music, 119–121
    success, 128
    Toronto concert, 131–133
    touring, 157

Canned Heat, 144
  creation, 157
Cannon (show), 259
Cannon, Freddy, 90
Canyon Records, MaryAnn signing, 291
Capitol Records, 34
  Dolenz, Jones, Boyce & Hart record deal,
    258
Carey, Macdonald, 91
Caron, Leslie, 42
Carr, Vikki, 252, 254, 256
Carter, A.P., 300–301
Casablanca (movie), 239
Cashbox charts, 124
Cash, Johnny, 198, 300–301
Cash, June Carter, 300–301
Cassidy, David, 238
Castro, Fidel, 179
Catch Me If You Can (movie), 179
"Catch Us If You Can," 101
CBS Television City, auditions, 205
Champion, Marge/Gower, 242
Charles, Ray, 129
  Palmer involvement, 17
"Chase, The," 101
Checker (record label), 7
Checker, Chubby, 38, 55
  single, chart climb, 57–58
  titles, examination, 56
Chelsea Records, 237, 251
Chess (record label), 7
Chesterfield Hotel, 73, 303
  Hart residence, 49, 56, 77
Chesterfields (cigarettes), 15
Chesterton, Jerry/Joan, 278
Chicago (Royal Albert Hall performance), 225
"Chicano," 256
Christie, Lou, 52–53
"Christmas Song, The," 288
Churchill, Winston, 187
Church of All Religions, 294
Circus Boy, 105
Circus Circus, 212
Clara Ward Singers, 163
Clark, Dick, 90
Clark, Sanford, 24
"Claudia Jennings," 241
Cline, Patsy, 197
Cloud, Christopher, 251
  See Tommy Boyce name change, 269

Coasters, The, 39
Coca-Cola, 15
Cocker, Joe, 221
Colgems Records, 112
  Kirschner/Sill, duties (exchange), 136
Colonel Tom Parker, 181–182, 206
Columbia Pictures, 83, 123
Columbia Records, 127
  Hart agreement, 253–254
"Come A Little Bit Closer," 61
  Kirshner favorite, 83
Comedy Store, 110
"Come On Let's Go," 18
Coming to America (movie), 205
Committee to Re-elect the President, 188
Cooke, Sam, 5, 140
Copacabana (nightclub), 74
Corday, Ken, 91
Corday, Ted/Betty (Hart/Boyce meeting),
    90–91
Cordell, Denny, 218
Corman, Roger, 243
Coronation Street, 105
Costa, Don, 38–39, 45, 63
  Little Anthony and the Imperials signing, 84
  money advance, 50
  studio, construction, 281
  unemployment news, impact, 71–72
Costa, Terry (Terri), 281, 306
Cow Palace, 128, 133
Craft, learning, 62
Crain, Jeanne, 209
Cranston, Alan, 189
  Hart/Boyce meeting, 187
Cream Records (Richards deal), 225
Creativity, usage, 62
Creedence Clearwater Revival, 154
Crickets, The, 95
"Cripple Creek," 129
Crosby, David, 144
Crossroads of the World, 35
Crossroads of the World, 11, 301
"Crowd, The," 26
"Crying," 26

D

Daily Variety, 104, 169, 185, 202
Dance Panorama (magazine), 63
"Dancing in the Streets," 149
Darin, Bobby, 40

Dark of the Moon, 233
Das, Baba Ram, 96
Dating Game, The, 225
Dave Clark Five, 101
Davis, Clive, 254, 315
Davis, Jr., Sammy, 177
"Daydream Believer," 138
Days of Our Lives (television show), 91–92
   theme, performance, 252
"Day Tripper," 116
Dazzlers (Dazzlers), 63, 70–73
DCP (record production company), 39
Dean, James, 22
Death Sport (movie), 259
Dee, Joey (and the Starliters), 38
Del-Fi (record label), 7
Della Reese Show, 205, 255
Delon, Alain, 142
Dern, Bill, 314
De Walden, Christian, 257–258, 263
   MaryAnn, interaction, 290–291
   MIDEM show, 268
Dharana, 308
   usage, 311–312
"Diamond Girl," 240
Diamond, Neil, 135
Dick Clark Productions, 90, 95
Dingman, Jimmy, 234–236
Dino, Desi & Billy, 93
Disk jockey school, 14
Dobro, Lonnie, 41
Dolenz, Micky, 105, 118, 209, 227
   "Last Train to Clarksville," recording,
     118–119
   tour. *See* Dolenz, Jones, Boyce & Hart tour.
     discussion, 257
   voice, 121–122
Dolenz, Samantha, 209
Domino, Fats, 5, 8, 32, 111, 170
Don Costa Productions, 45
Don Martin School of Radio, classes, 3
Donovan, 113
Don Quixote, 239–240
"Don't," 4
Doors, The, 93
Dougher, Cathy, 231
"Dream Weaver," 302
Drennan, Alan, 194
"Dr. Heartache," 33–34

Dunes Records, 36
   Lee release, 37
Duvall, Robert, 297, 300

E

Eastman, Dick, 314–315
Eastwood, Clint, 249
Eden, Barbara, 200
Eden Roc, 147
Ed Sullivan Show, The (Beatles appearance),
   130
Edwards, Vince, 109
Eldorado Studio, 91, 106
"El Paso," 59
Ember (record label), 7
Engel, John, 65, 69
Era Records, 7, 38, 141
Eric Burdon and the Animals, 90, 144
Erwin, Wayne, 113–114
   Monkees, music, 117–118
Estes, Gene, 118
Everly Brothers, 22, 224
   Palmer, involvement, 17

F

Fame, Ricky (Richard Hartley), 270
Farrell, Wes, 55–58, 237, 251
   divorce/marriage, 259
   Hart/Boyce, songwriting, 59–61
   working style, 59
Fats Domino, 5, 8, 32, 111, 170
   Palmer, Earl (involvement), 17
   soloist, 24
Faulkner, Dr., 265
Faulkner, Reverend, 311
Feliciano, Jose, 175
Fiddler on the Roof, 91
Fidelity Recorders, 8
Fidelity Studios (recording time), 12–13
Fields, W.C., 156
   voice, imitation, 40
First 500, The, 236
First Annual International Monterey Pop
   Festival, The, 143
First Bobby Hart Solo Album, The, 274
First Time Voters for Robert Kennedy, 164
Fisher, Eddie, 216
Five Easy Pieces (movie), 100
Flamingo Hotel, Hart/Boyce performances,
   184, 204

Flashdance (movie), 299

Fleetwoods, The (influence), 141

Florence, Bob, 252–253

Flores, Danny (Chuck Rio), 17

Fonda, Henry (voice, imitation), 40

Fontana, D.J. (drum licks), 13

Forge (lounge), 44

Fortune, Tommy, (*See* Tommy Boyce name
    change), 269, 270

Four Freshman, 70

Four Tops, The, 149

"Foxy Lady," 145

Freebie and the Bean (movie), 250

Freed, Alan, 82

Freedom Riders, 163

    beatings, 194

Friedman, Ron, 317

"Friends and Neighbors" (KHEP audience), 3

Frontiere, Dominic, 249–2540

Frontiere, Sicily, 250

Fugitive, The (show), 249

Funny Girl, 124

G

Gable, Clark (voice, imitation), 40

Gabor, Jolie, 208

Gabor, Zsa Zsa, 208–210, 212

    Hart/Boyce meeting, 204–205

    tour, offer, 214

Gallie, John, 157

"Galveston," 224

Garland, Judy, 287

Garrett, Snuff, 113, 120

Gary Lewis and the Playboys, 90, 93

Gatlin Brothers, The, 291

'*Gator Bait* (movie), 259

Gaye, Marvin, 71

Gentry, Bobby, 147

Gerry McGee and the Cajuns, 64–65, 70–71,
    76, 85, 111

    Candy Store Prophets (reincarnation), 113

Gibb, Maurice, 226–227

Gigiandet, Jay, 245

"Girl in the Window"

    copies, pressing, 34–35

    local hit, 39

    Pick to Click/Pick of the Week selection, 35

    recording, 34

"Girl of My Dreams," 27

"Girl, You Make My Day," 191

God

    love, 308, 311

    MaryAnn search, 292

    master plan, 310

    race, 304

Goffin, Gerry, 113, 138

Goffin & King, 82, 113

"Goin' Out of My Head," 85

Golden Gate Park, 95–96

Golden Globe Awards, 300

Golden Hotel and Casino, 70

Goldner, George, 81–83, 152

    death, 154

    Hudson, interaction, 82–84

Goldner, Linda, 82

Gone (record label), 7

"Gonna Build Me a Mountain," 129

Gonzalez, Henry (Hart/Boyce meeting), 187

Good Times (show), 205

Gourdine, Anthony, 84–85

Grace, gifts, 309

Graham, Don, 146–148, 244

Grand Canyon College, 31

Grand Central Station, 84

Grand Ole Opry, 197–199

Grant, Cary, 209

Grateful Dead, The, 144

Gratitude, 313–314

Great Golden Hits of The Monkees Show, The,
    258

Greenwood, Lee, 314

Gregory, Dick, 255

Griffith Park, 96

"Groovin'", 155

Gurdjieff, George Ivanovich, 79

Guyden Records, 27, 29

Guys Who Wrote 'Em, The, 317

Gypsy, 161

"Gypsy Cried, The," 52

H

Hagman, Larry, 200

Hammond B-3, 71

    usage, 16, 40, 91

Hang 'Em High (movie), 249

Happening (Clark show), 90

Happening '68 (show), 177

Hard Day's Night (movie), 100

Harper, Tess, 300

Harrison, George, 226, 302

Harshman, Bobby Jr., 215
  birth, 33
  move-in, 242–243
  visit, 172
Harshman, Bret
  birth, 36–37
  father/son Mexico trip, 259–261
  private school enrollment, 243
  visit, 172
Harshman, Robert (Bobby) Luke, 21, 302–303
  Becky, arguments, 44–47
  Bobby Hart, naming, 35
  car accident, 36
  fictitious career, 22
  house/car, purchase, 43
  New York City, attraction, 48–49
Hart, Bobby, 35
  alcohol, impact, 77
  Bell Sound recording session, 45–46
  Bishop warning, 185–186
  Boyce, cowriting, 49–51
  Boyce/Farrell, songwriting, 59–61
  Boyce problems, 173–174
  Boyce/Richards reunion, 88–89
  Brill, reuniting, 80
  Checker single, 57–58
  Chesterfield Hotel residence, 49, 56, 77
  Columbia Records, agreement, 253–254
  Copacabana performance, 74
  Corday meeting, 90–91
  Costa money advance, 50
  defensive rationalization, 287
  father, excitement, 302–303
  father/son Mexico trip, 259–261
  father, traditional relationship, 192–193
  Grace, gifts, 309
  Grand Ole Opry arrival, 197
  gratitude, 313–314
  homework tutor, service, 234–235
  Impala accident, 66–67
  Infinite, communication, 298–299
  Jennings breakup, 261
  Jennings meeting, 222–224
  Jennings relationship, 224–227, 246–248
  Joshua Tree National Monument trip,
    217–221
  Las Vegas
    lifestyle, 77–79
    performance decision, 64–65
  lyrics, change, 174–175

  MaryAnn
    introduction, 281–283
    marriage, 306–307
  meditations, 301–302
  Miami arrival, 147
  Monkees income, 247
  NARAS performance, 175
  Nashville recording, 84
  radio market tour, 146–151
  rent/child support, 75
  Savoy residence, 77
  Screen Gems-Columbia Music contract, 87
  Screen Gems Television agreement, 199
  solo album, 274
  sons, visit, 172
  Special Citation of Achievement (BMI
    presentation), 87
  spiritual nature, 248, 265–267
  Stagg, impact, 79–80
  tour. *See* Dolenz, Jones, Boyce & Hart tour.
    father accompaniment, 190–196
  unemployment/re-employment
    cycle, 76–77
    news, 71–73
  upbeat attitude, 159–160
  Warner Brothers Records solo deal, 225
  Weinstein meeting, 84
  WIXY, on-air interview, 158
Hartley, Richard (Ricky Fame), 270
Hart, MaryAnn, 291
  Canyon Records signing, 291
  De Walden, interaction, 290–291
  God search, 292
  Hart introduction, 281–283
  Hart sons, interaction, 284–285
  marriage, 306–307
  recording success, 295
Haskell, Jimmie, 241
Hassinger, David, 117
Headquarters (album), 138
Hefner, Hugh, 228–230, 246–247, 276
Heidelberg automatic presses, 6
Help (movie), 100
Hendrix, Jimi, 145, 150–151
"Here We Go Round the Mulberry Bush," 195
Herman's Hermits, 93, 103, 112–113, 125
Herman, Stan, 247, 275–278
"He Stopped Loving Her Today," 197
Hicklin, Ron, 118
Hilton, Conrad, 209–210

Hippies, 104, 116
"Hitch Hike," 71
Hodges, Jesse, 11–12, 31, 35
    business scheme, 14
    first-class studio, booking, 16–17
    marketing idea, 17–18
Ho, Don, 208
Hoffman, Heinrich, 294
Holiday House, performance, 72
Holliday, Johnny, 146–147
Hollies, The, 103
Holloway, Brenda, 231
Holloway, Patrice, 231
Holly, Buddy, 26
Hollywood Boulevard, 31, 54, 155
    Aldo's Coffee Shop, 35
    importance, 15
Hollywood Hills, 88
Hollywood Palace (show), 177
Hollywood Ranch Market, 7
Hollywood Reporter, The, 104, 185, 210
Hooker, John Lee, 64
How to Write a Hit Song and Sell It (Boyce), 50
Hudson, Susan, 48
    Boyce phone call (JFK assassination), 72
    Boyce relationship, description, 53, 81
    Boyce reunion, 152
    Goldner, interaction, 82–84
"Hurt So Bad," 286, 316
    recording, 86
    top ten hit, 87, 89
Hyland, Brian, 52, 209, 230
Hyland, Rosmari, 209

I

Identity thieves, 65
"I Don't Hurt Anymore," 198
"I Don't Know Why I Love Like I Do," 111
I Dream of Jeannie (show), 200
"If I Could Get to You," 315
"If You're Thinkin' What I'm Thinkin'", 125
"I Got a Woman," 39, 129
Ikettes, The, 90
"I'll Blow You a Kiss in the Wind," 202
"I Love You and I'm Glad I Said It," 264
"I'm a Believer," 134
"I'm Gonna Buy Me a Dog," 103
"I'm Hurtin'", 26
"I'm in the Mood for Love," 111

"I'm Not Your Stepping Stone," 93, 103, 111, 121, 124, 134, 316
    performance, 263
"I'm On The Outside (Looking In)", 85
Imperial (record label), 7
"I Need You," 314
In Search of Serenity, 222
"Instant Karma," 65
Integratron, The, 218–219
"In the Night (Where Your Dreams Are Waiting)", 89
Ishta, 266
"Is You Is or Is You Ain't My Baby," 27
"It Must Be Him," 252
"Itsy Bitsy Teenie Weenie Yellow Polka Dot Bikini," 52
"I Wanna Be Free," 100, 103, 124, 148, 166
    Las Vegas performance, 210
    Webb performance, 224
    writing, 127
"I Want to Hold Your Hand," 52
"I Wonder What She's Doing Tonight," 160, 191, 198
"I Would Fly," 315

J

Jackson, LaToya, 315
Jan & Dean, 39
Janeeza (smuggling), 239–240
Janssen, Danny, 230–232, 237, 245, 249–250
Japa, 308
Japa yoga, 311
Jay and the Americans, 59, 61
Jefferson Airplane, 144
Jennings, Claudia
    death, 276–278
    Hart breakup, 261
    Hart meeting, 222–224
    Hart relationship, 224–227, 246–248
    meditation, 275–276
Jim Crow segregation laws, 193–194
J-Love, 316
Joey Bishop Show, 167, 177
    Hart/Boyce appearance, 186
Joey Dee & the Starliters, 38, 70
John & Judy, 65
"Johnny B. Goode," 39
Johnny's Steak House, 31
Jones, David (Davy), 101, 105, 118
    Dolenz, Jones, Boyce & Hart tour, 258, 262–267

Far East tour, 262–267
    tour, discussion, 257
    voice, 121–122
    Singapore, airport security (impact),
        264–265
Jones, George, 197
Jones, Jack, 287–288
Jones, Tom, 184
Joplin, Janis, 144–145
Josie and the Pussycats (show), 230–231
"Journey of Love" (recording), 34

K

"Kansas City," 243
Karma, 308
Karma Yoga, 310
Kaye, Chuck, 89–90
"Keep on Singing," 238
Keller, Jack, 238
Kennedy, Bobby/Ted, 147
Kennedy, John F., 38
    assassination, 72, 187
Kennedy, Robert F.
    assassination, 167
    candidacy, 163–164
    death, 168
Kersh, Kathy, 109, 155
Keys, Alisha, 316
KFWB
    "Pick of the Week," 35
    rock 'n' show, 39
KHEP (country radio), 3, 6
Kidd, Bob, 8, 162
Kidd, Leota, 8, 290
Kiki's (restaurant), 110, 269
King, Carole, 113, 120, 138
King, Coretta Scott, 168–169
King, Jr., Martin Luther, 163
    assassination, 166
    Birmingham arrival, 194
    death, 168
Kinks, The, 103
Kirkland, Sally, 234, 261
Kirshner, Don, 82, 111–112
    creative control, 135
    Monkees revolt, 134–135
    operations, Columbia Pictures/Screen Gems
        Television acquisition, 83
Knox, Buddy, 24
Kohl, Phil, 56–58, 61

Kohlsky, Joe, 56, 57, 61
Kottish, Steve, 301
Krauss, Alison, 290
Kristofferson, Kris, 157
Kriya Yoga, 272, 280
    meditation, 313
Kriya yogi, 307
KRLA
    "Pick to Click," 35
    rock 'n' show, 39

L

"La La La (If I Had You)", 230
"Last Train to Clarksville," 115
    live performance, 130
    recording, 117–118
        problems, 118–119
    success, 119–120, 126, 134
    Wilson version, 316
Las Vegas Flamingo Hilton, 208–209
Lavang, Neil (guitar player), 17
Lawford, Peter, 177
"Law of Success, The" (Yogananda), 231
Lawrence Welk Show, The, 17
Lay Disciple Group, 317–318
Lazar, Swifty, 299–300
"Lazy Elsie Marley," 56
"Lazy Elsie Molly," 57
Leaves, The, 94
Lee, Arthur, 93
Lee, Curtis, 28–33, 269
    Boyce, musical accompaniment, 52
    performance, 36
    royalties, loss, 49
Leeds, Gary, 69
Lemmon, Jack, 170–171
Lennon, John, 65, 225
Leno, Jay, 203
"Let It Be Me," 224
"Let's All Take a Trip to Nashville," 198
"Let's Dance On," 114
"Letter from Birmingham Jail," 194
Lettermen, The, 87
Let Us Vote. See L.U.V. (Let Us Vote)
Lewis, Billy, 64, 77, 109, 111, 131
    Monkees, music, 117–118
Lewis, Gary, 90
Lewis, Jerry Lee, 111
    piano track, 7
Lewis, Mama, 301

Lewy, Henry, 97
Lichtman, Rachel, 317
Life and Teachings of the Masters of the (Far) East, The (Spalding), 80
Life, unique role, 296
Lindsay, Benny, 11
Little Anthony and the Imperials, 86
    DCP signing, 84
"Little Green Apples," 175
Little Richard, 5
Little Stevie Wonder, 149
"Little Woman," 230
Live at the Greek (album), 252, 253
Live in Japan (album), 264
Locklin, Hank, 6
Lomax, Louis, 169–170
Long Beach Municipal Auditorium, 36
"Long Way Home," 315
Lopez, Trini, 39, 291
Lorre, Peter, 78
Los Virgines High School, 40
Louie & the Rockets, 245
Love-ins, 95–96
Love Serve Remember Foundation, 96
"Love Whatcha Doin' To Me," 17, 21, 27
Lovin' Spoonful, The, 103
Lowenstein, Allan, 188
Loze, Don, 317
LSD, impact, 96–97
Lulu, 112, 226
L.U.V. (Let Us Vote), 188, 255
L.U.V. (Let Us Vote) campaign, 178–181
    Boyce/Hart, celebrity spokesmen, 186–187
Lynn, Loretta, 9, 290

M

"MacArthur Park," 224
Mad Dogs and Englishmen Tour, 221
Madison Square Garden (Beatles appearance), 130
Maharishi Mahesh Yogi, 97
Mahasaya, Lahiri, 248
Maltz, Maxwell, 97, 99
Mamas & the Papas, The, 143, 144
Mandela, Nelson, 38
"Maniac," 299
Manilow, Barry, 74
Mann & Weil, 82
Mantra, repetition, 97
Maple Leaf Stadium, 131

Marley, Elsie, 56
Martha and the Vandellas, 149
Martin, Dean, 177
Martin, George, 181
Marx Brothers, 101
MaryAnn. *See* Hart, MaryAnn
Mastery of Life, The, 10
Mathews, Kevin, 178–182
    advertising campaign, 185
    Bishop warning, 185–186
    disappearance, 211–214
    expectations, 183
    misappropriations, 212–213
    problems, 206–208
Maus, John, 65, 69
McCarran Airport (McCarran Field), 70, 87
McCartney, Paul, 94–95, 115, 225
McClanahan, Rue, 233
McGee, Gerry, 64, 70, 71, 85, 111
    Kristofferson tour, 157
    Monkees (music), 117–118
McGinnis, Don, 91
McGuire Sisters, 22
McQueen, Steve, 207
Meetings with Remarkable Men (Gurdjieff), 79
Megna, Vinnie, 85, 109, 111, 274
Melson, Joe, 25–27
Men in Trees (show), 205
Mercury, Freddie, 270
Merv Griffin Show, 177
Mesa Optimist Club, 235
MIDEM, 268
Midland-Odessa, arrival, 25–26
"Midsummer Night's Dream" gatherings, 246–247
Miller, Bill, 184
Miller, Roger, 126
Missing Links 2, 139
"Mission Bell," 17
Mitchell, Joni, 97
"Money (That's What I Want)", 41
Moni, Kashi, 248
Monkees, The, 94
    Canadian tour, 146
    Denver concert, 128–130
    Miami concert, 148
    photo shoot, 123
    revolt, 134–135
    success, 134–135
    Toronto concert, 131–133

Monkees, The (album), 123
Monkees, The (show), 100, 119–120, 315
   auditions, 104–105
   records, absence, 113
"Monkees, The" (song), creation, 101–103
Montgomery, Elizabeth, 201–203
Moody Blues, The, 167
Moonshine Country Express (movie), 261
Moor, Cherie, 231–232
More of the Monkees (album), 124
Morrison, Jim, 93
Morton, Shadow, 82
Moss, Jerry, 141–142, 149–150
Most, Mickey, 112–113, 120
Motown Records, 149
Motown Revue, 148
Ms. America (album), 252
Musicians Union, 41
   songs, recording, 117
Music Laden, 291
"My Boyfriend's Back," 46
"My Cherie Amour," 239
"My Secret," 315

N

Name for Evil, A (movie), 249
National Association of Recording Arts and
      Sciences (NARAS), Hart/Boyce
      performance, 175
"Natural Man, A," 256
Nazarene Church, 303
Nelson, Ricky, 8
Nesmith, Michael, 106, 128
   ringleader, status, 134
   theme song disagreements, 131
   touring, disinterest, 257
   voice, 121
"Never Again," 87
Nevil, Robbie, 315
New Edition, 314–315
"New York Mining Disaster 1941," 191
Nicholson, Jack, 124
Nicodemus, 303
Nilsson, Harry, 225–227
Nilsson Schmillson, 225
Nipper Caper (RCA mascot dog), 125
Nixon, Richard, 165–167
   enemies list, 188
   law and order political machine, 188

O

Oak Creek Canyon, 54
Ocean's Eleven (movie), 177
Ochs, Phil, 181
"Ode to Billy Joe," 147
Odom, Ray (deejay), 3, 24
Ohio Express, 167
"Oh, Susanna" (singing), 8
Oldham, Andrew Loog, 116
Old World Restaurant, 226
Oliver, 105
Omnipresent Good, power, 318
"One Dyin' and a Buryin'", 126
"Only the Lonely," 26
Orbison, Roy, 26
Osborn School, 10
"Out & About," 146, 148, 151
   charting, progress, 160
   singing, 201
Outer Limits (show), 249
"Out of the Picture," 89
"Over You," 297, 300
Ozzie and Harriet Show, 100

P

Pacino, Al, 300
Palmer, Earl (involvement), 17
Pandoras' Box, 65
"Paperback Writer," 115
Pariser, Alan, 226
Parkland Hospital (Dallas), 72
Parks, Rosa, 25
Partridge Family, The, 237
Partridge Family, The (theme song), 237–238
Pasadena College, 31
Pat Boone TV show, 226
Paul Butterfield Blues Band, 144
Paul Revere and the Raiders, 94, 95
   Allison, enlistment, 95
   producing, 253–254
Paul Revere & the Raiders Greatest Hits
      (album), 125
Peace Corps, establishment, 38
"Peaches and Cream," 90
Pease, Sharon, 16
Pentecostal Church (Phoenix), 15
People Will Talk (movie), 209
Peppermint Lounge, 38
Perkins, Anthony, 40

Perkins, Carl, 24
Perry, Richard, 225
Peter Gunn (show), 34
Peterson, Ray, 37, 94
Philbin, Regis, 167
Phillips, John, 143
Phoenix Christian High School, 11, 25, 70, 303
    attendance, 20
Phoenix Sky Harbor Airport, 4
Phoenix Temple, 302
Pickett, Wilson, 141
"Pick of the Week" designation, 35
"Pick to Click" designation, 35
Picturetone Music, 56, 61
Pierce, Web, 24
Pine Flats Camp Grounds, 8
Platters, The, 22
"Pleasant Valley Sunday," 138
"Please, Please Me," 52
Podell, Jules, 74
Point, The (play), 227
Poor People's Campaign, 169
"Poor People's March on Washington,"
    169–171
Pop Star Touring 101, 147
Postman Always Rings Twice, The (movie), 100
Practice of the Presence of God, The (Lawrence),
    298
Prelude Club, 63, 243
Prelude Lounge, performances, 42–44
Presley, Elvis, 4, 17, 207
    musical genre creation, 24
"Pretty Little Angel Eyes," 37
Prowse, Juliet, 211
Psychedelic Bubble Gum, 94
PsychoCybernetics (Maltz), 97, 99
Puerto Rico (Hart arrival), 75
"Purple Haze," 145
    Billboard Hot 100 Bound charting, 151

Q

Queen, 270

R

Race music, 25
"Race" music, 162
Radio Recorders, 16–17
Radio Records, contract, 21
Rafelson, Bob, 100, 104, 124
Raiders, The, 103

Rainbow Studios, 113
Randazzo, Teddy, 39, 63, 262, 274
    band, performance, 63–64
    Boyce, hiring, 71–72
    Dazzlers, 63
    Hart job, 68
    Nashville recording, 84
    string section conducting, 84
Rascals, The, 103
Rawhide (show), 249
Rawls, Lou, 256
Raybert Productions, 100, 124, 128
RCA, record distribution, 112
RCA Studios, 116
RCA Victor Records (mascot dog), 125
Record Labels, Inc., 6, 24
Record promotion, television (impact), 177
Redding, Otis, 144
Reddy, Helen, 238
"Red River Valley" (singing), 8
Redwood Lounge, 44
Reeves, Alan, 314
"Remember Me," 24
"Reputation," 46, 86–87
Revere, Paul, 94
Rhino Records LP, 315
"Rhythm & Blues," 162–163
Richards, Barry, 40–44, 63, 76, 110, 146–147,
    209
    best man, 306
    Boat House occupation, 211
    Cream Records deal, 225
    gifts, 239
    Grand Ole Opry arrival, 197
    Joshua Tree National Monument trip,
        217–221
    problems, 149–150
    Russia trip, 225
Rico, Tony, 258
Righteous Brothers, The, 39
    Bill Medley, 175
Rio, Chuck (Danny Flores), 17
Ripp, Artie, 57, 61
Rivers, Johnny, 144, 170
Robbins, Marty, 59
Roberts, Austin, 237–238, 297–298
Robinson, Fabor, 21, 22, 27
Rock 'n' roll (breeding ground), 15
Rodgers, Jimmie, 30
Rolling Stones, the, 103, 116, 128

Rondor Music, 269
Ronstadt, Linda, 87, 286
Roosevelt, Franklin Delano (death announcement), 72
Roots, 205
Ross, Diana, 290, 291
Rosser, Brenda Lewis, 301
Rosser, John/Brenda, 301
Rousos, Demis, 314
Royal Albert Hall, 225
Rubini, Michel, 118
"Runaway," 52
Russell, Johnny, 24
Russell, Leon, 157, 218–221
Russell, Rosalind, 161, 170, 171
Ryman Auditorium, 197

S

Sandoval, Andrew, 317
Sands, Tommy, 34
San Juan (Hart arrival), 75
Santa Monica Boulevard, 31
"Satisfied," 315
Saturday Night Live, 203
Savoy (Hart residence), 77, 85
Schlachter, Marvin, 244–245
Schneider, Abe, 83
Schneider, Bert, 83, 100–101, 112, 124
    Monkees revolt, 134–136
Schulman, Stan, 36
    Boyce, interaction, 37
Scooby Doo (show), 230
Scorsese, Martin, 244
Screen Gems/Columbia, Hart contract termination, 214–215
Screen Gems-Columbia Music, 135
    Hart/Boyce contract expiration, 183
    Hart contract/paycheck, 87, 109
Screen Gems/Columbia Music offer (Boyce), 83
Screen Gems, Monkees royalties (retention), 135
Screen Gems Music, 297
Screen Gems Television, 83
    Hart/Boyce agreement, 199
"Sealed with a Kiss," 52
Sedaka & Greenfield, 82
Seeger, Pete, 181
"See See Rider," 130
Self Realization Fellowship (Self-Realization Fellowship), 226, 272, 294

church, 301
    International Headquarters, 279
    Temple, 317–318
Sembello, Michael, 299–300, 314
"Send Me the Pillow That You Dream on," 6
Sergeant Pepper's Lonely Hearts Club Band, 226
Sex Pistols, 316
Shankar, Ravi, 144
Shannon, Del (Charlie Westover), 52, 98, 209
Shannon, Shirley, 209
"She," 93, 103, 111, 124
Shebang! (television show), 90
"She Loves You," 52
Shelton, Louie, 113–114
    Monkees, music, 116–118
Sherman, Bobby, 230
Shondells, The, 103
Showaddywaddy, 269
Shroedel, Klay, 317
Sid the Virginia Kid, 30, 110, 190–196
Sill, Joel, 154
Sill, Lester, 35–36, 89, 111–112, 297
    Monkees photo shoot, 123
    Monkees revolt, 134–135
    renegotiation, avoidance, 184
    songs, arrival, 157
Silver, Lee, 34
Simon, Carly, 227
Simon & Garfunkel, 144
Simon, Paul, 144
Sinatra, Frank, 39, 177, 207
Sinatra, Nancy, 287
Sinatra, Tina, 259
Sixth Army Band (emceeing), 5
"Slow Down," 41
Smathers, George, 179
Smith, Keely, 76, 233
Snow, Singing Ranger Hank, 198
"Soap Opera Music," 253
Somer, Abe, 140, 143, 182
    exclusive writer's agreement, 269
    record deal, testing, 258
"Something's Wrong with Me," 237
"Sometimes She's A Little Girl," 146
Sonny & Cher, 113, 167
Sound Factory West, The, 172
Sousa, John Philip, 5, 191
Southern Christian Leadership Conference (SCLC), 168
    support, 169–171

South Mountain Music, 39
writing, 50, 58
Specialty (record label), 7
Spector, Phil, 35, 69, 89, 200
Spirit houses, 265
SRF Convocation, 301–302
SRF Temple, attendance, 294, 303
Stagg, Warren (impact), 79–80
Staples Singers, 181
Starr, Ringo, 225
Star Track, 274
State Fair, 209
Stay Hungry (movie), 100
"Stepping Stone," 125
Steve Allen Show, 177
Steve Miller Band, 144
Stevens, April, 38
Stewart, Jimmy (voice, imitation), 40
Stewart, John, 138
Stills, Steven, 105, 144
Stopplemoor, Cheryl Jean (Cherie Moor), 231–232
"Stop Talkin, Start Lovin," 17
"Strawberry Girl," 174
Streets of San Francisco (show), 259
Streisand, Barbra, 124
Stylistics, The, 274
Success, zigzag, 99
"Sunrise, Sunset," 91
Sunset Strip, 93, 95
Sunshine Acres, 235–236
Sunshine Park (home), 153
Supremes, The, 209
Surfaris, 65, 66
Swinger, The (club), 111
Sylvester, Ward, 128, 129

T
"Take a Giant Step," 119
Tarantino, Quentin, 203
Taylor, Derek, 142, 225
Taylor, Larry (the Mole), 64, 109, 274
    Canned Heat creation, 157
    Monkees, music, 117–118
Teddy Bears, The, 35
Teddy Randazzo and the Dazzlers, 70
    Copacabana performance, 74
Teddy Randazzo Show, 63–64, 69
"Tell Me Why," 291
Tempo, Nino, 34, 38
    musical taste, respect, 39

Temptations, The, 149
Tender Mercies (movie), 297–298, 300
"Tequila," 17
Test Patterns (album), 142
"That'll Be the Day," 86
"Theme from Days of Our Lives," 91
"Theme from the Monkees," 103, 114, 119
    Nesmith argument, 134
    recording process, 107–108
The Presidio, 5
"There Stands the Glass," 24
"This Just Doesn't Seem To Be My Day," 103, 113–114
Thoughts, impact, 176
Thunderbird Hotel and Casino, 70
Thunderbird Lounge, 63, 68, 77, 85, 95
Tin Pan Alley, 48, 56
"To Know Him Is to Love Him" (Spector), 35
"Tomorrow's Gonna' Be Another Day," 119
Tonight Show, 203
Tork, Peter, 105
    reappearance, 263
    voice, 121
"To Sir With Love," 226
Trammell, Bobby Lee, 24
Transcendental meditation (TM), 220
Truck Stop Women (movie), 259
True Adventure TV series, 179
True Rock House of Prayer, 162
Tubb, Ernest, 30
Tucker, David, 216
Turner, Ike/Tina, 90
"Turn on Your Love Light," 42, 86, 221
Turtles, The, 103
Twenty-Sixth Amendment, 189
Twilight Zone, The, 66
"Twistin' the Night Away," 141
Twist music, 41
"Two Faces Have I," 52
Tyler, T. Texas, 24

U
"Under the Moon of Love," 37, 269
Unholy Rollers, The (movie), 243–245, 259
Uni Records, 230
Upbeat (show), 158, 177
Uprising, the Musical, 317
"Uptown," 26
Uptown (Orbison record), 26
"Up, Up and Away," 224

V

Valens, Ritchie, 18, 22
"Valleri," 137–139
Van Tassel, George, 218–221, 231
Vee, Bobby, 45, 113
    influence, 141
"Velvet Fog, The," 288
Venet, Steve, 90
Vietnam War, 116, 187, 189
Vincent, Gene, 17, 24
Visualization, 99

W

Wald, Jeff, 238
Walker Brothers, The, 69
"Walking to D.C.", 181
"Walk the Line," 198
Wallace, Marcia, 233–234
    homework tutor, service, 234–235
Warner Brothers Records, 225
Warren, Dennis, 181
    Mathews arrangements, 186–187
Watts, Alan, 79
Wayne, John, 106
Webb, Jack, 179
Webb, Jimmy, 223–224
Weinstein, Bobby, 75, 86, 274
    Hart meeting, 84
Wells, Kitty, 198
"We Never Close" (Hollywood Ranch Market), 7
"We're All Going Along to the Same Place," 174
"We Shall Overcome," 181
Western Recorders, 97
Western Studios, 128
Westover, Charlie (Del Shannon), 52
West Wing (show), 205
"Whad I Say," 41
"What a Feeling," 299
"Where Angels Go Trouble Follows," 240
Where Angels Go, Trouble Follows (movie), 160
Where the Action Is (Clark show), 90
    Allison, signing, 95
    Boyce appearance, 94
Whisky a Go Go, 93, 94
"Whole Lot of Shakin' Goin' On," 26
Who, The, 144
"Wichita Lineman," 224

William Morris Agency, 157–158, 164
Williams, Andy, 124
    "I Wanna Be Free" recording, 127
Williams, Hank, 30, 197, 269
Williams, Roger, 124
Willie and Scratch (movie), 230
Willpower, 289
Wilson, Cassandra, 316
Wilson, Jackie, 73, 148
Wilson, Mary, 209
"Wind Me Up and Watch Me Cry," 45
Winters, Jonathan, 105
"Wipe Out," 65
Wisdom of Insecurity, The (Watts), 79
"With Every Beat of My Heart," 231–232
"With Pen In Hand," 252
WIXY, on-air interview, 158
Woodrow Wilson Drive, 88, 242
Woodrow Wilson Park, walkthrough, 193–195
Woodward, Bob, 188
"Words," 94, 103, 111
Wright, Gary, 301–302, 315
Wright, Rose, 315
Wynette, Tammy, 9

Y

Yama-niyama, 273
Yeszin, Bernie, 123
Yogananda, Paramahansa, 160, 174, 220–221, 226, 272
    disciples, 305
    God, spiritual path, 308
    SRF lessons, 272, 292
    teachings, 287
    writings, reading, 234
"You Are My Sunshine," 7, 12
"You Can't Judge A Book By Its Cover," 129
Young, Andrew, 168–169
Young Rascals, 155
"(You're Still My Girlfriend) Alice Long," 172, 175
"Your Eyes," 315
"You've Come a Long Way, Baby," 231
"You Win Again," 269

Z

Zimmerman, Vernon, 244
Zutrubies, 263–264